A GHOSTHUNTER'S GUIDE

TO HAUNTED LANDMARKS, PARKS, CHURCHES, AND OTHER PUBLIC PLACES

ARTHUR MYERS

CB

CONTEMPORARY
BOOKS

CHICAGO

Library of Congress Cataloging-in-Publication Data

Myers, Arthur.
    A ghosthunter's guide : to haunted landmarks, parks,
churches, and other public places / Arthur Myers.
        p.   cm.
    ISBN 0-8092-4288-5
    1. Ghosts—United States.   2. Haunted houses—United
States.   I. Title.   II. Title: Ghost hunter's guide.
    BF1472.U6M9   1992
    133.1'0973—dc20   92-10505
                                                                             CIP

Published by Contemporary Books, Inc.
Two Prudential Plaza, Chicago, Illinois 60601-6790
Manufactured in the United States of America
International Standard Book Number: 0-8092-4288-5
10   9   8   7   6   5   4   3

This book is dedicated to
Bert Holtje, literary agent,
who called me up one day and said,
"How would you like to write some books
about hauntings?"

Contents

But First, a Few
Afterthoughts . . .

And so, fellow devotees of hauntings, we are off on another excursion through the supernatural. This is the fourth book on hauntings that I have written in the past six years, and I sometimes feel I am spending more time in the next world than in this one. Actually, I rather like it that way.

   If I were to pick the one paragraph from this book that I find most meaningful, I'd choose a quote from Melissa Baker, who with her husband owns a restaurant in Texas that is so haunted they pass out leaflets to their patrons, urging them to report anything unusual they become aware of while dining—the odd apparition, the unexplained touch, the flying cup, or whatever. This is what Melissa said to me:

> I always had a fear of death. It really disturbed me to think of dying, or my parents dying. And now I truly believe that there is life after death, that there is some-

thing that continues on, that this body is strictly physical. There is a spiritual world after we die. It's much
easier for me now to deal with someone dying, because
it's not final.

I constantly run across indications, both in the press
and in the course of my work, that our superficial, mate-
rialistic American culture is beginning to accept the possibility that there may be a few other dimensions floating
around. About a year ago, my literary agent sent me a story
from the *New York Times* about a house in Nyack, New
York. A buyer had put down $32,500 on it, then found out
it was haunted and wanted the money back. No soap, said
the state supreme court. But while I was writing this book
a psychic friend, Suzanne Jauchius, sent me an updated
story about the same house from the *Portland Oregonian*.
The reluctant buyer had appealed the decision, and the
court of appeals had reversed it. "As a matter of fact, the
house is haunted," the new decision said.

About a year ago, I was on a radio show with a Minne-
sota storyteller named Duke Addicks, who had quite a
repertoire of ghost stories of the upper Midwest. I like to
spread cases around geographically, so I asked Duke what
possibilities he had up his way. He said he knew of a
haunted hospital in Minneapolis, which delighted me—I
didn't have a hospital. However, my hopes were dashed
when he said the building had been sold and that the new
owner was going to use the building for business offices.
That wouldn't fit my purposes, since this book is exclusively about public sites, places anyone can walk into.
However, I was intrigued when Duke said the project had
been delayed while the new owner looked for a good psychic to get rid of the ghost before the renovation work
began. It's encouraging when entrepreneurs take such
things seriously.

I have before me stories from the *Washington Post* and the *Boston Globe* to the effect that Senator Patrick Leahy of Vermont may have a haunted office. Not his official Senate quarters, apparently, but a "hideaway" office he—like many other senators—has in a hidden crevice in the Capitol building. Leahy's Capitol office once belonged to Daniel Webster. In fact, when the rundown quarters were being renovated for Leahy a few years ago, workers told him they had had a conversation or two with Webster, but Leahy scoffed, it says here. But a heavy marble coffee table in the place tends to vibrate and wiggle itself across the room. Leahy saw it do that one night while working late. And now, he says, he occasionally comes into the hidden office and finds the table has moved. He isn't worried. "I'm sure there's some totally natural explanation," he says. Well, I suppose recognition of anything else wouldn't play well in Montpelier.

How refreshing to see an item from England, a more mature society, where ghosts are made welcome. London's Transport Museum is asking the public for evidence of ghostly sightings in the Tube—their quaint expression for London's subway. The museum wants to mount a haunting exhibition. Now that's what I called sophistication.

I am constantly reminded that the older countries are more with it, supernaturally. While doing the chapter on the haunted Vokes Theatre near my home in Massachusetts, I interviewed a member of the theater. Unfortunately, she hadn't seen any ghosts around the place, but she cheered me up by telling me of a relative who had visited England. Her relative had stayed in an old house where people were wont to say, "Did you see Colonel Fotheringay this morning?" It took a while for the Yankee visitor to find out that Colonel Fotheringay had been dead for a couple hundred years.

However, I must admit that even a crass scoffer can occasionally come up with a good line. I was trying to work up a chapter on the Capitol building in Raleigh, North Carolina, but could find only one witness. He was a retired night watchman who told me he had seen a ghost in a blue and white bathrobe go into the men's room without opening the door. He didn't follow it in, apparently. But later that evening, he said, he saw the same ghost go out the east door of the building, again without opening it. This sounded promising, so I went back to Ray Beck, the Capitol historian who had referred me to the watchman, for some more good witnesses. Unfortunately, my hoped-for chapter didn't pan out. "The new watchman hasn't had any experiences," Beck said. "I guess he's using a different brand."

While trying to get a handle on who the spirit or spirits might be in the Sise Inn, in Portsmouth, New Hampshire, I contacted various local historians. One cooperative scholar, Richard Winslow, did his darnedest but couldn't come up with anything that might indicate who was responsible for the highjinks at the hotel. But he sent me a consolation prize, an item from the *Portsmouth Morning Chronicle*, August 3, 1863, which is herewith reproduced:

Morning Chronicle.

☞ Solomon Shaw, a miser, who died last winter while being conveyed to an insane asylum at Northampton, Mass., has appeared through a spirit medium, and declares that Clark, the officer who had him in charge, took over $20,000 from his clothing after he was dead, and kept it. Clark says if this sort of talk is continued he shall prosecute the medium, which is as near as he can get to the spirit.

I hesitated about including the following story. I don't want to come across as a homophobe. I couldn't care less how people express themselves sexually. But let's face it, almost any kind of sex is sort of funny, so here is the story.

Sometimes I get letters from readers, sent to me through my publisher. One day I got a letter from a woman who, it seemed obvious, was a natural psychic. Like many such people, she lived in a milieu that was ignorant and fearful of such gifts, and she was floundering around for some advice. It so happened that she lived in the Boston area, and when I replied to her she wrote back enthusiastically, offering to take me to lunch at a restaurant of my choice. That is not the kind of offer I am likely to refuse.

The lady proved quite delightful. She had been brought up in a conventional family, and although she had long since left behind many of their religious notions, she still had a few guilt feelings and a lot of confusion. Many such people are very much in need of a sympathetic ear, and I provided one.

She lived in an apartment in a house and was friendly with another tenant. The house was haunted, and they both would see the ghost. He was a man, and they took to calling him Murphy. Sometimes, my new friend said, she would hear Murphy calling her name.

Then she got married, and her husband moved in with her. He was very macho. A ghost? How absurd, what a womanish reaction! As a red-blooded American male, he had been taught that there are no such things as ghosts, and he had bought the package.

So my friend—and Murphy—suffered a lot of ridicule. But there came a reckoning day.

"One morning," she chortled, "my husband was in the kitchen, painting the walls. All of a sudden, I heard him scream. He was not the screaming type. I ran to the kitchen. He was white as a sheet. He said, 'Somebody put their hands on my rear end! I thought it was you, but I turned around and there was no one there!' "

With giggling satisfaction, we discussed a couple of possibilities. Murphy has a sense of humor. Or he's gay. Or maybe both.

Have you ever read a novel or seen a movie and wondered what happened to the characters after the story ended? Further adventures of spirits in two of my earlier books have recently come to my attention.

One concerned Cyrus, a deceased night desk clerk, watchman, and bookkeeper who worked most of his life at the Kennebunk Inn in Kennebunk, Maine, and who, it seemed, was still hanging around, tossing the odd glass, tipping the odd tray, doing whatever his fancy dictated when he was displeased or just wanted a little attention. Cyrus's antics, and the reactions of the live people at the inn, were duly recorded in *The Ghostly Register*.

The last chapter I wrote for this present book was about the East Wind Inn up in Tenants Harbor, Maine. Accompanying me was my friend Ginny Cutler, who also came along when I checked out the Kennebunk Inn about six years before. While driving back down the Maine Turnpike we saw an exit sign for Kennebunk and decided to drop by for lunch at the inn and say hello to the people we had met there.

Our waiter, John Bowker, had been there before, but most of the staff had changed. New ownership had taken over a couple of months earlier. Cyrus had quieted down in recent years, John told us, but in the past few weeks he was really acting up—turning lights on and off, opening and closing guests' doors, tossing things around, and so on. John told us, "You go down in the cellar, and he waits till you get your arms full and then he flicks the lights out."

This sort of thing does tend to happen when there is

any change in a place. Earthbound spirits are conservative, and get nervous when their familiar environment is altered. Another item of interest, John told us, was that Cyrus was not the spirit's correct name. It was Silas—Silas Perkins. The psychic waitress who had identified the spirit some years before had gotten the name slightly wrong. The two names do sound similar. This was discovered when a niece of Silas's saw an account of the haunting that gave the ghost's name as Cyrus. She came to the inn with the information that they were not addressing her uncle correctly. Silas was also a poet, she said, and brought along some of his published poetry.

The previous owners of the inn were Arthur and Angela LeBlanc, who had just established a new restaurant, Seascapes, in nearby Cape Porpoise. There I spoke with their daughter, Elise, a summer waitress and opera singer in training. A couple of years before, Elise had been in contact with Silas by Ouija board.

"These young sisters came to the inn because they had heard of the ghost," she told me, "and they brought a Ouija board. I had never heard of a Ouija board. I was waiting tables and got friendly with them. We took it down to the basement, where most of the activity has taken place. The rule was no hands on the thing; we just held our hands about half an inch above the planchette. And it really moved. It was freaky. It scared me, and I've never used a Ouija board except for that one time.

"We asked him how old he was when he died. It wouldn't move. I got an idea; I said maybe he doesn't know he's dead. So we asked him if he was dead, and the planchette went to NO."

The other sequel to a spirit's adventures concerns Elizabeth, one of the sweetest ghosts I've encountered. She is the star of a chapter in *The Ghostly Gazetteer*, and her

venue—as the current jargon has it—was the Country
Tavern in Nashua, New Hampshire. Elizabeth had left this
life suddenly and violently about two hundred years ago,
when her sea captain husband murdered her and her infant
on the premises, their home. The captain had been on a sea
voyage for well over a year, so obviously the baby was not
his. Elizabeth, a pretty young woman, manifested as an
apparition to a number of people. She was playful, liked to
toss cups around, dematerialize things, lift women's long
hair, and generally act the cutup. She was lovable, and
many people at the restaurant felt close to her.

When I inquired about putting her in my book, about
three years ago, Meri Reid, a member of the family that
owns the restaurant, asked if I could bring along a medium
who might urge Elizabeth to get on her way. I brought
Annika Hurwitt, now of Gloucester. A large group of restaurant staffers, my friends, and Annika's friends were
present. Annika, after asking the group if they agreed to
asking Elizabeth to leave and getting no negative response,
went about convincing the spirit to go on, telling her that
her infant, whom she had been seeking all those years, was
no longer there, and had probably already had a couple of
new incarnations.

Six months later, before sending in my manuscript to
the publisher, I checked back to see what had happened,
and Bonnie Gamache, a manager who had had a particularly close relationship with Elizabeth, told me tearfully
that Elizabeth was no longer there. "I wish we had never
held that seance," she said. "I didn't even get to say good-
bye." Bonnie had avoided the seance, sorrowing over the
possibility of her friend's departure.

Two years went by, and I got a call from a producer at
the tabloid TV show, "Hard Copy." They wanted to do a
case from one of my books, and we settled on the Nashua
restaurant because there had been so many witnesses and

the ghost had been so attractive. Annika and I were invited to the shoot, and we hadn't been there five minutes when Annika whispered to me, "Elizabeth's back."

I asked Bonnie Gamache, and she smiled happily and said, "Oh yes, she's back." Annika meditated further, and said that Elizabeth is no longer an earthbound spirit, she now knows she is dead and has been on to higher spiritual planes. She just likes to visit her old earthly haunt.

Annika told me that Elizabeth said she comes back for two reasons: her friends at the restaurant miss her, and she likes to demonstrate to them that death is not oblivion, that life goes on.

1
Spooky Doings in the Bird Cage Theatre
As Well as Big Nose Kate's Saloon and Other Spots in Onetime Wild and Woolly Tombstone, Arizona

Location: Tombstone is a town in southeastern Arizona, about thirty miles from the Mexican border. It's about seventy miles southeast of Tucson and—perhaps of interest to devotees of haunted habitations—about ten miles from Fort Huachuca. A haunted house on officers' row at Fort Huachuca figures in *The Ghostly Gazetteer*, and so does a church in Nogales, about thirty miles farther west.

Description of Place: Tombstone is one of the most famous of the silver boomtowns of the Old West. During the 1880s, the eyes of the world were on this violent, colorful expression of American Westward Ho. Beginning with the first silver strike in 1879, the town had a decade of glory. Gunfighters such as Doc Holliday, Johnny Ringo, Wyatt Earp and his brothers, Bill Hickok, and Jesse James made their contributions to the famous local cemetery, Boot Hill. Some of the residents of Boot Hill hit the dust at the OK Corral, where the Earps took on the Clantons and the McLaurys in a gunfight long celebrated in song and story.

The town's population mushroomed to ten thousand people, larger than Los Angeles or San Francisco in its day. But in 1889 the mines closed, and the population dropped to a handful. There are now about 1,600 residents. But the tourist influx, according to a booster, totals hundreds of thousands of people a year.

As seems the case with many a once-violent locale, the number of ghosts may outnumber the live permanent population, although taking a census might be difficult. As in the gold rush town of Skagway, Alaska, or the old gold town—now a state park—of Bodie, California (both of which figure in *The Ghostly Gazetteer*), every other nook and cranny seems to house a disembodied spirit. Parapsychological wisdom indicates that many of these spirits left this dimension so suddenly that they don't quite realize they're gone, and they're still looking for another drink, another roll of the dice, another try for the big strike—or whatever it was they were looking for when they were so abruptly and unhappily terminated.

One of the central attractions of Tombstone is the Bird Cage Theatre, and if it weren't haunted it would just lay down its head and die. But it sure seems to be. The Bird Cage, a National Historic Site, is a long, narrow building one and three-quarters stories high, with a basement. It's 48 feet wide and 150 feet long. Fronting it, as throughout downtown Tombstone, are board sidewalks and gas lights.

The Bird Cage is open for tourists every day. Admission is $2. Preserved as they were the day the place closed for real-life business, in 1889, when the town itself pretty much closed, are the barroom, the gambling casino, the wine cellar, the dance hall, and the stage where can-can girls titillated prospectors, cowboys, and outlaws, where famed performers such as Eddie Foy and Lotte Crabtree strutted their stuff. Big-time gamblers from all over the nation flocked to the Bird Cage's poker room, which is still intact.

In its heyday, the place was also a bordello; few entertainments were neglected at the Bird Cage. Fourteen bird-cage cribs hung from the ceiling, and in these compartments the ladies of the evening plied their trade. The cages remain today, with their original red velvet drapes and all the trimmings.

There's a coin-operated music box that still works. Carved from rosewood in Germany more than one hundred years ago, it still gives out the tunes of its day from nickel-plated steel disks.

The Bird Cage was the most famous honky-tonk in America, and it doesn't take much imagination to see it as it was when it was thronged with Wild Westerners looking for a good time. In fact, in Tombstone they say there's a distinct possibility that you won't have to use any imagination at all—the sights, sounds, smells, artifacts, and people of a hundred years ago can manifest right in front of you when you least expect it. And unless the whole town is lying, they seem to be right.

Ghostly Manifestations: The chief honcho of the Bird Cage Theatre is Bill Hunley, whose family has owned the place for four generations. His great-grandfather built it in 1881. When Hunley begins talking about the Bird Cage he goes into overdrive. The man has enthusiasm—he talks about spooky doings with such elan that you feel this can't be just a publicity ploy.

As an example of the ubiquity of the ordinarily unseen dimension in Tombstone, Hunley immediately overflows the Bird Cage into the house he lives in, built in what he terms a rare architectural style, Spanish Victorian, behind the theater. "I've recently restored it to all its

Jim Kidd

The Bird Cage Theatre.

former glory," he says. "It has two ghosts; one is a little boy who died of yellow fever in 1882. He's been horsing around here this morning. The other is my aunt, who died in this house in 1958. But when you've got a place like the Bird Cage, where something happens every day, you don't pay any attention to things like this.

"One of the most common incidents at the Bird Cage," he said, "is a woman singing. You can't hear the words but you can hear her real clear and you can hear the music and you can hear the crowd. Hundreds and hundreds of people have heard this. I have no idea who it might be."

Although Hunley's enthusiasm was rather convincing in itself, I need more than my own convincing when I write these books; I want to convince my readers too. So I interview as many witnesses as I can find. Here are a few who testify to the mysterious music and crowd noises at the Bird Cage:

- Susan Baldwin of Mesa, Arizona, who is in the marketing department of a large medical laboratory. "I could hear, faintly, singing and voices in the background." I asked her if it could possibly be some kind of tape recording. "I don't think so," she replied. "And I've always been skeptical of this sort of thing. I'm an acquaintance of Bill Hunley and I was with him at the time."
- Sandra Sheppard of Blythe, California. Her husband, Lefty, is a very big man in lettuce. They also have a house in Wilcox, Arizona, and are friends of Hunley's. "Lefty and I were at dinner with Bill, and late at night we went over to the Bird Cage because he said things might happen. We were the only people in there, just the three of us. We heard some music. I wasn't sure about it because I don't really believe in that kind of stuff, but I don't know where it was coming from. It was some old music, real faint."

  Sandra also told me of another experience she had had on that evening's jaunt to the Bird Cage. "We were sitting at an old table where they used to deal cards," she said. "We were talking, and I felt something underneath my chair, like a thumping. I thought it was those guys giving me a bad time. I said, 'OK, you guys, quit it,' and I looked down and it wasn't either one of them; they weren't anywhere near me. So I moved the chair and the thumping, real loud, continued, as though somebody was on the floor with a pipe underneath my chair, but there was nothing there. And there's no basement underneath there, so there was no way anybody could be down there thumping. When I moved the chair it moved with me. Lefty and Bill both heard it. It really got my attention."
- Nancy Hunley, Bill Hunley's daughter. A college student, she is now living with her mother in Tucson. "I lived in Tombstone for nineteen years. I'd notice things in the winter when my brother and I were in the Bird Cage.

Once when I was small we were turning out the lights and it was raining, and we heard like a muffled noise, a little bit of faint music in the background, and the sound of people, as though they were having fun. I thought my brother Bill was doing something to spook me. Later, I found out that other people heard this too. I heard it several times, usually when I was with either Billy or my Mom, and they would hear it too."

• Marilyn Hunley, Bill's ex-wife. "I was working in the office one slow day. It was around ten in the morning and no one had come in yet. I could hear talking and laughter, and the clink of dice. It sounded as though it was in the back part of the place, the museum. I went to the door and opened it and yelled, 'Is anyone back in there?' There was no answer. I went and looked and there was no one there. I went back to the office, and I could hear it again."

"This sort of thing is nothing new," Bill Hunley says. "The Bird Cage was boarded up for about fifty years. We reopened it as a tourist attraction in 1934 when it was made a historic site. The high school was built across the street in 1921, when they tore down the red-light district and built the school over it. Many old-timers today were students there during the time the Bird Cage was closed, and they tell of walking by and hearing people singing— the same thing that we hear today."

The Bird Cage features smells as well as sounds—old-time macho smells such as cigar smoke. Victoria O'Shaughnessy Dewitt, who was the manager for three years, says that sometimes when she opened the old music box a cigar smell would come out of it. Who knows, it might have been blown in there by Billy the Kid while he was playing a tune. Paula Jean Reed, Hunley's fiancee, also says she is sometimes aware of a heavy cigar odor in the place when nobody among the living is smoking.

Poltergeist activities are also reasonably rampant at the Bird Cage. Things pop up where they don't belong, things that belong to a different time or place. Stories of this sort are close to Hunley's heart. He tells of the hundred-dollar Bird Cage poker chip that a tourist found lying on a table in the casino, although there is no such chip now in existence—or there wasn't until the tourist found it. Hunley studied it and found it genuine. He locked it in the drawer of his old rolltop desk and put in a call to historians. When the Western scholars came roaring in a couple of days later, the chip was not there, although Hunley has the only key to the desk. "Those guys drove seventy miles," Hunley relates. They gave him distinctly dirty looks. "They left," Hunley says, "and I opened this oak file cabinet, and it's in there."

He put it in a lock box in the bank across the street. "More historians came to see it," he says, "and that son of a gun was gone again!" He found it once again in his desk. "The last time I looked, it was in the lock box across the street. That was four months ago. My ex-wife has seen it, my fiancee has seen it, all the employees who were there when the tourist found it saw it. It just keeps jumping around."

(This account is quite convincing to a ghost writer who, when he is working on a book about hauntings, finds film rolls, sheafs of research, tape cassettes, and finished chapters of books missing from his office. Gone into thin air! They usually reappear, but not always. The spirits seem to like to play. *See*, they're nudging the living, *I'm here!*)

Hunley suspects that his grandfather, to whom he was very close as a child, is saying hello in this way.

Here's another jumping around story. Back in the 1920s, when cigarette lighters were new, my grandfather had made about a dozen or two distinctive lighters. They were shaped like a horse, and they had his name on them. He would give them away. I had never seen one. A couple of years ago when I opened my hundred-year-old rolltop desk there was one of these lighters lying on the desk just like it was brand-new. On it was "Best wishes, Harry F. Ohm." Grandfather died in 1964 just short of being a hundred. I put this lighter in a glass case.

About six months later, I came into the Bird Cage one night. No one else was there. I laid the lock down on the same glass case while I went to pick up something. I wasn't in there thirty seconds. I came back to pick up the lock and right next to the lock was this lighter; it looked like the same lighter. It wasn't there thirty seconds before. The original lighter was still in the case. Now I've got two lighters. I put the second lighter in there with the first one.

About a year ago I had some guests who were involved in parapsychology, and I told them about this, and they wanted to see the lighters. So we went into the Bird Cage and I opened the glass case and there were three lighters in there. These things were breeding!

So three or four months later my fiancee, Paula, and I are taking a steam bath in my house behind the Bird Cage. She walks out, and I hear her screaming. I run out and she says, "Look what's in my makeup kit!" And here was one of these lighters. I immediately called my manager, Victoria, and asked her to look in the case, and the three lighters were there, so now we've got the fourth lighter.

Three weeks ago, the fifth lighter showed up in Beaumont, Texas. Paula owns a Holiday Inn there. The fifth lighter showed up in a jacket, something she hadn't been wearing, a jacket she'd left in Beaumont, and that's twelve hundred miles away. By now we're not even getting excited. Paula had some unusual luck on that trip in selling her Holiday Inn, so now she thinks my late grandfather is her guardian angel.

One of Hunley's favorite poltergeist anecdotes dates from about fifteen years ago, when he had a well-known Indian artist, Jay White Eagle, carve statues of some of the historical characters who had hung out at the Bird Cage. Among these were Wyatt Earp, Johnny Ringo, Doc Holliday, and the Clantons. The Clantons had met their end in the shoot-out at the OK Corral, coming in second to the Earp brothers.

I put the statues in the various bird-cage cubicles that overlook the main room. The cubicles had been used by the girls in the old days. You couldn't get into these cubicles; they are screened off. Wyatt Earp was in one cubicle. His hat would be constantly off. It would be lying on the table. This went on for six or seven months. Sometimes it would happen for several days in a row. Then the hat began to be thrown out on the casino floor. Sometimes the statue would be turned around.

A historian came by and told us that the cubicle we had put Earp into was the one that the Clantons had always rented. It was the best-placed cubicle, overlooking the casino. I had put Earp in there because it was the most visible from the floor. So we moved him into the cubicle that Earp himself used to rent, and that incident has never happened since.

(To an experienced chronicler of spooky doings, this has the ring of truth. It reminds me of an incident in my book *Ghosts of the Rich and Famous*, in a chapter on the Flagler Museum in Palm Beach, Florida. The director of the museum mentioned, among other parapsychological happenings there, peculiarities concerning a certain locked

glass case. There were two factions of Flagler family dece-
dents. The loathing between the groups was mutual. Each
side seemed to have laid claim to certain shelves in this
case. If artifacts—a dressing table set of mirror, comb, and
brush, or asparagus tongs—belonging to one faction were
placed on a shelf claimed by the other faction, they would
later be found on the "right" shelf, although only two
people, the director and his assistant, had keys to the case.)

Apparitions also are claimed to abound in the Bird
Cage. "People come out of the Bird Cage saying they saw
people standing around in old-time dress," Hunley says.
"They looked around, and the figure was gone. This has
happened hundreds of times.

"One of the visual things," Hunley says, "is the man
who walks across the stage. He has on a celluloid visor
like a stage manager, green pants, a shirt with no collar,
and suspenders. You see him for a split second. He's got a
clipboard in his hand and a pencil behind his ear. I have
seen it many times in my life. I first saw it when I was
about eight years old. Several of my employees have seen
it, and nobody knows how many tourists."

Apparitions are said to manifest all over town. Hunley says, "There's a man who's crossing the street who
never gets to the other side. He's dressed in a frock-type
deal with a black hat. I've seen that twice. Many tourists
have seen the same thing.

"There's the woman in the white gown who blocks
cars off the road. Her child died of yellow fever back in the
1880s and she committed suicide. She's seen around town
all the time. I've seen her a dozen times. My kids have seen
her, everybody's seen her. She's been seen as far as nine
miles away."

I interviewed several people who work or used to
work at the Bird Cage, and they came up with the same
stories. One former employee, Beverly Black, told me she
had never seen any ghosts but she was still afraid of them.

"I was told," she said, "that when I locked up at night I should walk back through and make sure that the place was empty. There was no way in hell that I was going to walk back through that place. I'd just yell, 'Is anybody here?' and then turn out the lights."

Jim Kidd of Tombstone is a professional photographer and says he has taken four psychic pictures—photos with ghosts in them. "The first one," he says, "before I was aware of the value of it I wore it out showing it to people, but I've still got the other three. My wife, Jeanne, and I have studied parapsychology a bit because of strange events that have happened, which is an entirely different story. The films are just something that have shown up over a three-

Jim Kidd

Is that a headless ghost standing just to the left of the wagon? Photographer Jim Kidd says it is. For a discussion of headless ghosts, see Chapter 3.

year period. We don't go out looking for ghosts to photograph. The photos have been gone over by Eastman Kodak
in Rochester and Duke University."

Jim mentioned a ghost in a photo of a house on a hill
outside Tombstone. "It had been used as a home and head-
quarters for a mining company," he said. "Some friends of
ours bought it and wanted us to take a picture before they
fixed it up. I took a picture of them in front of the house,
and there's the ghost of a young woman in the picture. She
has an old Gibson girl hairdo. My mother explained to me
what the hairstyle was."

(While taking photos of haunted places, I have often
had strange things happen to the film. Negatives tend to
come out black, although I usually manage to get something that can be printed with a little loving care. But the
pictures are dark. Sometimes people have complimented
me on the "spooky" photographs I have taken for my
books. It was inadvertent, however.)

Jeanne Kidd mentioned that pebbles had been mysteriously thrown at them while they were in Big Nose Kate's
Saloon in Tombstone. "And there was somebody touching
my hair," she says.

Jeanne also mentioned other haunted buildings in
Tombstone—Shieffelin Hall, a building used for town
council meetings, plays, and offices; Aztec House, now an
antique shop; Nellie Cashman's Restaurant; the Wells
Fargo building.

At Big Nose Kate's, I talked with the manager, Bob
Passehl. Bob is a young Philadelphian who came to Tombstone in 1988. "My dreams were always to come out West
and be a cowboy," he said. He's thrown himself heart and
soul into the environment. He's the Warden of the Tombstone Vigilantes, and the Hanging Chairman. "We go
through a full procedure of a hanging," he explains, "with
a judge, prosecutor, and so on. We have a protester who

comes in, and he gets shot. If it's a guy we're hanging, the girls of the Vigilantes start a fight over him. He's usually somebody who left town without paying the madam. At the end of the hanging we award him a plaque. I need a two-day notice for a hanging. I've done seven in the past two weeks. Oh no, we don't actually hoist them up."

Bob was enthusiastic and informative about Big Nose Kate's Saloon. "It's only been called Big Nose Kate's for the past fifteen years," he admits. "It was called the Grand Hotel when it was first built. It was three stories high, and the largest building from here to San Francisco.

"Doc Holliday lived here, in Room 201. He was Big Nose Kate's boyfriend. Her name was Mary Kathrine Harony. The story was that she loved Doc Holliday, and everyone else when Doc wasn't in town."

The place still has its original bar, Bob said, and some of the original walls and floors.

I shifted the conversation to ghosts, and Bob offered that the Clantons and the McLaurys were believed to have quaffed there the night before their ill-fated rendezvous with the Earps at the OK Corral. "They used to come here all the time," Bob says. "It's thought that one of them is still roaming the bar."

Bob offers that "a real-estate lady" once mistook a cowboy in full dress as a member of her retinue. As she was leaving the place, she turned at the door and asked, "Are you coming?" whereupon the cowboy disappeared.

Bob says, "Since I've been here, sometimes we'll be closing and the bartender will have a drink on the bar and he'll go back to the office for a moment and when he comes back the glass will be empty."

They have a photograph on the wall, taken by Jim Kidd, that is fondly believed to include the image of a ghostly cowboy sitting at the bar. "It's just a cloud," Bob says, "but it's shaped like a person."

Jim Kidd

The interior of Big Nose Kate's Saloon. Photographer Jim Kidd says that the image of a ghostly figure seated at the bar can be seen at the lower left.

Bob says he's heard noises in the back and gone back there to find beer cans knocked all over. "You get a little worried sometimes," he says. "Who's knocking over six cases of beer? Unless somebody's unhappy because they can't get a bottle open."

You could write a book about ghosts in Tombstone— and people have.

History: Tombstone got its start in 1877 when a prospector named Ed Schieffelin discovered silver deposits. He had been told that all he would find in that desolate area was his tombstone, so in a gesture of triumphant irony, that's what he called the place. Within four years thousands of people had swarmed in, some of them prospectors and businessmen, many of them outlaws, adventurers, and gunslingers. The place riveted the attention of the nation, and much of the world. The *New York Times* had a permanent correspondent in Tombstone. Platoons of journalists came booming in from the eastern United States and from Europe.

"Tombstone was the epitome of the Wild West," Bill Hunley says. "Wyatt Earp, Bill Hickok, Jesse James were like the astronauts are today, people about whom every kid dreamed a hundred years ago."

In 1882, President Chester A. Arthur threatened to declare martial law in Tombstone, but he relented.

Identities of Ghosts: They appear to be mainly the denizens of the town's palmy days, although there are also more modern ghosts around, such as Bill Hunley's aunt, who only left this sphere of activity in 1958.

Personalities of Ghosts: Many that I heard of do not seem to react with living people, so they may be what parapsychologists sometimes call place memories. These are merely apparitions that are implanted in space, not the real spirits of the people who put them there. They are more like TV or movie images, unaware.

But many others seem to have minds of their own. Hunley's grandfather, for example, if it is indeed he who is materializing the cigarette lighters and the poker chip. And the irate Clanton who kept knocking the hat off the statue of Wyatt Earp. And whoever is knocking over the beer cases at Big Nose Kate's. And possibly the lady with the Gibson girl hairdo who had her photograph taken with Jim Kidd's friends. None of them seems to be doing anyone any real harm, aside from an experience that Bill Hunley had during a seance—read on.

Witnesses: Bill Hunley, owner of the Bird Cage Theatre; Marilyn, his ex-wife; Nancy, his daughter; Paula Jean Reed, his fiancee; Sandra and Lefty Sheppard, visitors to the Bird Cage; Susan Baldwin, visitor; Victoria O'Shaughnessy Dewitt, former manager of the Bird Cage; Marie Traywick and Beverly Black, former employees at the Bird Cage; Jim Kidd, photographer, and his wife, Jeanne; Bob Passehl, manager of Big Nose Kate's.

Best Time to Witness: About any time will serve, it appears.

Still Haunted?: Seems to be.

Investigations: "We had one seance at the Bird Cage," Bill Hunley says. "Sybil Jones (a friend) was the medium. I almost got choked. When they turned the lights on I was almost unconscious and totally purple. So we just decided never to do that again. Maybe it was one of the Clantons, mad because I put Wyatt Earp in their cubicle."

Hunley says that about thirty years ago Duke University parapsychologists did research at the Bird Cage and counted twenty-seven spirits.

He says a spirit photographer took photos in the Bird Cage that had ghosts in them, and that the *Tombstone Epitaph*, the local newspaper, has taken photos there with ghosts and has published them. The *Epitaph* is now used as a teaching tool by the journalism department of the University of Arizona, and Bill Green, a professor there, confirmed that many a story about the Tombstone ghosts has been run by the paper. "The kids love ghosts," Green told me. "They get very enthusiastic about ghost research."

Concerning informal, unrecorded investigations, a ballpark guess might be that the psychics and parapsychologists who have rattled around Tombstone over the years might well outnumber the ghostly population.

Data Submitted By: The people listed as witnesses; material provided by the Bird Cage Theatre; the *Encyclopedia Americana,* and the *Encyclopaedia Britannica.*

Where Harriet is rumored to roam.

2
The Haunted Elementary School

A Little Girl's Ghost Plays Games in a School Built over Her Grave

Location: Gorman School is in Gorman, California, a village in the extreme northeast corner of Los Angeles County.

Description of Place: "Gorman is a town of about a hundred and some people," says Wesley Thomas, superintendent of Gorman School District. "We're the smallest school district of all the school districts in Los Angeles. We only have sixty-four students in the whole district, and only the one school. It's like a one-room schoolhouse, except we have three rooms now. We have students from kindergarten to the eighth grade.

"We're at 4,100 feet elevation, at the top of the mountains that rise above L.A. It's basically a truck-stop town. It has a market, a post office, a couple of gas stations, a restaurant, a motor inn with a swimming pool, and that's about it."

The school building is one-story and of Spanish design—white stucco with a red tile roof.

Ghostly Manifestations: Thomas has been at the school for five years, and he's heard most of the stories of the little girl ghost, whose name is Harriet. He has no reluctance about passing them on. He and his secretary have heard doors shutting after school is over and presumably everyone else has left. "We walked out into the hallway," he says, "and there was nobody in the school. We had locked it up from the inside; nobody could have gotten in."

A favorite local legend about Harriet concerns her effort to keep a woman from walking out into the snow and breaking her hip. That's one version of the story. In another, it was a different lady, and she broke her leg. Thomas told it this way:

> Many years ago, back in the 1940s, there was a women's club that met here for tea. The women were leaving. It had snowed the night before and there was snow on the ground. Most of the women had walked out. One woman was walking to the door when she saw this person, a girl about twelve. And the girl said, "Don't go outside, there's danger. If you go outside something will happen to you." The woman did a double take and this person, or vision, was gone. And the woman walked outside, slipped in the snow, and broke her hip in two places.

Mary Jane Fuller is a custodian at the school and has worked there about seven years. Her story of the slip in the snow is slightly different from Thomas's.

According to Mary Jane, it was a secretary named Barbara who was leaving, and this was shortly before Mary Jane had come to work there. "The little girl's ghost," says Mary Jane, "warned Barbara not to leave, that something was going to happen to her. She went on outside, slipped in the snow, and broke her leg. She never came back; she quit."

Mary Jane, who usually schedules her time so that she

is working when the children and the teachers are out of the building and she is alone, has several firsthand stories to tell. The piece de resistance is the time she and Harriet went round and around in an eerie combination of tag and hide-and-go-seek. She describes it this way:

One time I was cleaning up in the principal's office and I heard doors slamming at the other end of the hall. There's a classroom down there that has a stage at one end of it. There's a stairway that goes up onto the stage. Then it comes down the back of the stage to a smaller classroom, the room for primary students, kindergarten through second-grade kids. There is carpeting on the stage, but I could hear someone going up and down those stairs—they're wood.

I walked into the larger classroom and I go, "Somebody here?" Nobody said anything. I started going up onto the stage, and I heard footsteps going down the steps at the back side of the stage and into the primary room. There was a door there, and it slammed. I kept following the footsteps, trying to see something. I was scared, but I had a crowbar in my hand. I figured if it was some vagrant from off the street I could hit him or something.

But I didn't see anything. It was like there was something with me that day and I was following it. It was like it was getting a big kick out of it. It would go up the stairs, across the stage, down the back steps, slam the door, and then go through the classroom, open that door, and slam it. Every time I would get to a door it was shut. After about three trips around, I decided to double back. I was really getting the willies. As I opened the door to the little room I just felt so creepy. Maybe whatever it was just went through me, I don't know. I just went, "That's it for me," and I grabbed my purse and bailed. I had to go back to the principal's office to get my purse, and I heard the footsteps and the door slam one more time before I got out of there. It never happened again.

Mary Jane is a brave young woman, but enough is enough. The day after her merry-go-round with Harriet or whoever, she brought with her one of her two dogs—the biggest one. "She's part timber wolf, part malamute, and part Great Dane," Mary Jane said. "She's very protective. But she wouldn't go into the building. Her fur was standing straight up on the back of her neck. I thought, 'That's enough for me, let's go home.'"

I was told that Mary Jane had actually seen the ghost, but her firsthand version was a bit tamer. "One time when I was vacuuming," she told me, "I thought something was standing behind me. I thought a teacher had come back. I turned around and nobody was there. It was in that same room, the primary room. That room was pretty active. There would be times when Joanne, the teacher, and I would be standing in there talking, after the kids had left, and a whole stack of papers would just go flying across the room."

Joanne is Joanne Yolton-Pouder. "Harriet stuck mostly around my room," she told me. "I think it's because she's buried under the stage area, and the stage and my room share a common wall. Sometimes things would get kind of weird. For example, there would be days when the heater made strange noises. It would bang even when it wasn't on. We would talk to Harriet. I'd ask her how she was doing, not expecting an answer or anything. But when I talked to her, things would sort of settle down."

Perhaps Joanne's most intriguing experience, shared with her son, Robbie, was the day Harriet played cards. "This was last year, when Robbie was seven," Joanne related. "He was in my room with me because he got kicked out of music. We were putting away the game center, and the cards started dealing themselves."

Joanne explained that these were cards that had a puzzle on the reverse side. They had been lying on the floor when they began to lift up and deal themselves into four hands.

"About half a dozen dealt themselves," Joanne told me. "When I moved, they stopped. Robbie and I went 'Uh-huhhh.' Robbie got a little bit nervous. *I* got a little bit nervous. But we were no worse for wear. We knew she was there. 'Okay, Harriet,' we'd say. 'It's fine.' We'd talk to her."

Joanne said that Harriet played other tricks, such as locking her classroom door. The only person who had keys to the classroom doors was the principal. He was not a suspect.

Joanne's favorite story concerns a papier-mache tree she had in her room. "It's a huge tree," she says, "eight feet high. Nobody could put decorations on the tree without a ladder, least of all me. I'm only four feet eleven. Every month I'd change the decorations—September it would be paper apples—welcome back to school—October would be pumpkins, November, turkeys, and so on.

"I had nineteen students. One morning I came in and counted the apples and there were twenty apples on the tree. And one had Harriet's name on it."

I hardly had the heart to suggest that somebody might have been playing a joke on her, but I did. Absolutely not, she insisted. She was the last to leave the night before, and she's always the first one into the school in the morning.

I believe it. It was Harriet.

History: "This was farmland back in the 1930s," Wesley Thomas told me. "There were a lot of ranches. The girl lived on a wheat farm. She was running around and her father accidentally hit her with a tractor and killed her. The school was built on the property in 1938. The girl is buried under what is now the stage portion of the school."

Identity of Ghost: Harriet?

Personality of Ghost: Playful, childlike, seeking communication and attention.

Witnesses: Wesley Thomas, superintendent; Mary Jane Fuller, custodian; Joanne Yolton-Pouder, teacher; some of the staff at the school as well as residents of the town.

Do the children see Harriet, or have other experiences with her? Thomas says, "Kids say they have seen her, but you know how little rumors with kids go."

Best Time to Witness: Most of the manifestations seem to occur when few people are around, such as late afternoon or evening.

Still Haunted?: Seems to be.

Investigations: Thomas says there have been no psychic investigations.

Data Submitted By: Wesley Thomas, Mary Jane Fuller, Joanne Yolton-Pouder. Suggested by an account in *Globe* magazine. Tip from Richard Bolton.

3
A Haunted Mission in a Remote California Valley
Ghostly Friars, a Headless Horsewoman, and Violets on a Little Girl's Grave

Location: The Mission San Antonio de Padua is situated fifteen miles from the Pacific Ocean, about 250 miles north of Los Angeles by way of Route 101, and about twenty miles south of King City. The nearest place on the map is the small village of Jolon.

Description of Place: One of my two prime informants, Richard Senate, described the place as follows:

> It's in a long, dry valley, with a few oak trees dotting the lower hills. The mission stands stark, by itself. That's one of the things that makes it so charming, the remoteness of it, like stepping back in time. They like visitors. They have a nice museum, but being off the beaten track they don't get many tourists, although a few people attend mass out there.

My other chief informant, Franciscan Brother Timothy Arthur, lived at the mission for fifteen years and acted as historian there. He is now at a mission in Santa Barbara. He described the Mission San Antonio, built in 1771, as Spanish in design, with tile roofs, arches, and fountains, similar to Mediterranean buildings from Greece to Spain and across the sea to Central and South America. "Mission San Antonio is a very special and spiritual place to me," he said.

On a more mundane note, the mission acreage is completely surrounded by Hunter Liggett Military Reservation, a huge U.S. Army training base.

Ghostly Manifestations: I first heard about the Mission San Antonio from a reader, Richard Bolton of San Diego, who sent me a clipping from a supermarket tabloid. The account was inaccurate in detail, it turned out, but the general assumption seems correct—the place is haunted. The tabloid story was based on an interview with Brother Timothy, who corrected for me some of the reporter's inadvertent or deliberate distortions.

I was particularly interested when Brother Timothy mentioned a man I know, Richard Senate, an investigator of the psychic who has helped me in the past. Senate, who is manager of the Albinger Archeological Museum in Ventura, California, told me he has been interested in the mystical since late one night in April 1978 when he saw a ghost at the Mission San Antonio.

"That's what got me involved in all this nonsense," he said. "Before that, I was relatively sane."

He was staying at the mission for two weeks, part of an archeological group from California Polytechnic State University at San Luis Obispo.

> Several of the team had bizarre things happen to them, and I am fully convinced these things resulted from far more than overactive imaginations. The reason I feel that way is that I saw something.

In the dozen years that I've been doing investigative work since then, I've only seen a handful of things, maybe five or seven. And this is after going out *looking* for things—spending nights in haunted houses, going to seances. But at the mission I was not thinking about ghosts.

I was up at 12:30 one night, and I was exhausted. I had been involved in cataloging a collection of Spanish axe heads. I left the museum and decided to go to the kitchen to raid the icebox. I walked out into the courtyard, a typical Spanish courtyard, a quadrangle— church on one side, rose garden, gravel pathways, huge fountain tinkling in the center. I walked to the fountain. It was a dark night; the stars were out but without any moon.

I saw to my extreme left, on another pathway, a candle moving, as if someone were carrying it. It didn't shock me or anything like that. I figured it was someone else up late at night, an archeologist or one of the

The Mission San Antonio de Padua.

friars. I decided to see who it was. I took the path that would intersect with his path. I had been observing him for well over a minute, and as he got closer I could see that it was the figure of a monk in a cowl, carrying a candle. Monks are much more apt to wear T-shirts or sweatshirts and jeans today than robes and such, though they do still wear robes on occasion. I got about twelve feet away from him, and he vanished. Gone! No trapdoor, no nothing. All of a sudden it dawned on me—this was a ghost.

I became frightened at that point, lost my appetite, forgot about the cold chicken in the kitchen, and went to bed. And by the way, I left the light on in my room.

The next morning I asked about ghosts and Brother Tim mentioned all sorts of supernatural events. Since then I have learned that monks did use to get up about 12:30, take a candle, go to the chapel, and pray for a time. So I may have encountered a spectre following his habitual path of 150 years ago.

Interestingly enough, the figure did not glow, it did not hover, it looked very much like a solid, regular person wearing a monk's habit, carrying a candle. It didn't do anything abnormal until it disappeared.

Senate also told me about a headless woman riding a ghostly horse. "They know the rider is a woman," he said, "because she's not wearing anything from the waist up. She has on a white petticoat from the waist down."

Having gained my attention, Senate continued. "The story is that she was an Indian squaw who married a gold miner. He went off to make his fortune and left her in Jolon. He struck it rich and came back in the middle of the night to find his sweet young Indian bride in bed with some other fellow. He took an axe and killed the woman, her lover, and her prize horse. He knew the Indian legend that if the body is incomplete one can never find rest in the Happy Hunting Ground, so he chopped her head off and took it with him. He buried it somewhere unknown, and ever since then she has been riding on her ghostly horse, looking for her head, and vanishing in front of the mission."

This is a very romantic tale. I also heard a variation to the effect that the Indian lass was married to another Indian but took to slipping off to carry on with a prospector. In both stories it was her husband who did her in.

(This is not the first time I have encountered a ghost without a head. In this book, Chapter 1, which recounts the ghostly glories of Tombstone, Arizona, is illustrated by a photograph of the headless ghost of a figure dressed as a miner. It was taken by Jim Kidd, a well-known Western photographer, whom I have talked with at length and who seems to be a quite solid citizen, above fakery.)

Headless ghosts are not new to Richard Senate, who has been an inveterate ghost chaser since that night that changed his life. "I've recorded," he said, "more ghosts without heads than can be accounted for by decapitation or accident. People have seen them where there was no history of anyone being decapitated there. And a lot of ghosts have no feet. I think that whatever is manifesting goofs; sometimes it doesn't fully manifest, at one end or the other."

In fact, most of the books I have written have poltergeist happenings involving disturbed Indian graveyards, or collections of scattered Indian skeletons. Perhaps like Ronald Reagan they're asking, "Where's the rest of me?"

Brother Timothy is also a devotee of the headless lady galloping through the night. Some witnesses are said to be soldiers at Hunter Liggett. "MPs have told me that they've seen her," Brother Tim said, "way out in the middle of the night, or GIs tell me that when they were sitting in some guard station she rode by and scared the living daylights out of them. Once I was told about two Jeeps that took off after her, with two MPs in each car, and she disappeared over the horizon."

I contacted the army base and was referred to Harriet Grindstaff, who is the safety officer there. She is a civilian, born and living in King City. She was a bit skeptical, as might be expected of a safety officer when confronted with something that can't be accounted for or controlled. (This reminds me of the stage manager of a theater in Albuquerque who was radically discombobulated by an apparition she saw on stage during a show's intermission, recounted in *The Ghostly Register*. She told me that anything that can't be controlled is very upsetting to a stage manager.)

"I don't know of anyone," Ms. Grindstaff told me, "who has seen it other than after they became aware of the story, so I don't know how much these sightings are self-induced."

But whether the headless horsewoman really rides or

An aerial view of the Mission San Antonio de Padua.

not, there are other manifestations at the mission that seem reasonably well attested. The tabloid story recounted Brother Timothy's seeing what appeared to be a wispy apparition of a fellow friar who had died that day sixty miles away, unknown yet at the mission, but Brother Tim told me that was not quite correct. Actually, he said, he was told this by some students who were staying at the mission.

"The students," he said, "told me they had just seen a cloud that floated out from underneath an arch, went out to the center of the garden to the fountain, then in the side door of the church. That's exactly what Father John Baptist used to do every day. Old people kind of do the same thing every day at a certain time. He'd go out and see the goldfish, and then walk with his breviary into the church and say his prayers. Other people have also told me of seeing dead friars."

The tabloid story said that the friars often heard footsteps across the floor of the empty attic above their dining room. Brother Tim said that to his knowledge this has happened only once. "We went upstairs and looked," he told me, "and found nothing."

His favorite story involves a seven-year-old girl, Gigi Giardino. She was suffering from cancer, and her mother had brought her to the mission. The little girl liked the place so much she asked to be buried there, and the day before she died permission was granted. "This happened during my time there," Brother Timothy said. "Violets sprang up on the girl's grave. Violets don't usually do well in the heat. It gets to be 100° F there in the summer, too hot for those dainty little flowers. Some years later, I remember walking by the grave with Father Joe and seeing a white violet among the purple ones. I asked him if he had not said something on Sunday about Mrs. Giardino and he said yes he had, that she had just died."

History: The mission was built in 1771, the third church in a mission chain founded by Father Junipero Serra. Brother Timothy told me the first wedding in California was performed there. Richard Senate said, "The mission system fell apart in the 1830s when the mission lands were given out to settlers by the Mexican government to encourage people to come to California. While on that archeological dig we discovered Spanish axe heads that were hundreds of years old. This indicated that the mission once had an extensive logging operation. The trees were no longer standing because they had chopped them down to send to Monterey to help build the then-capital of California."

Identities of Ghosts: Various friars, including Father John Baptist; the headless horsewoman; manifestations involving Gigi Giardino and her mother.

Personalities of Ghosts: All seem to be tending to their own business.

Witnesses: Brother Timothy Arthur; Richard Senate and others in the archeological team from California Polytechnic; various friars and students at the mission; possibly soldiers at the surrounding army base and residents in the area.

Best Time to Witness: Sightings are reported both day and night.

Still Haunted?: Probably.

Investigations: Brother Timothy said he knew of no psychic investigations.

Data Submitted By: Brother Timothy Arthur; Richard Senate; Father Leo Sprietsma, present head of the mission; Harriet Grindstaff, safety officer of Hunter Liggett Military Reservation. I also talked with an eighty-five-year-old friar at the mission who said he has never seen anything there and doesn't believe any of this. Tip from Richard Bolton.

A stone fence in Dudleytown.

4
Is the Ghost Village of Dudleytown Really Haunted?
The Locals Claim Such Stories Are Ridiculous, but Strange Tales Keep Filtering Through

Location: Dudleytown is a deserted village on a wooded plateau about fifteen hundred feet above the Housatonic River Valley in northwestern Connecticut. It has always been a part of Cornwall, one of several settlements within the boundaries of that township.

One way to get there is to go to Cornwall Bridge on Route 7. Turn eastward and go up Route 4 for about two miles. Turn right on Pine Street into Cornwall. At a fork take a left on Bolton Hill Road. Go past two facing churches and a school, where the road ends in a *T* at Pine Street. Take a right on Pine, past the Cornwall library. After a short distance, take a left onto Dark Entry Road, which winds upward for a couple of miles, changing from asphalt to dirt. The road is blocked off where the general area of Dudleytown begins. You can walk in on a narrow dirt road.

Another approach is to go eastward on Route 45 off Route 7 and take the first road on the left up into Dudleytown.

Description of Place: The area of Dudleytown, once cleared farming land, is now covered with hardwood forest. Tumbled-down rock walls line the main dirt path through the abandoned village. Occasionally there is a break in the wall marking the entrance to a onetime farm, and nearby is a stone-lined cellar hole of a vanished house, sometimes with an adjacent, small cellar hole of an outbuilding.

The secluded, deserted atmosphere seems peaceful and pleasant, although if one were psychic, open, or sensitive—whatever you wish to call it—perhaps it might not seem so.

Ghostly Manifestations: Dudleytown was first settled in the mid-1700s, and more than one informant told me that this was a mistake from the beginning. The altitude was not conducive to profitable farming. It was too cold up there. The area was constantly in the shadow of the small mountains surrounding it. The soil was rocky, and the earth itself was not particularly suitable for cultivation, nothing like the rich loam of the neighboring valleys.

And things kept getting worse.

Nearby, in Cornwall and elsewhere, iron furnaces were developed. The hills, Dudleytown included, were stripped of timber, which was burned into charcoal to feed the smelters. This was not healthful work. There is a theory that there was much insanity in those hills because of the oxygen deprivation that charcoalers are subject to. When the Dudleytowners came down from their domain, they were easily recognized by their blackened faces. They tended to act awkwardly, although that may have been only the natural uneasiness of the rustic in town. Further complicating life in Dudleytown, the constant denuding of the land invited rains to wash away topsoil.

When the Bessemer process came along in the late nineteenth century, the iron and steel industry moved west, pulling the rug from under the charcoal economy of places like Dudleytown. The people themselves were moving west as the nation expanded, to less stony and more fertile, easily acquired land.

People began to notice that untoward things kept happening to people in Dudleytown. In 1792 Gershom Hollister, while assisting in a barn raising, fell to his death. This could happen anywhere, say realists. In 1804, Sarah Faye Swift was fatally struck by lightning. Could happen anywhere. A native of Dudleytown, Mary Cheney, met Horace Greeley in a vegetarian boardinghouse and married him. Things seemed to be looking up for a Dudleytowner. Greeley became a famous man. But Mary committed suicide one week before her husband was defeated for the presidency of the United States. A family named Carter had a run of bad luck. A band of Indians killed Mrs. Carter and an infant child. Nathanial Carter himself was killed as he returned to his cabin. Two daughters and a son were kidnapped by the Indians. The girls were eventually rescued, but the boy joined the Indians and refused to return to Dudleytown.

Within living memory, in the early twentieth century, a New York City physician named William Clarke built a house in or on the border of Dudleytown. Legend has it that he returned from business in New York to find his wife had either lost her mind or committed suicide. The stories vary. His son, William, told me that neither was true; his mother committed suicide in New York.

Possibly things were no worse than they are in most hill towns, but that did not prevent the development of the legend of the Dudleytown Curse. For a place with a bumpkin background, the village's curse has considerable class. Soon after the village's beginning in the 1740s, four Dudley families came to the settlement, and from sheer numbers gave the place their name. They were from Guilford,

on the Long Island shore of Connecticut, but they were
descendants of a noble English family. The English Dudleys were prone to displease kings and to lose their heads.
One Dudley became known to posterity as Edmund the
Headless. Another married his son to Lady Jane Grey, who
after the briefest of reigns on the English throne lost her
head, as did her husband and father-in-law. A subsequent
Dudley, the Earl of Leicester, became a favorite of Queen
Elizabeth. He managed to keep his head by the expedient
of leaving England. It was his progeny that came to Connecticut. The adversities that seemed characteristic of
Dudleytown began to be laid to the Dudley name—it was
the Dudley Curse.

Was this a viable explanation? Was there some mystical reason for the haplessness of the place? Or was it just
normal human bad luck, abetted by an ill-chosen environment? No one seems to deny that Dudleytown was one
melancholy excuse for a hamlet. It should never have been
started where it was. But the reasons for its afflictions are
where people part company. The majority of late-twen-
tieth-century Cornwall residents put little stock in any
talk of curses or ghosts. They particularly dislike people
coming to thrash about in the forest. I spoke with many
people who live on the edge of the Dudleytown area. A
typical reaction is that of John Leich, president of the Dark
Entry Forest Association, which maintains Dudleytown as
a nature preserve, who said:

> We don't mind people writing about the place if they
> don't entice other people to come and visit. We've had a
> great problem with people coming and having witch-
> craft things and building fires in our forest. We've been
> very distressed that over the years Dudleytown has
> been more and more in the news as a place where
> ghosts are, which is absolutely untrue. There's nothing
> there but some very-difficult-to-find cellar holes.

Art Myers

The foundation of a vanished home.

Another neighbor, Susan Kochman, told me, "We've been here for six years and there's been absolutely nothing supernatural. Nor have I heard of anybody who has had any such experiences. I've heard of people who come in and hold seances and things like that. People come in by the busload. But whatever is here doesn't bother us."

I talked with a ninety-six-year-old woman named Harriet Lydia Clark, who wrote a pamphlet titled *True Facts About Dudleytown*, which she ends as follows:

> Dark Entry is too dangerous for cars and motorcycles. Please do not come. There are no ghosts, no spirits, and no curse.

In Cornwall Bridge one woman told me, "Dudleytown is a very mellow place."

Another said, "I've heard a lot, but I don't know anyone who has had a hands-on experience."

But if you talk with enough people hither and yon, you begin to build up another side to the story. An example of this sort of respondent is Paul Smith of New Milford. I came across Smith's name in a newspaper article that reported talks on Dudleytown given by two historian types, who had said nothing in their program about parapsychological doings up that way. I happen to have interviewed both these people, and neither had closed minds— they just couldn't come up with anything supernatural. But Smith and some other people at the gathering were irritated that the mystical aspects of Dudleytown had been ignored.

A man after my own heart, I thought, and I sought him out. It developed that he is a member of an occupation with such a reputation for conservatism that he spoke to me only on my word that I not reveal what he did for a living.

"In my opinion," he said, "there have been too many people who have come back after a visit to the area who have experienced some sort of emotional or physical phenomenon. I've been there three times, and I guess the best way to describe my reaction would be a gut feeling. The Appalachian Trail touches upon Dudleytown. There have been many, many incidents when dogs accompanying their owners have refused to go into the confines of the area. Horses have been taken on the Appalachian Trail, and they'll shy in that immediate vicinity."

(One of the speakers, on the evening when Smith objected to the neglect of the occult, was Bill Bader of Washington, Connecticut. I had interviewed Bader and he told me that while in college he had investigated Dudleytown for a course in civilization, but had had no experiences with the supernatural. "As far as I'm concerned," he said, "it was an environmental thing that happened up there." But, he added, "A friend of mine named Joe Young told me that he went up there with a dog, and the dog just got to the edge of Dudleytown and that was it. He kept barking and charging and hollering and just wouldn't go any farther. He told me that he went up there with some psychic, and the psychic kept saying, 'I hear voices in here, and I hear wagon wheels squeaking.' ")

Paul Smith went on. "I've heard stories that people have gone there and left with a piece of stone from a foundation or something, and within a day or two they start having undesirable events befalling them. And when they return the item these events stop occurring. The last time I was there it was an incredibly warm, oppressive day, but there were unmistakable wind noises in Dudleytown. When I got back on the Appalachian Trail, it was quite quiet."

I kept running into people who began by pooh-poohing anything supernatural in Dudleytown, but as they conversed they seemed to talk themselves into something different; they began to remember things.

One such was Jeff Johnson. Jeff is a young man who worked in the Dudleytown area for two years logging. The Clarke family had a sawmill there. "We never saw anything too much out of the ordinary," he told me. "I used to go up there camping. In high school, we went up there in a folklore class, just about the history of the place and the people who once lived there. Supposedly the last person who lived there, Calvin Brophy, raised goats, and Brophy was last seen walking on all fours like his goats. This was back many years ago."

As Johnson, who now does carpentry and furniture restoration, talked he began to shift gears. Perhaps he was just trying to give me what he thought I wanted to hear, but he came up with a number of details for such short notice. Or he might have realized he had a sympathetic ear for some of the strange tales about Dudleytown that had been kicking around in his memory of the place.

> I met one guy who told me he was hiking up there and a stick came flying out of the woods and hit him in the leg. There was nobody up there, so that was kind of strange. A week later he fell and broke his leg in the place that the stick had hit it.
>
> One time when I was logging up there I went out drinking in a bar, and it got late, so instead of going home to Falls Village I decided to go straight up to Dudleytown. I was camped out behind the corral where we used to keep the horses. I had my sleeping bag and I was lying on the ground. And in the middle of the night I could swear that something nudged me, reached down and pushed me. It grabbed my shoulder and wiggled me and woke me up out of a sound sleep. That really freaked me out. That next morning one of the horses was loose and we spent the next two days walking the mountain looking for him. Finally we found him down the road, hanging out in the pasture.
>
> I found a tiny horseshoe up there and for good luck I threw it under the seat of my Toyota Land Cruiser. The following weekend I got into a bad car accident. I had three friends in the truck. I rolled it three times. They all walked away; I was the only one who got hurt. I broke my back. I've always wondered if that horseshoe had something to do with my accident—the Dudleytown Curse and all.
>
> It was a weird place. When I was working there I began to feel it was a great place, there were no bad feelings. But I don't know if today I'd want to go up there and sleep by myself.

After talking with Johnson, I looked up Dody Clarke of Cornwall Bridge. She has done logging with Johnson, and with her father, William, and brother, Steve. She is the granddaughter of the New York doctor and his unfortunate wife who built a house there.

"I'm pretty convinced," she said, "that the curse of Dudleytown is the ghost hunters.

"I've been written up as a ghost, by the way. I was riding through on my horse one time and one of those groups saw me. So I just took off across a hill to go around them. Later, somebody sent me this newspaper article from Danbury about the ghost on the horse. So I'm one of the ghosts, I guess.

"The stories are pretty outrageous. We've had all sorts of weird people come in, people who are into ghosts and so on."

Among people I contacted was Paul Chamberlain, who wrote a booklet for the Cornwall Historical Society with the no-nonsense title *Dudleytown*. It is a sophisticated, amusingly written historical footnote. Chamberlain came down hard on the reality side of the issue. "I have mixed emotions about that booklet," he said. "Sometimes I wish I hadn't written the damn thing. All the publicity Dudleytown has received has done a great disservice to the area ecologically. They've had a great deal of trouble with trail bikes and snow machines, which tear the roads all to pieces. People have come in with metal detectors and pretty well torn the foundations to pieces. It has become the popular thing to go ghost hunting up there."

Chamberlain once told a *New York Times* reporter that he drew on "grandfather knowledge." His great-grandfather had farmed in Dudleytown. Though a highly sophisticated man—he was a radio and TV writer in Connecticut and an advertising writer in New York City—he has some of the characteristics of a local Yankee: he believes people don't really belong in a place till their ancestors have lived there for a century, or better, two. For example, the Clarke family arrived early in the twentieth century—William Clarke told me he first came to Dudleytown as an infant, in 1911, and his children still live in the vicinity. But Chamberlain took pains in our conversation to distinguish these Clarkes from the aforementioned Harriet Lydia Clark, whose forefathers lived in Dudleytown from its early days.

"Actually," Chamberlain said, "the old-timers didn't know there were ghosts there. There are an awful lot of come-latelies and they've blown it all out of proportion. There are very few people left in Cornwall who, if I may use the term, belong in Cornwall. They sit around and dream up things like this so that they can entertain their summer guests."

While researching this chapter I was perusing a ten-year-old feature article in the *New York Times* and came across a familiar name, William DeVoti. I lived in nearby Berkshire County, in Massachusetts, for some years and I belonged to a meditation group that included Bill DeVoti and his wife. He was an English teacher at the Housatonic Valley Regional High School in Falls Village, and was teaching a course in American folklore. The *Times* article said, in part:

> DeVoti . . . told of students of his who were "frightened by glowing apparitions" one night during a Dudleytown camping trip. The campers "saw 'a glow in the woods,' as they described it to me," said Mr. DeVoti. "And as they got closer, it separated. One went one way, and the other went another way, around them, and just disappeared."
> "The mother of a student who took his folklore class 'had an intuition' that Dudleytown was important to her," said Mr. DeVoti. While searching in daylight

for the village's as yet unfound graveyard, the woman saw "a hooded figure riding on a dark horse. It charged across the road into the brush," reported DeVoti. The woman called to her husband, but by the time he arrived the apparition had vanished.

I called Bill DeVoti and found he was still living in Sheffield, Massachusetts, just north of the Connecticut state line, and was still teaching in Falls Village. He said the *Times* quotes were correct, but he felt the story had not made it clear enough that "these stories were told to me, I wasn't selling them.

"I got the job of teaching a course on folklore," he said, "because I was absent on the day they were handing out assignments. I was a newcomer from New York City. I got very interested in folklore. I taught it for eight years and got to be considered an expert on some places around here. I've been to Dudleytown many times."

I asked if he had had any outre experiences there.

"Aahh, I almost hesitate to mention it . . ."

"Aw, go ahead . . ."

"Well, it was nothing you would call scientific, nothing you could separate from psychology and emotions. A ghost never walked up to me and said hello."

"What *did* happen?"

"Well, I took a puffball mushroom that I found one time and it just bothered me so much that I brought it back and put it in the same spot I found it. Because part of the story is that you're not supposed to take anything away from Dudleytown unless it's a gift. The mushroom bothered me so much as the story started working on me that I could actually feel it throbbing in my pocket, so I said the hell with that and I brought it back, about a mile back up the road, superstitious or not."

On the other hand, Bill said, "In my fireplace, the top

stone came from Dudleytown. It was given to me by Steve Clarke, the grandson of the New York doctor who settled there. Steve was a student of mine, and that's brought nothing but good luck to my life."

I told Bill the stories I'd heard about animals refusing to go into Dudleytown, and he pointed out that the Clarkes had logged the place with horses. "I've taken my golden retriever there a few times," he said. "I've always found it a very peaceful place."

He echoed Paul Chamberlain's comment that the ghost stories seem to be relatively new. "I never could find anyone who could remember ghost stories prior to the 1940s," DeVoti said. "There were two books around that time, *Ghost Towns of New England* and *They Found a Way*, that just happened to pick up some of this stuff, and

Another part of the forest.

Art Myers

then it got into the oral stream and then started leaching out into other stories, similar to Ichabod Crane and stuff like that.

"But the thing about folklore is that the truth of the matter is not important, the existence of the story is the important thing."

As I interviewed person after person, being recipient of a high incidence of blank stares, occasional indignation, and little that would fit into a book on the supernatural, I began to feel I was seeking witnesses in the wrong way. Perhaps what I needed were a few psychic people who had been to Dudleytown. So I began beating the bushes of Connecticut for psychics who had heard of the place or, even better, visited it. Perhaps I might start with a pertinent quote from one of these people, Bonnie Nadeau. Bonnie lives in New Haven, says she is a sensitive, studied astrophysics in college, and runs an herbal tea business. She said:

> I've lived in a haunted house all my life. It's my grand-mother's house; I've been here since I was a child. We have a couple of inhabitants, entities, who aren't quite here. But some people can walk into this house and you could hit them with a Mack truck and they wouldn't know they've been hit. It's the same with Dudleytown. People who are sensitive had immediate impressions. The people who weren't sensitive either didn't know something was going on, didn't feel whatever was there, or their personalities changed but they didn't know why.
>
> A friend of mine, who is sensitive, walked through this barrier thing [the Dudleytown perimeter] and immediately felt very cold. He started looking behind him as though someone was out to get him. He almost had a paranoia. But when he stepped back outside he didn't feel that.

On subsequent visits we felt the same coldness, the same feeling of airlessness, of oppression. You keep feeling there is something behind you. We always go up in groups. I wouldn't go up there alone for anything.

(I went up there alone and walked around for an hour and didn't feel a thing except for the buzzing of swarms of insects. Which may go to show that ignorance can be bliss.)

"We used to go up there when I was in high school and college," Bonnie said. "The first time I went there was with a bunch of kids from North Branford High School. We didn't see anything, but personalities changed. Someone who was happy-go-lucky all of a sudden was very morose. It was very dark and oppressive there, although it was a sunny day. There's a point where you go into the area where the village was. You cross this point and it's like crossing a bridge. If you're sensitive at all, it's like you're walking through a doorway, and once you've got through the door, the air is thick."

In my quest for psychics I called the Soulmate Bookstore in Woodbury, Connecticut, and spoke with the owner, Debbie Miles. "When we were growing up, Dudleytown was kind of a hot place to go," Debbie told me, but said she had never had strange experiences there. But she referred me to her sister, Susan Kelly, whom she said had. Susan said:

Nothing personally happened to me, but I was with a group of people that things did happen to. We went in with four-wheel-drive vehicles—Jeeps. We stopped near what were apparently original foundations. And what we found near one of the foundations was the head of a dead horse. That was very strange. I have heard that people who practice black magic sometimes sacrifice live animals, but a horse seems a little large.

As we walked, one of the gals broke her foot, someone else cut himself severely on a broken bottle, somebody else fell and sprained his ankle. In fact, my husband and I were the only ones who came out totally unscathed. It was really odd. There were four couples. We were people in our twenties.

At the time, I hadn't heard anything about the place being haunted. I thought I was just going on a hike. By now, I've heard the legend that if you spend too much time wandering around there, the insanity that seems to have gripped the people of Dudleytown can also take hold of you.

If I were to leave it at that, the current neighbors of Dudleytown would probably be delighted. They might even forgive me for this chapter. However, I must mention a conversation with Jo Smith, a librarian in Woodbury, who used to lead hikes into Dudleytown for her library every fall around Halloween. "It was for the historical interest," she said, "although I'd tell everybody about the legends and so forth. But my experiences were very mundane. We never had any unusual number of injuries, and one time I had sixty people on a hike."

I have been working my way up to the person I consider my heaviest hitter. Her name is Lynn Bouchey. She lives in Old Lyme, and she is now a full-time psychic. She told me that in 1982 she and her sister, Dawn Oulette, tramped through Dudleytown and had some memorable experiences. They went again a couple of years later, and "nothing happened at all." Her sister, she said, "is very intuitive, but she's never wanted to develop it to any extent." This is Lynn's account of their first visit:

Lynn Bouchey.

We were walking along, and I had gone on a little ahead. I turned around and saw Dawn sitting on the ground. I went back and asked her if she had fallen. She said she was sitting on a rock and suddenly something pushed her forward. Her rear end went off the rock and she landed on the ground, and she also hit her head on the rock.

A short time later we were walking along and some force seemed to catapult me head over heels. I wasn't hurt, and I brushed off the dirt. My sister saw it and I experienced it. But it was like it didn't happen, like I was playing games with my head or something. We decided, let's get out of here and go back to the car.

On the way back to the car I took a snapshot of Dawn, and she took a picture of me standing by an old cellar hole. Then I took another picture of Dawn. This was with a one-step Polaroid camera. In one of the pictures I had taken of Dawn, you could clearly see an energy with a head on top of it, in front of her. The energy sort of trailed off.

On the one she took of me, there were two of me in the picture. One was of me facing forward, and the other figure, in the same photograph, was me standing sideways. I showed this to a professional photographer, and he couldn't explain it. He got very nervous and didn't want to know any more about the story.

The other picture I took of Dawn was by a cellar hole. There was a circle of light on the ground where the front entrance of the house would have been, and a bright red spot. On the drive home we stopped in a diner, and we showed this picture to a waitress, and she said she saw the circle and the red light. By the time we got home, the ring of light was still there but the red light had disappeared from the photograph.

At one point in our walk, I heard a high frequency noise that didn't seem to be coming from anywhere.

When we got to the vicinity of the car we heard a car door slam, but when we got there the car seemed untouched. However, we had carefully locked the car and now it was unlocked.

Lynn said that, although their second visit was comparatively uneventful, "there was a bird, a black bird, that followed us."

"Did it say, 'Nevermore'?" I asked.

"No, it didn't do anything," she said, "it was just there all the time, wherever we went."

What does all this amount to? Is Dudleytown haunted, and if so, why? After I had mulled Lynn's account for a few days, I called her up and asked if she had any theories about why she and her sister had had these experiences there, and why so many other people have. She gave me this answer:

Throughout the earth there are positive and negative energy columns. In the old days, religious people used to seek out positive places of high energy and build temples. People who were into black magic would seek out negative ones. In that Dudleytown area, for some reason, there are an unusual number of negative columns. You find such columns in haunted houses to which a lot of negative spirits have been drawn, houses that happen to have been built on one of these negative energy columns. Dudleytown is full of them, and they're quite close together.

There are also positive columns, and some are very powerful. Sedona, Arizona, is an example of a place that has a lot of positive energy, and there's a place in the Hawaiian Islands and some in England. They're all over the world. Those are the major ones. There are major negative ones, too. And there are also minor positive and negative columns. If you're in the middle of a negative one you can be bothered by the kind of stuff we experienced at Dudleytown.

Like attracts like, and negative columns can attract not only negative spirits but the kind of living people who want to do that sort of thing. Somebody who is into black magic will be attracted to a place like that because they can feed off the negative energy.

At this point I mentioned that I had been told that people were going into Dudleytown to do black magic, and she said, "Aha!" She said she hadn't known that.

I have an additional theory. In my investigations, I have been told more than once that people who have had difficult, unhappy lives can tend to remain earthbound. Instead of their spirits going on to higher spiritual planes, they may hang in on the physical plane. They become discernible as ghosts. If the people of Dudleytown were affected by negative columns, I mused, it might have made their lives so miserable that they would remain as earthbound spirits, thus adding to the strange manifestations in the area. And when news of these phenomena brings in people involved in black magic, you have a vicious—or at least a negative—circle. It might be a sort of self-feeding situation.

I decided to call the person who had directed me to Lynn Bouchey, Roger Pile, a mystic who lives in Branford and who has trained many psychics. He was Lynn's teacher. I knew he had had experience with energy columns, thought forms, elementals, demons, and such manifestations. He said:

> In one house Lynn and I found five earthbounds. Now why in hell were they there? We also found in the house a column of energy. You can feel them; they come out of the earth. The earth is basically like a porcupine; these columns come up all over the place. Some are negative and some positive. In anything, alternation works the same way as electricity; it's a constant vibration between the positive poles and the negative poles. So it would make sense that the earth would have things like this.

Roger Pile.

These columns are like beacons; they attract earthbounds. So it would stand to reason that if there are negative energy columns they would attract negative energies, like earthbounds who have a negative bent. It would also affect the people who live there.

I mentioned to Roger that I had been told that dogs and horses resisted going into the Dudleytown area, and was also told that there seems to be no wildlife up there, and he said, "Yes, animals pick up on these energy patterns."

History: The first settlers came to Dudleytown, a section of high land in the southern part of Cornwall township, in 1738. Thomas Griffis, a farmer, bought the first parcel of real estate soon after, and in 1747 Abiel and Barzillai Dudley, who had been soldiers in the French and Indian War, took title to land. As part of the general movement inland in the middle of the eighteenth century, other settlers also came—Carters, Joneses, Porters, Pattersons, Tanners, Rogerses, Dibbles, and others—and they formed a farming community. At one time, thirty to thirty-five families lived in Dudleytown.

To quote the book *Ghost Towns of Connecticut*, a work detested by some modern residents of Cornwall:

> Dark forces were at work, bringing to the inhabitants of Dudleytown more than their due share of misfortune. Some of the people were struck down by epidemics, others lost their minds; there was a much publicized murder and when some of the inhabitants, becoming restless, tried to escape by moving away, a malevolent jinx appeared to follow them down from the hills.

That's one point of view. More historically verifiable is the story that the Dudleys were descended from a noble

English family noted for their tendency to fall out with monarchs and lose their heads, and that the general bad luck of this tiny hill hamlet in America began to be attributed to the Dudley Curse.

Farming was difficult at Dudleytown's high altitude, and when the iron industry developed in northwestern Connecticut many Dudleytowners turned to charcoaling, denuding their plateau of trees to feed the iron furnaces. Producing charcoal is today considered an unhealthful occupation in itself, but in any case this economic prop slipped away when the Bessemer process came into use and the iron and steel industry moved westward.

And so did many of the people of Dudleytown, along with many other New Englanders, to the more fertile, easily cultivated land of the Midwest. By the twentieth century, Dudleytown was virtually a deserted village. It is now private property, administered as a nature preserve by a group of local residents called the Dark Entry Forest Association, founded in the 1920s.

Identities of Ghosts: During my travels, I heard no mention of apparitions. The manifestations in Dudleytown don't seem to be visual unless you count the reported sighting of a ghostly rider on a ghostly horse, which Dody Clarke says was only her, out for a ride in the woods. Jeff Johnson told me of being shaken while sleeping there one night, and mentioned a man who told him he was hit by a stick propelled from the deserted woods. Most of the manifestations seem to take the form of a vague sense of negative energy felt by some people and not felt by others.

Dody Clarke, who has spent much time in Dudleytown camping and logging, told me that tools and artifacts went missing regularly, which she attributed to the trespassing tourists. But almost any psychic person, or simply someone like myself who sometimes writes books about spirits, can testify to constant mysterious disappearances of objects from where they are supposed to be, sometimes never to return.

Personalities of Ghosts: A sense of negativity is commonly reported.

Witnesses: Lynn Bouchey, psychic; Dawn Oulette, Lynn's sister; Bonnie Nadeau, sensitive; Susan Kelly, visitor to Dudleytown; Debbie Miles, visitor; Jo Smith, visitor; Dody Clarke, worker and camper in Dudleytown; Jeff Johnson, worker in Dudleytown; Paul Smith, visitor; Bill DeVoti, folklorist and visitor.

Best Time to Witness: Almost all of the witnesses reported experiences during the daylight hours. The only person I met who was venturesome enough to go there at night was Jeff Johnson.

Still Haunted?: If it ever was, it probably still is.

Investigations: Hundreds of people, perhaps a few thousand, have rooted around in the woods and cellar holes of Dudleytown. A certain percentage of them must be consciously psychic, and it is said that we all are to some extent.

Data Submitted By: The above witnesses, plus Roger Pile, psychic and medium; Kent Library; Cornwall Library; Paul H. Chamberlain, Jr., author and Cornwall native; Jerome Bacca, historian; Bill Bader, historian; John Leich, president of the Dark Entry Forest Association; Bob Bury, member of the association; Clifton Read, member of the association; William Clarke, who has lived and logged in

Dudleytown; Rob Daalhuyzen, sometime logger in Dudleytown; Susan Kochman, neighbor of Dudleytown; Polly Calhoun, Cornwall resident; Harriet Lydia Clark, author and Cornwall resident; various Cornwall people informally interviewed.

True Facts About Dudleytown, by Harriet Lydia Clark; *Dudleytown*, by Paul H. Chamberlain, Jr.; *Ghost Towns of New England*, by Fessenden S. Blanchard; article in the magazine *Connecticut*, October 1982; article in *Yankee* magazine, March 1962; article in the *New York Times*, October 26, 1980; articles in various Connecticut newspapers.

The Artist House.

5
The Strange Doll
in a Key West House
Does It Have Magic Power
or Is It Just a Very Large Doll?

Location: The Artist House is at 534 Eaton Street in what is called the Old Town section of Key West. Key West is the westernmost of the small islands that stretch some 120 miles across the Gulf of Mexico from the southern tip of mainland Florida. Key West is the ultimate end of Route 1 on its progress down the East Coast from Maine. Some spectacular bridges link the tiny patches of land.

Description of Place: Key West is a town of 26,000 permanent residents and is also a tourist center. A sophisticated, colorful place, the town includes many artists, writers, and free spirits of various persuasions. Many people famous in the arts have lived there—Ernest Hemingway and Tennessee Williams, for example.

The Artist House, now a bed and breakfast establishment, was built at the end of the nineteenth century and until the mid-1970s was the home of the Otto family. It derives its name from the last of the Ottos to live there,

Robert Eugene Otto, a painter. The current owner, Ed Cox, describes the house as follows:

> It's West Indies Victorian, built by shipbuilders for the Ottos. It's got the columns and the runaround veranda. There are two stories, with a big turret, or cupola, on the front. The rooms have twelve-foot ceilings. Upstairs there are three bedrooms, and downstairs there are three more bedrooms, originally a parlor, a library, and a studio. The upstairs front room, the one under the turret, was once Gene Otto's nursery, and in later years his studio and bedchamber. The upstairs rear room was the bedroom of his wife, Ann.

The house, its exterior now painted lavender with white trimming, has been elegantly restored. Many of the furnishings are antique, including four-poster beds, oriental rugs, and original pictures.

Ghostly Manifestations: I first heard of the Artist House from Poochie Myers. Poochie is no relation to me, and as to the other half of her name, she says a lot of people in West Virginia, where she comes from, are called Poochie. Poochie is psychically sensitive and is currently working with the well-known psychic Pat Hayes, who has a school in Georgia. Poochie is also an artist. Among other things, she teaches creative knitting.

About ten years ago, Poochie was living in Key West and was a friend of the then-owner of the Artist House, Nancy Tazwell. For several weeks, she took care of the place when Nancy was away, and she became aware of things that psychic people are prone to become aware of.

"A little girl sits on the staircase," she told me. "She didn't materialize so that somebody else could see her but I could sense her energy. She sits all scrunched up in a little white, old-fashioned nightgown. She has long, light brown curls. She seems to be about five years old. She's very angry about something. I think she may have been kept in the front room for punishment. I think if I had been a male she would have been fierce or something. I'd just say, 'Good-night, see you later.'

"In the big back bedroom on the second floor there's a feminine presence, a very warm, loving energy. That was Ann Otto's room, and her loving energy is still there."

Poochie was the only person to mention a little girl ghost to me, but most of Key West seems to know about Ann Otto and her husband, Gene. Gene Otto's grandfather, Thomas, had built the house only a few years before Gene was born. Most of the Otto men were doctors; Gene, however, became an artist. He studied in France, where he met his wife, Ann, who came from Concord, Massachusetts, and was a concert pianist. When Dr. Thomas Otto died, the family let Gene inherit the house and he and Ann came there to live.

Gene appears to have become cruel and abusive toward his wife. The Ottos were an old-time and well-known local family and some Key Westers clam up about this aspect of the Ottos' life. But other people do not. William Reuter and his wife, Myrt, bought the house and lived in it for a few years, and they had considerable contact with the Ottos.

"What was Gene like?" I asked Reuter.

"Well, he was an artist."

"What was his disposition like?"

"Not too good."

"He was supposed to have been very cruel to Ann. Is that true?"

"Well, in the last few years, yes."

Gene died in 1974. Ann went back to Massachusetts, where she died two years later and where she is buried.

But the most fascinating character in the tales of this

house is Robert. Robert is not human; he is a doll the size of a child.

"Gene had a doll that people said was haunted," is the way William Reuter puts it. "It was made as an effigy of him when he was a five-year-old boy. That was the style around 1903 or 1904. It was his doll. It was supposed to have some magical property."

"What do you think about that?" I asked.

"A lot of people feel that way about it," Reuter replied. "It didn't give us any magic, plus or minus."

The Reuters are now divorced and no longer live at the Artist House. Myrt Reuter has the doll, which was given to her by Ann Otto. "Everybody says it's voodoo," Myrt told me, "but I've never had any trouble with the doll."

Nancy Tazwell, who bought the house from the Reuters, told me, "That's what Myrt would say. She's a real down-to-earth woman."

But Key West has never been accused of being excessively down-to-earth. Tom Hambright, a local historian, told me, "A lot of Key Westers are very much into what is something of a combination of voodoo and Catholicism. It's practiced quite heavily, particularly in Miami, but also here. There's a Cuban influence but it's practiced by people of all sorts. The doll that Gene Otto had was supposed to be something like his alter ego."

"The story I heard," Nancy Tazwell said, "was that Gene Otto had a doll when he was a little boy that was his mirror image. It was supposedly made to look like Gene. It wore the same clothes. I've seen it. It had several outfits, supposedly the same outfits that Gene had when he was a little boy.

"All the bad things that Gene did were blamed on the doll, so that the doll took on all the kind of negative karma of Gene as he was growing up. He was the bad doll.

So that later on when things happened in the house it was supposedly the spirit of the doll. Gene would always say he hadn't done it, the doll had done it. Everything that was negative was put onto the doll."

Many tales are told of the doll, and some go back to when Gene Otto was alive. Some of them are rather outlandish, folklorish. An article in a Key West newspaper, *Island Life*, tells of a plumber who heard the doll giggle, and who found it sitting in different spots when no one had moved it. Other people have also told of the doll's moving.

Nancy Tazwell felt there was an energy in the house, and that it was centered in the cupola. "It's my understanding," she said, "that this was where the doll was kept. The cupola was Gene Otto's place in the house when he was a child and later on it was his studio. When I would walk up the steps there would sometimes be like a cold wind, and the windows would shake as though there were a storm going on. I didn't find it frightening. I would say things like, 'Don't worry, I am a friendly spirit.' I wish now I had been more aware. It seems that I was always so busy rushing around that I didn't take very much time to experience the sensations of the house."

However, some guests in the house have noticed sensations. Ed Cox, the present owner, says:

> I had a couple who stayed up in the front bedroom and the woman came down and said the house is haunted, and the more you go up that staircase the worse it is. She was a German girl, and she was terrified. Her husband didn't notice anything at all. And there have been other guests who have spoken about things.
>
> The boys who lived here before me said that pictures would come off the wall and smash on the floor. Doors would lock up on them and they couldn't get out. Nothing like that has happened to me, and I've been here two years now. I did have one strange thing.

The door of a bookcase flew open. It's never happened since, but that door winged right out in front of me, and that was kind of odd.

The Ottos had separate bedrooms. She had the back room on the second floor, where I now stay. He had the front room on the second floor. I've brought a lot of Gene Otto's artwork back into the house. I've got a picture of her hanging in his room.

You know, there's a strange religion down here like a sort of voodoo. Eugene being an artist, I think he probably experimented with these things. Local people won't talk much about this, so I haven't gotten many answers.

I asked Myrt Reuter what the doll looked like, and she said:

It's a large doll, as big as a child. I don't know if it was made in the image of Gene, because I never knew him as a child. It has hair on it like a real child. It has buttons for eyes. It has different kinds of clothes. It was in a pixie outfit when I got it, but they were termiting so I put Gene's little sailor suit on him. I had a sailor suit that was left there in a cedar chest. I dress him in that, and at Christmas Eve I used to put him in pajamas and set him by the Christmas tree. A neighbor told me that Ann told him that whenever Gene did anything mean or hateful he always blamed it on the doll.

People around Key West don't like the doll. They believe in voodoo, and they don't want to come in contact with it. But it does not bother me, and I've never had any problems.

Myrt told me about an article that appeared in a Key West weekly paper, *Solares Hill*, about the doll, a few years ago. I tried to get a copy of the story but was unsuccessful, so we'll have to go with Myrt's version of it:

We went up north for the summer one year, and we left a man who was studying to be a lawyer to live in the house while we were gone. He wrote this fantastic story that the doll was voodoo and it locked him up in the attic and he caught yellow fever. I don't remember his name. To me, he was some kind of a nut.

The doll's name was Robert. It's not clear who gave him the name—possibly little Gene. Gene's full name was Robert Eugene Otto.

I came across two versions of how the doll came into Gene's life.

One story is that his great-grandfather, Dr. Joseph Otto, went to Fort Jefferson, about sixteen miles off Key West, to help fight a yellow fever epidemic, and on the boat met a man who made such dolls, and had one made for little Gene. The problem with that story is that Dr. Joseph, according to the research and memories of people I spoke with, seems to have died some years before Gene was born. An alternate donor might be Gene's father, also named Eugene. However, Thomas Otto III, a nephew, told me that the elder Eugene was a pharmacist, not a physician, so it would be unlikely that he had gone off to fight an epidemic. However, other people said that at that time pharmacists did practice medicine to some extent.

The other story is that a black girl who was somehow connected with the house had given the doll to little Gene.

While I was researching this chapter, I went to a party given by a group of dowsers. Dowsing is basically a method of releasing one's psychic powers. There were two well-known psychics at the party, so I asked them what they thought of the doll.

One was Enid Hoffman, now of Bradenton, Florida. She has written a number of books on the psychic, including one on Huna, the Hawaiian mystical tradition.

"It could be," Enid said, "what the Hawaiians call Mana. Mana is creative intelligence. It carries ideas, qualities, and intentions. It can be stored in certain things— wood and silk in particular. Or water. Mana goes where your focus goes. It flows in ways that are hard for us to understand. The doll has possibly infected the atmosphere of the house."

The other psychic is Carl Carpenter of Penacook, New Hampshire, who specializes in hypnotism and healing. He told me of something that had happened to him.

I had a small statue on my front lawn. I had taken it out of a house in Manchester because there had been a lot of negative energy in the house. The statue had been noticed by a psychic person behind the furnace, so I took it out of the house and put it on my lawn.

Three years ago I was at the national dowsers convention at Danville, Vermont, and there was a fellow who was dowsing people's property from maps and drawings. He pointed to the outline of my place that I had drawn, and he said, "There's something negative right there." And he pointed right to where that thing was.

What I'm assuming is that whoever made that statue pounded it out of rock, and got his anger out into that rock. You can put energy into an object and the thought form of that energy will affect people. Thought forms are energy fields that have a physical existence.

To turn from eerie, bizarre Robert the Doll to a relatively mundane human spiritual entity may seem something of a letdown, but we cannot neglect the positive energy that Poochie Myers felt in the second floor back, which she attributes to Ann Otto. Other people have reported a similar awareness. One is Susan Olsen, a local historian, who said, "I've heard about the house being haunted from the people who painted the building when Nancy Tazwell restored it. I think it's haunted by the wife of Gene Otto. They said they heard crying all the time. Apparently she was very unhappy."

I contacted one of the painters, Alec Harvey, who denied hearing crying. But he said, "I just had this omnipresent sort of feeling of misery and evil. I don't often say that about places, but that place was odd. There's something there for sure."

History: The first member of the Otto family to come to America was Dr. Joseph Otto, who fled his native Prussia during the rebellions of 1848. He was a contract physician for the Union Army during the Civil War, and later came to Key West. His son, Thomas Otto, built the house, probably around 1890. Gene Otto died in 1974. His wife, Ann, went back to her family home in Massachusetts and died there two years later. Since then several people have owned the house and operated it as a bed and breakfast.

Identities of Ghosts: There is the conjecture that negative energy is being radiated from Robert, Gene's doll. This energy seems concentrated in the upstairs front of the house, particularly in the cupola.

People have also reported a positive energy, possibly that of Ann Otto, in the second floor back.

Poochie Myers spoke of repeatedly sensing the spirit of a five-year-old girl sitting on the back staircase. No one I spoke with, including Thomas Otto III, a marine engineer who lives in Miami and who has often visited the house, had any recollection of the death of a young girl in the house. However, Ed Cox, who has made a study of the history of the house and the Otto family, told me that in the Otto plot in the city cemetery there is a small grave identified as that of the daughter of E. O. and R. R. Locke, who died in 1893 at the age of ten months. The present Thomas Otto told me that there was a "Locke connection," that a Locke had married into a branch of the Otto family. It has been said that sometimes when children die they remain close to the physical plane and mature.

Personalities of Ghosts: The supposed energy of Robert the Doll seems negative. The energy of Ann Otto seems unhappy, but warm and loving. Poochie Myers says the little girl is angry.

Witnesses: Poochie Myers, house sitter; Nancy Tazwell, former owner; William Reuter, former owner; Myrtle Reuter, former owner; Ed Cox, present owner; Addie Lamberson, grounds keeper at the city cemetery; Alec Harvey, painter and decorator. More than once I was told of friends and neighbors who had had experiences in the house, but when I questioned them they denied everything.

Best Time to Witness: Most of the reported incidents seem to have happened during the day or evening, when people were up and about.

Still Haunted?: Most of the reports have been fairly recent.

Investigations: There were no reports of formal inquiries, but there seem to have been plenty of informal ones. The house is known as a haunted place—a sight-seeing bus goes by the place and the Artist House is pointed out to tourists—so occasionally those inclined may come back for a look. "A lot of people come in who don't identify themselves as psychic," Ed Cox told me.

Nancy Tazwell said, "I had a woman come to the

house and ask to be shown around. She said she was interested in old houses. She said she wanted to go through the house and feel the energy. When we got to the back part of the house, where Ann had lived, the hair on her arms was standing straight up, and she was quite struck with the sensation she had of a presence. She told me she had been involved in exorcisms. I have no idea what her name was."

Data Submitted By: In addition to the above-named witnesses: Enid Hoffman, psychic; Carl Carpenter, psychic; Sharon Wells, historian and occasional helper to Nancy Tazwell at the Artist House; Frank Taylor, publisher of the *Solares Hill* newspaper; Peggy Hicks, neighbor; Bill Gieser, neighbor; Susan Olsen, historian; Tom Hambright, historian; Thomas Otto III, nephew of Gene Otto.

Willard Library, about 1890.

6
The Lady Who Haunts
the Library
She's Been Known to Go Home with
Her Favorite Librarian

Location: The Willard Library is at 21 First Avenue in Evansville, Indiana. Evansville, a city with a population of 136,000, is in the southwest corner of Indiana, across the Wabash River from Kentucky. It's about one hundred miles west of Louisville and 160 miles east of St. Louis, by way of Route 64.

Description of Place: The Willard Library was built in 1885 and is touted by locals as the oldest library in Indiana that is still open to the public. It's on the National Register of Historic Places. It's a privately endowed library, helped by grants.

Don Baker, former librarian, described the architecture as Italianate Gothic, a tall, two-story brick building with stone trim. "There's a large tower on one corner," he said. "You feel it ought to be a clock tower or a bell tower, but it's not, it's decorative, the standard Victorian corner tower. The ceilings are high and the windows are large. It was originally lit by kerosene."

Ghostly Manifestations: This is the sort of case that comes as a relief to the weary ghost hunter. There is no beating the bushes for witnesses, many of whom saw nothing, heard nothing, smelled nothing. Most of the people who work or once worked at the Willard have either seen, heard, or smelled this ghost. In fact, a few years ago, the Governor of Indiana presided over, to quote from the invi-

---

Governor and Mrs. Robert D. Orr

on behalf of

the Trustees and Friends of Willard Library

request the pleasure of your company

at a High-Spirited Dinner Dance

to celebrate the Library's 100th year and

in honour of its Resident Spirit,

The Lady in Gray

Friday, the eighteenth of October

nineteen hundred eighty five

seven o'clock in the evening

at Willard Library

$25.00 per person	Black Tie
Spirits available at cash bar	(Long Gray Veil Optional)
Reservations limited to 250	Valet Parking
Music by the Temple Airs	

---

tation, "a High Spirited Dinner Dance to celebrate the Library's one hundredth year and in honour of its Resident Spirit, The Lady in Gray."

My first interviewee at the Willard was Anita Glover, a children's librarian. She told me about the ghost's favorite librarian, Margaret Maier, who in 1989 relinquished this dimension herself after fifty years at the library. "There was another long-term staff employee named Helen Kamm," Anita said, "who is also now dead. They both believed in this ghost. They told me they would be sitting in the children's room and they could see this . . . whatever it was. One time Miss Margaret told me she came in from lunch and Miss Helen had the doors to the children's room locked. 'She's down here, I saw her,' Miss Helen said. Miss Margaret said, 'Well, locking the doors isn't going to keep her out if she wants to come in.' It went on like that."

Anita had some tales of her own. "In 1980," she said, "the room was remodeled and we had monitors put in so we could see the hall outside. One day I was sitting at the desk and I happened to glance at the monitors. There was something in one of them. I couldn't tell if it was a man or a woman, it was just a mass. It was moving. We have four monitors; first it was in one and then in another. Then after three or four minutes it went away."

"Did you go out in the hall and check?" I asked.

"NO!" she exclaimed.

"And then there's this perfume," she went on. "One Saturday morning I was working by myself, and every once in a while I'd get this whiff of perfume. It'd be there and then it would go away, and then it would be back again.

"When they were remodeling here in the basement it was very noisy. One morning, Miss Margaret came in and said, 'I've taken the ghost home.' I asked, 'Why would you say that?' She said, 'It's just that some of the oddest things are happening.' She and her sister, Ruth—they never married and they lived together—they had various things happen, and they could smell that perfume in the house."

I called Ruth Maier and got an enthusiastic response.

I'm glad to help, because my sister always loved telling about the ghost. Margaret would see something, but she never saw the form definitely until they started remodeling the children's room in the basement and the ghost came to our house for a while.

Margaret went there in 1939, and one of the janitors had seen it shortly before that. He would encounter it when he went to the library in the middle of the night to stoke the furnace. He was so frightened that when he went there he would take one or two of his children with him. He finally quit.

They got another janitor, and he too quit because of the ghost. He said he bumped into it, and then it was gone. He described the ghost as a lady in gray, with a gray veil and a gray hat. He said it was often there.

While they were remodeling, nobody saw the ghost at the library. One evening my sister and I were sitting in our living room and she said to me, "Boy, whoever that was who just went down the street had a lot of perfume." I said, "Yes, I smell it too." We each had wondered if the other was wearing it; sometimes in a store they'll spray it on you. But it was just invasive, it was all over. We laughed and decided the ghost had come home with Margaret because of the dust and noise of the remodeling. Margaret was her best friend.

Another evening we were sitting in the living room watching TV and we heard the static ball going around in our dryer. We went and looked and found it had been set on sixty minutes. Neither of us had set it, and there was no one else in the house.

One Saturday morning I was here in the house and one of my nephews was with me. He was a teenager at the time. I put him in the dining room and went back into the kitchen. When I came back, he said, "What were you doing in there? I thought you went upstairs." Then he thought a minute and said, "But those were high-topped shoes I saw. I just saw somebody going up the stairs. But those weren't your shoes at all."

It was when the ghost was with us that Margaret got her first clear sighting of her. We had come into the house from the back and Margaret said, "Ruth, I saw something down the hall." Then she said, "Oh it's just the lady in gray." She said there was no veil but she had a long gray dress and button-top shoes. Margaret followed her down the hall but by the time she got into the living room the form was no longer there.

She was only here for a period of three or four months. Margaret was never upset. She always talked kindly about the ghost. After the remodeling was over the ghost went back to the library, and was seen around there again.

We had parties in the children's room, and one time a mother brought a child of three. He wouldn't stay with his mother, he was all over the library. All at once, the child ran from the front hall outside and into the parking lot, and he was crying. Several of us ran after him, but he wouldn't come back in because he said he had seen a ghost. The mother said she had never discussed ghosts with him. The only ghost he had ever heard of might have been Caspar the Ghost. When we got him back in, he wouldn't let go of his mother. He sat in her lap. He had seen a ghost.

For a while there was a group of women who met in a room on the top floor of the library. This was about ten years ago. There was a door at the south end of the room. One time it opened, and there was nobody there. Then it closed. No group has wanted to meet there since.

Women from a church would use the microfilm on the third floor on Mondays when the library was closed. One day one of them came downstairs and said to Mr. Baker that there was a perfume smell up there. They wondered if something was leaking.

A few years ago the library ran out of space for its sale books. A plastics company granted the library some space in their warehouse across the street, so

they put some books in that building. The books were
in boxes. The report to the library was that someone
over there had seen the ghost near the books. The
employee didn't want to work at night after that. There
were other reports that this figure was seen in that
area. There were several sightings.

Frank Chandler, a genealogist at the library, takes the
ghost in stride. In fact, as far as he's concerned, it's much
ado about nothing.

Ghosts are really very boring. They don't *do* anything.
They just stand there. I've seen her a couple of times.
All of a sudden, there it is. Then it spots you, and it
just vanishes. It doesn't "poof" disappear, it like retreats
very quickly, goes around a corner. It's no shape at all.
It looks like a lot of black, chiffon handkerchiefs hanging in the air.

You're doing a book on this? Oh God, that means
more people will call.

They used to see her all the time in the basement.
They remodeled the basement, so then she came up
here, on the second floor. And then she was back in the
stacks.

She's pulled a few tricks. She turned on all the
lights one night. She turned on water faucets a couple
of times. The only one who ever ran into her face-to-
face was the head of our department, Joan Elliott. She
ran into her when she turned a corner downstairs.

I'm so bored with that ghost.

Joan Elliott Parker, special collections librarian, told
me that she did indeed run into the ghost. "I always read on
a break," she told me, "so I had my head in a book and I was
going to the staff room in the basement. I was just walking
into the room with my head down when I felt I was going
to run into someone. I looked up and had a clear impres-

sion of a lady in gray. I thought, 'Wait a minute, this can't be.' I just kind of closed my eyes and looked away, and when I looked back there was nothing. It was just for a second, but it was just as real as though she were standing in front of me. I always thought it would be frightening to see a ghost, but it was not frightening at all, which surprised me."

Joan had another eerie experience, the prototypical case of the ghost in the bathroom, fooling around with the water faucets. "I was in the bathroom downstairs," she told me. "This was back in the late seventies, before they did the remodeling. The door was locked, and while I was in the stall I heard the water start running. When I came out, it was still running. And those old-fashioned taps weren't easy to turn on or off."

(See the Spy House haunting—Chapter 18—for some more-or-less educated guesses on why spirits like water, and why they so often turn it on in bathrooms.)

Betty Miller Faba, retired head librarian, gave me another water story. "The library is closed on Monday," she said, "but I frequently worked then, and I'd be alone in the building. Once I heard water running upstairs. Then it turned off. It only did it the one time. I went upstairs, and nobody was there. I'll tell you, it was a spooky building to be alone in."

"I've never seen the ghost," said Don Baker, who was head of the library from 1976 to 1989. "I never heard the ghost, never felt the ghost, never smelled the ghost. So I'm no expert on the ghost. But ghost lore is rampant. I've heard about mysterious footsteps, water turned on—all that sort of thing. But nothing ever jumped out and said 'Boo!' to me.

"But I used to give talks to groups, and one time I asked for questions and a woman asked, how about the

Rachel Yokel

The Willard Library.

ghost? So I told some of the stories. At that time there hadn't been a lot of publicity about the ghost, so later on I asked her how she had known about the ghost. She said when she was a little girl she went to the library and saw it."

History: The library was built in 1885 by a prominent local businessman named Willard Carpenter. The story of the ghost did not gain currency, it appears, until the mid-1930s, when a janitor resigned after constantly encountering the apparition of a lady dressed in gray when he arrived to stoke the furnace in the basement in the dead of night. The ghost's dress indicates she goes back well into the 1800s, but Don Baker says, "Maybe it took that long for people to take notice of it and begin to talk about it."

Identity of Ghost: For half a century, some staffers at the library speculated that the ghost might be Louise Carpenter, one of Willard's daughters, who felt the library had been given money that should rightfully have been hers. She had sued the library and lost on both the local and appeals level. She must have been a pretty disgruntled lady.

But other staffers, although they had no definite candidate, did not feel it was Louise Carpenter who was haunting the place. Margaret Maier, for example, felt the ghost was too nice, that Louise would have been a troublesome, vindictive spirit.

Don Baker agrees. He said, "I think Louise would be just terrible if she were around, because she did lose her case." He had another reason for believing that the ghost was not Louise. He felt that the dress of the ghost did not fit the period when Louise was living, particularly when her lawsuit was being tried, in the 1890s. The high-button shoes and shorter skirt seemed to predate that time, Baker felt.

Then one evening in 1985 an itinerant psychic made a very public inspection of the library in search of the ghost. She was Lucille Warren of Monroe, Connecticut, who with her husband, Ed, tours the country giving talks on parapsychology. The Warrens had been appearing in Evanstown for the Students Association at the University of Southern Illinois.

Don Baker gave me this account of the evening:

They showed up about ten in the evening, with about fifty students, and a lot of our staff was also there. Mrs. Warren wandered down to the children's room and said she did indeed see something there, but she couldn't communicate with it. It wouldn't talk with her. She proceeded to describe the ghost. She said the woman's

clothing looked early nineteenth century. She described the hair, that it was split in the middle and
braided down the back. I had heard that the ghost
always wore a veil and a hat, and I thought, Ah, I have
her, because in the stories I had heard no one had ever
seen the ghost's hair. Margaret had become separated
from the group and was about two rooms away, so I
called her and asked if anyone had ever seen the ghost
without a veil on her head. And she said, "Oh yes, it
doesn't have a veil, it has a shawl." And she proceeded
to describe the hair in the same way Mrs. Warren had.

Mrs. Warren said she did not see the ghost in a
building at all, but in an open meadow, staring down
into a pool of water. The site of the building was indeed
once an open meadow, originally called Carpenter's
Field. Mrs. Warren indicated that the ghost was not
haunting the building at all, it was haunting the preex-
isting property. And that the spirit was somewhat confused by the fact that it could sense a building had
been built around it but couldn't understand what was
going on. There is still no clue as to who the ghost is.

I spoke with Lucille Warren, and she said she couldn't
remember much of the details, except that she felt the
ghost had drowned, possibly as a suicide.

Could the ghost have drowned in the pool of water
into which Lucille saw her staring? Baker said there is a
canal near the library and there is some conjecture the
woman might have drowned in the canal.

Personality of Ghost: She seems shy, confused, harmless.

Witnesses: Anita Glover, assistant children's librarian;
Margaret Maier, head children's librarian (deceased); Ruth
Maier, Margaret's sister; Helen Kamm, children's librarian

(deceased); Joan Elliott Parker, special collections librarian; Frank Chandler, genealogist at library; Betty Miller Faba, former head librarian; Don Baker, former head librarian; two custodians in the mid-1930s, and some children of one of them; a little boy visiting the library with his mother; a woman who saw the ghost as a child; the women who saw the opening and closing door; the women who smelled perfume; a nephew of Ruth and Margaret Maier who prefers to maintain a low profile. Lucille Warren, psychic.

Best Time to Witness: The spirit seemed to roam both day and night.

Still Haunted?: Frank Chandler thinks the ghost hasn't been around for the past three or four years, but then he found her boring, anyway. "I'm so glad she left," he said.

Investigations: The Warrens' visit was the only psychic inquiry reported.

Data Submitted By: Anita Glover, Ruth Maier, Frank Chandler, Don Baker, Joan Elliot Parker, Betty Miller Faba, Lucille Warren. Material from the *Evansville Courier & Press*.

7
The Haunted World War II Airplane Hangar
They Say It's the Spirit of a Young Navy Pilot Who Crashed There

Location: Hangar 43, situated at what is now the Johnson County Industrial Airport, is about eight miles southwest of Olathe, Kansas, a city just southwest of Kansas City. The airport is on Interstate Highway 35.

Description of Place: The airport, built as a World War II Navy flight training base, is in a largely unpopulated area. Tina Volek, a public relations person for Johnson County, said, "We're turning the airport into an industrial park, so a lot of the old buildings that were neglected before we took it over are being replaced by more modern buildings. Some hangars out there are still in use by local National Guard units. It's a county facility, but they use some of the space."

Hangar 43 is something of a historical structure according to Tom Hampton, a retired aviation mechanic who has worked there off and on since 1943. "There were three hangars like this put up here during World War II, and this is the only one left," he said. "Those wooden hangars had two hundred-foot bays, one on each side. They were the largest wooden structures that had ever been built. Forty-three is going to be completely renovated."

John Nave, who is gathering materials for a naval museum at the old base, said, "It's one of the last hangars built for World War II that is still standing. It's in pretty bad shape right now. It's going to take about $200,000 to renovate."

It is currently used to house army helicopters and, as Nave says, "The county park's snow plows and so on in it."

Ghostly Manifestations: It is a documented fact that a young navy pilot, flying a training plane, crashed into the administration building of the then navy air base, early during the Cold War. Just who he was has been lost in the mists of time and military paperwork. He did not belong to the base and the plane was in transit when it crashed, so there was no reason for people connected to the base to keep any special record of the unfortunate pilot's name.

But gradually it began to seem that someone had settled in at Hangar 43—and before long folk wisdom settled on this particular young navy pilot. Quite convincing ghostly manifestations have been observed for some years now in the cavernous old structure. If it isn't the navy pilot, *somebody* certainly seems to be haunting the place.

The ghost is usually called the Commander, the navy equivalent to an air force colonel. The pilot was only a lieutenant when he died, but his groupies have promoted him regularly as time goes on. It's only fair, they feel. He wouldn't be a lieutenant now if he had stayed in the navy, and he certainly seems to be staying in, on his own terms.

If you visit Hangar 43, you'll find plenty of people with stories of the ghost—Al Pennington, for example, who's been a civilian airplane mechanic there for thirteen years.

Don Delphia, *Kansas City Business Journal*

Al Pennington hangs in there.

"If anyone had told me that some day I'd believe in ghosts, I'd have told 'em they're full of crap," he said. "But I know the Commander's still here. I hear him knocking. He closes doors on you, right in front of your face. We have a catwalk up there and you can hear him walking around it and whistling.

"When I first took a job here, I slept in this hangar for six months. I lived right in here till my wife moved here from Woodson and we got a house. I had plenty of experiences with him then. One night I went upstairs, had to go to the bathroom, and the door of the bathroom wouldn't open up. The guys don't believe that, but it's true."

I asked if he ever got in.

"Yes, about half an hour later," he said, "I guess he took pity on me. I never believed in ghosts, but I do now."

I first heard of the ghost of Hangar 43 when a friend who lives in Kansas sent me a feature story from a rather unlikely publication, the *Kansas City Business Journal*. In his story, reporter Tom Bassing quoted a civilian employee who asked that his name not be printed: "I don't want anyone to know I believe in ghosts, but this hangar is definitely haunted."

When I called there, I may have reached the same guy. He said he had had experiences but didn't want to talk about them. However, he was cooperative enough to put me in touch with someone who would talk for the record—Norman Weaver, who has been a quality control inspector at the hangar for eighteen years. Weaver said:

> There have been a lot of things. One that sticks out in my mind was when we were playing cards on our break time. I had a coffee cup setting on the table. There was no rowdiness, and nobody was sitting near the cup, but all of a sudden the coffee cup just turned upside down. There was about half a cup of coffee in it, and it went all over the table.
>
> We've got a catwalk that goes around the hangar and you'd hear footsteps up on that catwalk. I've gone up and looked and there was nobody there. But you could still hear the footsteps going up and down it.
>
> One time there was nobody in the hangar—this was about one or two in the morning. I was sitting in what we call the watch room, and all of a sudden a door opened. Not one of the big hangar doors but one of the walk-through doors. I could hear whistling. I thought, there's somebody coming in, I'd better check and see who it is. I walked out into the hangar to where that door was and there was nobody there. But you could hear that whistling going from one side of the hangar to the other, as though somebody was walking back and forth. I'd heard these stories about the flier who was killed out here, and I thought it must be him. I just kind of shook it off.
>
> Another time, this was in the middle of an after-

noon, I had gone into the restroom to wash my hands.
I turned the faucet off and walked back out. I remembered that I'd left a coffee cup in there, so I walked back
in—it hadn't been two minutes—and the faucet was
back on again. I know I had turned that faucet off. And
there was nobody around.

Another witness is Olivario Rico, who has worked in
Hangar 43 since the mid-1970s. He is employed as an
aircraft mechanic, and until 1989 he also worked part-time
at night as supervisor of the security guards. He told me:

You constantly hear unexplained noises, basically footsteps and there's nobody there, doors closing and opening and there's nobody there and no wind draft. Stuff
like that.

There's one passage that, after I'd gone through it,
I'd hear a door close behind me. I'd go back and look,
and the door would still be standing wide open. We
have a catwalk that goes all around the hangar, and the
only time it will move is when somebody is on it. But it
will vibrate every once in a while like somebody is
walking around it, and there's no one there. The wind,
as such, cannot do that.

One night my wife and daughter were here and
there were very definite, distinct footsteps upstairs on
the second level. We all heard these footsteps. I went
upstairs and checked everything out and there was
nobody there. But the whole family heard these footsteps, like somebody pacing back and forth from one
side of the place to the other.

Rico was the only person to tell me about an apparition, and although the report is essentially thirdhand it
has a ring of truth about it. "One of the security guards,"
Rico said, "he's no longer here, he went on to a higher-
paying job, told me this after we had had some visitors stay

overnight. We used to have transit quarters here, although we don't anymore. Supposedly, in the early morning hours, about one or two o'clock, the visitors heard somebody walking down the hallway. So one guy got up and looked out, and he saw what he described as a person dressed in white, like a military uniform. He asked the security guard in the morning if some more visitors had come in. He said the figure was heading down the hallway toward the latrine. But the building had been locked up after duty hours."

Identity of Ghosts: The legend of Hangar 43 seems to take it for granted that the ghost is the young navy pilot. As I progressed with my research and found nobody, except the overnight visitor, who claimed to have actually seen anything, I began to wonder why they were so sure the ghost is that pilot. Tom Hampton gave me some food for thought.

Hampton began work at Hangar 43 in 1943, and worked there off and on for many years. He helped clean up the wreckage when the pilot crashed into the administration building. Hampton said he has never had any strange experiences in the hangar. "I don't believe that stuff until it's proven to me," he said. But he had some other interesting observations.

"I helped clean up the wreckage of that training plane that hit the building," he said. "I was home when it happened and came in to work the next morning. It was still foggy."

Although Hampton is not sure there is *any* ghost, if there is one he too wonders why it must be the pilot. "He ran into the administration building," he said. "That building is about three blocks north of Hangar 43, and there's a fuel dump and another big hangar in between it and 43."

I asked if the plane had been housed in 43.

"No," he said, "it wasn't one of ours, it was a transit plane. It was in transit."

Hampton had another intriguing bit of information to offer. "He had a hitchhiker in the rear seat," he said. "I think he was an army man, but I don't remember. He was killed too."

So why couldn't it be the passenger? Or somebody else?

"I know of two people who have been killed in Hangar 43 by falling from the overhead while they were doing maintenance," Hampton said. "One of them I saw fall. In fact, I was working on the plane that he hit the nose of, and fell off onto the ground. He was a civilian."

Hampton also pointed out that there were many plane crashes during the base's time as a training facility. According to navy records, there were thirty-two fatalities.

If it *is* the navy pilot who hit the administration building haunting Hangar 43, I wondered if it would be worthwhile to try to dig out his identity from the military records. John Nave had told reporter Tom Bassing that the records had been taken to a navy air station in Tennessee. I told Bassing I was thinking of making a slight effort to check out who the pilot was.

"I made a *hell* of an effort," he said, "and flat out it's going to be impossible to find out who the guy was. They had lousy record keeping back then. They moved all the stuff, and the stuff just got dispersed and lost. You know how the military is. This was precomputer and a lot of it just got thrown in boxes and it's somewhere and no one knows where."

History: The original field, the U.S. Naval Reserve Air Base, Olathe, Kansas, was commissioned in 1942. Approximately forty-five hundred naval cadets trained there during World War II. The area is currently part of the Johnson County Industrial Airport.

Personalities of Ghosts: Whoever he, or they, may be, there's no trouble being caused, aside from the slight scary factor.

Witnesses: Al Pennington, aircraft mechanic; Norman Weaver, quality control inspector; Tom Hampton, retired aircraft mechanic; Olivario Rico, aircraft mechanic and former security supervisor. Two employees who wished to remain unidentified.

Best Time to Witness: Apparently day or night.

Still Haunted?: Seems to be.

Investigations: No record of any formal psychic inquiries.

Data Submitted By: The above-named witnesses, plus Tina Volek, Johnson County spokesperson; Tom Bassing, *Kansas City Business Journal* reporter; John Nave, curator of projected naval museum. Article in *Kansas City Business Journal*, October 29, 1990. History of U.S. Naval Air Station, Olathe, Kansas. Tip from Scott Idlet of Lenexa, Kansas.

8
Are There Ghosts in Famous Mammoth Cave?
If There Aren't, a Lot of People Are Hallucinating

Location: Mammoth Cave National Park is in the south-central part of Kentucky. Via Route 65, the park is about twenty miles northeast of Bowling Green and about seventy-five miles southwest of Louisville.

Description of Place: Mammoth Cave is the largest cave in the world, with 330 miles of passageways on five levels. Some of its caverns are two-hundred feet wide and almost that high. Although Mammoth is the best-known cave in this national park, there are a number of others, which are not currently open to the general public. Some two million tourists visit the park each year. Hotel and other lodgings are available, as well as campgrounds. The park employs some two hundred full-time and seasonal guides and other staff.

Mammoth Cave contains various types of exotic wildlife, some eyeless and colorless—although their names are colorful—the Rough Pig Toe Mussel, the Spectacle Case

National Park Service

A large cave passageway.

Mussel, and the Cracking Pearly Mussel, for example. Plus an undetermined number of ghosts, some named, others not.

Ghostly Manifestations: I spoke with about twenty-five people who have worked in the various caves in the park, and by now can divide my interviewees into distinct categories:

1. The nonbelievers, just on the principle of the thing
2. The good old boys, who aren't likely to tell much, if anything, to a carpetbagger from Boston
3. The younger, well-educated guides who are eager to communicate whatever they've heard or experienced themselves
4. The high-powered scientists, most of them with doctorates in geology or other earth sciences, who are professors at universities and who surprised me with some of the most striking and believable accounts of all. To quote one member of this persuasion, "We're a bunch of hard-nosed people. Most of us who have had these experiences are essentially not believers in ghosts; we just describe the facts as we know them and let others conclude."

So as they say in show business, let's take 'em from the top.

Becky Dahle, a supervisor of guides at Mammoth Cave, put the no-ghost case well:

> I really don't agree with the precept that it's haunted. I'm afraid that a lot of the stories that are circulating are based on fictional accounts from the past. Like the gal who murdered her boyfriend, that's a completely fictional account. Once a story like that gets circulating among the guide force, people start thinking they've experienced things. If there ever was a place under the earth where people's imaginations could play tricks on them, it's Mammoth Cave. It's a deprivational thing. There's no natural light, no natural sound. We have a huge guide force, well over one hundred people, and it's almost a fad, there's a ripple effect, a funny-thing-happened-on-the-way-to-the-cave sort of thing.

Jim Norris, a retired science teacher and a part-time guide, said, "I'm a scientist. I've had some unusual experiences, but I write them off as bad ideas on my part."

Bill Ritter, a school principal and summer guide for eighteen years: "I think it's mostly imagination. When you walk through the darkness of the caves you can't help but think of these things. It's easy to begin to hallucinate."

Shorty Coates, an old-time guide, now retired, gave me short shrift. I was told he had all sorts of stories, but it seemed he wasn't giving me any. "I've never seen ghosts," he said, "never heard noises or anything like that, and I don't know anyone who has. I knew a man who lived in the cave for twelve years; if there had been haunts in the cave he'd had heard them."

An old-timer who was a bit more forthcoming was Lewis Cutliss. Cutliss's story was told me by a number of people and is standard fare at the park. I'm not sure it's such a great story, but here it is, direct from Lewis:

> My daddy, Lyman Cutliss, he and Grover Campbell had worked in that section of the cave. Grover was looking for mummies and artifacts. He found some mummified bats. They went to look around the back side of a big boulder. Grover asked my daddy, "What is that?" And my daddy said, "That's a skull, of a human mummy." It was an Indian man. This five-ton boulder had fallen on him. They worked on removing the big boulder. They had to stay down there at night to guard the mummy. During this time, they were exploring nearby, and about a quarter of a mile away they found a hole. They put their hands down in the hole, and they heard three knocks, like a rock hitting on another rock. Down in the hole, all they could feel was something real fine, like pumice stone.
>
> Three years after that, Grover Campbell died. Six years later, Daddy lost his job. In thirty years, my sister

had heart surgery, and three years later, thirty-three years from the time of the knocking, she died. My daddy always felt it was strange that these things came in series of three."

Joy Lyons, a guide at the cave for the past twelve years, told me, "That's what we call 'the Three Knocks Story.' It's a traditional story that we tell here sometimes, especially on Halloween."

Maybe Lewis Cutliss has something there, but actually, I like Joy's own stories better. She told me of conducting a group of tourists with two other park rangers and pausing at a place in the big cave called the Church. "Traditionally," she said, "we do a blackout there and have a sensory experience." This time, she had more of a sensory experience than she bargained for.

"The lead ranger, Red Langley, called for the lights to be turned out, and we did that. We were standing there quietly and Red was rambling on in the darkness, and I felt this strong shove on my right shoulder, strong enough so that I had to put my leg forward to keep from falling over. I said to the other ranger, 'Cut it out.' At that moment, Red lit a lantern and I saw that the other ranger was about seventy feet away from me. There was no way he could have shoved me and then gotten to where he was standing. There was no one near me. It was a very playful shove."

Joy also told me of a startling experience she had above ground at the park.

Chris Handly, who also works here, and I were walking across the bridge from the Visitors Center to the hotel. It was in the late summer, and in a grassy hillside to the right of the bridge I saw two sets of legs, but nothing attached to them. From the thighs down you could see the pants legs and the shoes, but there was nothing above that. The shoes looked like old work boots. They were walking down this little hill. Chris was talking to me and we both stopped our conversation at the same time. I saw it briefly. They moved two or three steps, and then they disappeared. Chris didn't say anything and I didn't. I wasn't going to say anything, but then she said, "Did you see anything?" I said, "Did you see two of them?" She said, "Yeah, two of them." It was like two people walking along, and we both saw it at the same time.

We've had discussions about different planes and times, when you see someone who's lived a hundred years ago and they see you in your time, that kind of situation. There are a number of us who feel things in various parts of the cave. It's not frightening, but it's something else.

A fascinating, firsthand account was told me by Larry Purcell, who is a science teacher at Bowling Green High School and who was a summer guide at Mammoth Cave for many years. The story involves a famous guide of years gone by, Stephen Bishop. Bishop, who was a black man and a slave, began guiding at the cave in 1838. In those days, a number of the guides were slaves. Bishop was the ultimate guide, and produced maps of the cave that are considered accurate today, with all the scientific resources for underground mapping that are now available. He discovered many parts of the cave. At one time, he was offered his freedom, but he refused it because it would mean he would have to go north into nonslavery territory, thus leaving his beloved cave.

Larry Purcell told me of an encounter he had that might indicate that Bishop still has not left. "One time," Purcell said, "I was on a tour and happened to be by myself for a moment as another guide was speaking to the group. The lights were off, and my job was to go and turn them back on. I was walking along and I saw a black man with a

Stephen Bishop,
a famous cave guide.

woman and two children. The man had on white pants, a dark shirt, a white vest, and a white Panama hat. They were real enough so that I walked around them. I went and turned the lights on and there were no people like that there. There were no black people on the trip."

Purcell mentioned that there have been many instances of people in groups asking, who is that person there, and no one is over there. "Too many things happen in the caves that just cannot be explained," Purcell said. "Fifteen years ago I would have thought all this was crazy."

This sentiment is similar to that voiced by Joe McGown, a guide supervisor who has worked in the caves since 1969. Although he was reluctant to go on record concerning specific experiences, he said, "I can tell you this, I came in here a nonbeliever in ghosts, and although I don't believe in them now, I'm not a doubter. I've got a lot more open-minded about the subject as time's gone by."

The apparition story is a distinct genre in the Mammoth Cave mystique. Other examples are a couple told to me by Charlie Hanion, a former guide who is now a writer on environmental subjects. Charlie said:

> We had a lantern tour, and a friend and I were scheduled on the tour. He was leading the tour. You light up the cave with torches. About two-thirds of the way through, you come to a place called Chief City. My friend was giving a talk, and I was standing off to a side. A girl of about fourteen stood up and asked, "Who is that person standing over by the rocks?" I looked and it was about forty feet away. It looked like someone from the turn of the century, with a black and white outfit, with a cummerbund—formal dress, the way people used to dress then when they went on tours.
>
> But the really weird part came the following week when we were on the same tour. We got to the same point, and when the other guide asked if there were any questions, a lady stood up and asked if strange things had been seen in this part of the cave. We wondered if she could be a ranger's wife, who they had put up to asking this question because they knew of the experience we'd had the week before. But it turned out that she was genuine, just a tourist. She said she was psychic and felt things. She asked who the person was standing over there among the rocks, almost in the same spot where we'd seen it before. I didn't see it at all this time.

Perhaps the most celebrated of the apparition stories is that of Melissa, the lovelorn Southern belle, who did to the man who rejected her what no lady should do, but then, as they say, hell hath no fury. . . . The Melissa story has already been referred to—sniffily—by guide supervisor Becky Dahle as "a completely fictional account."

The saga of Melissa burgeoned a few years ago after someone found an old magazine story in some forgotten file. The article, "A Tragedy of the Mammoth Cave," was published in the February 1858 issue of *The Knickerbocker*, a popular magazine of the day. Gary Bremer, a guide who worked at Mammoth Cave for five summers and who now is a park ranger at Indiana Dunes National Park, sent me a copy of the article after having told me of experiences he had had that might involve Melissa. The prose might be described as Victorian droll. The byline is "A New Contributor." The first sentence gives an idea of the flavor:

> For fifteen long years I have carried a dark secret buried in my heart, until it has worn away my life; but now that I am tottering on the brink of the grave, I am impelled to make a confession, which tardy as it is, I hope may render more tranquil my last sad hours."

The "new contributor" is billed as Melissa, who reportedly succumbed to tuberculosis. She—or some imaginative ghost writer—tells how she fell in love with her tutor, a handsome young Yankee from Boston, name of Beverleigh, who rebuffed her in favor of a neighboring planter's daughter. Being a local girl, she was expert in the twists and turns of Mammoth Cave. Through a series of complicated events, she ended up in the cave with Mr. Beverleigh. She conducted him to a place on the Echo River called Purgatory, and then faded off into one of the cave's passageways, leaving poor Beverleigh to find his own way out. He never was seen again. And she never got over her guilt.

There will be a pause while we dry our tears.

But let's not brush off this great story too lightly. Gary Bremer has a few modern riffs on the old melody. He told me:

We were down at the Echo River, a group of four employees, all men. We were in a boat. One fellow had
gone to get another paddle, because we were going to
explore the river a little further. The three of us in the
boat all heard a woman calling out. It wasn't a screaming, it was as though she was looking for someone. We
all looked at each other, wide-eyed.

The next day we asked if anyone had ever had such
an experience. We talked with one of the older guides,
Larry Purcell, and he said, "Well, there's a murder that
was supposed to have happened down there." And he
told us the Melissa story. None of us had heard of the
story before that.

Two summers ago, I took a new employee, Laura
Appler, who had never seen the river, down there. She
suddenly stopped and grabbed onto my shoulder. I
asked her what was wrong, and she insisted nothing.
But when we came out, she asked, "Did you hear a
woman cough down there?" Melissa was supposed to
have died of tuberculosis.

Gary had yet another Melissa experience. "I was walking along the Echo River once," he said, "and heard a sound
over my right shoulder and there was nothing there. It was
a very weak, rustling kind of sound. It happened after I
knew the story, so maybe I'm putting things together, but
it sounded to me like petticoats would sound."

I checked with Laura Appler, now a park ranger at
Chickamaugua, Chattanooga, Military Park, and she gave
me the same account that Gary had. She added that at
various times she has heard garbled voices in the cave, and
that once she heard someone whisper her name.

Some of the most intriguing accounts of strange doings involve not Mammoth Cave but Crystal Cave, about
five miles away in the park. Crystal Cave was owned by a
young man named Floyd Collins. Until well into the twen-

tieth century the various caves were owned by individuals. In the winter of 1925, Collins was exploring nearby Sand Cave and became wedged under a rock overhang sixty feet below the surface. For sixteen days, efforts to free Collins dominated the press. The story was a gigantic media circus, much as the kidnapping of the Lindbergh baby was to be a few years later. Collins was finally cut off from rescuers by a cave-in, and died soon after.

The Collins family buried Floyd in the family plot, but the spirit of American free enterprise then erupted, and the embalmed body was disinterred and displayed in Crystal Cave. Larry Purcell relates:

> The coffin had a glass top and you could go by and look at Floyd. Well, it worked extremely well. In Floyd's life, Crystal Cave had been an economic failure because it was so far back up the ridge. But now people were flocking from all over to see Floyd in Crystal Cave. This didn't go over so well with some of the other cave owners. They broke in one night and stole the body. However, they went to a tavern and got to drinking and told people what they had done, so Floyd was found, minus his left leg, and he was put back in Crystal Cave. He stayed there until a couple of years ago. He's buried now in the Baptist Church cemetery up on Flint Ridge."

Floyd's grisly odyssey was typical of the "cave wars" of the time, when rival owners fought for advantage in the tourist trade. McNeill van Meter, the assistant principal of an area school who was a summer guide for twenty-two years, told me, "This stuff about the cave wars you won't read in any of the Park Service pamphlets. They only put in the little things they want you to read. They don't put in the real, human stories. These cave wars made the Hatfields and McCoys look like a chicken fight. They shot each other. At that time, back in the 1930s, people owned different parts of caves, and if you were touring a cave there'd be a place where you'd come to another guide with his hand out, very much like a highway toll booth."

Gary Bremer told me of an odd happening in Crystal Cave.

> A group of park employees were on an after-hours trip in Crystal Cave, which is closed to the public. We went down a passageway and we noticed an old whiskey bottle stuck on a rock ledge. We stopped and looked at it. One fellow took it in his hand, and then placed it back on the shelf. We all continued down the passageway and then came back about fifteen minutes later. I had just come up to the whiskey bottle, I was just past it, and just behind my right ear I heard a sound as though someone had flicked a finger against a glass—a clink. I turned around just in time to see the bottle hit the ground. The guy behind me was absolutely wide-eyed, because he said the bottle didn't just tumble off the wall, it came straight out and dropped to the ground."

The guy behind him was Charlie Hanion, and he told me, "Yes, the little clink sound was enough to make me look over toward the ledge, and as I did the bottle actually came out and then went down in front of me. It was very bizarre."

Now, whether that was Floyd Collins flipping the whiskey bottle is anybody's guess, but ghost stories cluster around Floyd incessantly. If anyone is eligible to be an earthbound spirit, according to parapsychological wisdom—and there are those who would consider that last phrase a contradiction in terms—Floyd should be. He might well still be tramping and hollering around the place he owned, lived in, died in, and which made him famous.

In addition to sending me the original story of Melissa, hot from the pages of *The Knickerbocker*, Gary Bremer also sent me an account he had pulled from some file or other at the park. It is ascribed to someone named George Wood, who wrote, in part:

> Last June [1976] Bill Cobb and I spent a day checking springs as part of a study of the groundwater flow in central Kentucky. We didn't get to the last spring until after dark.
>
> I parked by the old Austin and Floyd Collins houses. They stand empty now except for one weekend a month when the folks of the Cave Research Foundation use them.
>
> Bill went down the side of the ridge to Pike Spring. I stayed up at the top in the truck. The night was pleasantly warm as I rolled down the driver's window and sat there thinking how pleasant it was to be so far from any human noises.
>
> My reverie was broken by a man shouting in the distance. At first I thought it was Bill calling for help, but the voice wasn't pitched low enough. The sound was so faint that I had to listen carefully in order to understand what was being said.
>
> Whoever it was was crying, "Help! Help me! Help me, I'm trapped. Johnny, help me!" over and over again.
>
> Then I remembered that Floyd Collins was supposed to have been trapped in a cave and began to wonder if it was in the cave off to my right and down the side of the ridge, which was the direction the calling had come from.
>
> [This was Crystal Cave, although Wood says he did not know that at the time.]
>
> Eventually, Bill returned. I asked him if he had heard any shouting and he replied that he hadn't. We were both a little spooked then and Bill entertained me the rest of the way home with Floyd Collins ghost stories."

National Park Service

An intersection of two passageways.

(Wood adds that research indicated that the "Johnny" heard in the mysterious cry might have referred to Johnny Gerald, a friend of Floyd's, and the last person to talk with him before the cave collapse sealed him off from further rescue attempts.)

The Cave Research Foundation (CRF) Wood referred to is an organization of highly educated, dedicated cave crawlers, formed in 1957. It has about 650 members nation-wide and investigates caves all over the country, but Mammoth Cave park is their main squeeze. CRF maintains quarters for its visiting members on Flint Ridge, where Crystal Cave and Sand Cave are located.

Mel Park, a neurophysicist at the University of Tennessee and the operations manager for CRF at Mammoth Cave park, told me he doesn't believe in ghosts, but spoke of a mysterious explosion he experienced while exploring a passageway. "You hear strange sounds in the cave all the time," he said, "like conversations. Sometimes you hear what sounds like a very active cocktail party, but it's probably just a waterfall."

Roger Brucker, co-owner of an advertising agency in Yellow Springs, Ohio, is an author of books on caves. One is titled *The Cave Beyond*, and it includes an experience Brucker had.

"I was surveying with another fellow down a passageway," Brucker told me, "and we heard someone call, 'Wait!' So we sat down and waited, but no one showed up. So we began yelling, but still nobody showed. So we went on, figuring that when we got back to the base camp we'd check the log and see who else was in that part of the cave. And when we did we discovered that nobody was in that part of the cave. Now this story by itself doesn't mean very much, but other people reported similar experiences when we described ours."

Brucker is also co-author of a book titled *Trapped!*, an account of the ordeal of Floyd Collins. Brucker is a past president of CRF.

There seems to be a mystique connected to Floyd Collins and his harrowing experience, particularly to the display of his body in Crystal Cave. Larry Purcell tells of a phenomenon that recurred when he was conducting tours at Crystal Cave, in the early 1980s when it was still open to the public.

"Candles would do strange things," he told me. "I was on a tight schedule, and the candle would flame up when it was time to leave. This has happened to other guides, and some feel that it is Floyd telling them it's time to move on. I never felt uncomfortable about the way the candles would blaze up. I always felt it was a helpful thing. Floyd was saying, 'It's time to go, Larry, you've got the lights out and told a pretty good story.' No matter what kind of candle I used—big, small, fat, skinny—it always did that. And it wasn't a burst of air; these candles were in a corner where it was dead air. The candles would almost go out, and then they would go up when it was time to leave."

Greer Price, a geologist, worked at Mammoth Cave park a number of years ago. He told me:

> I lived in Flint Ridge, where the old Collins house is. Across the road was a house built by Bill Austin, who owned Crystal Cave back in the 1950s. The CRF around 1970 leased the two houses, the Austin house as camp headquarters and the Collins house as a bunkhouse. There was also a little shed that Bill Austin had used as a ticket office.
>
> In the mid-seventies I moved into the Austin house as caretaker, working part-time for the park and part-time for the CRF. I heard a lot of stories about things that happened there. The old-time guides would look at me and say, "I wouldn't live out there for anything; you're crazy."
>
> I lived there in the dead of winter. The houses were very isolated. You had to walk a mile from the gate to get to the house. I was the only person on the site who had keys. The first thing I noticed was that several nights the lights would go on in the ticket office. We knew that the main chamber of Crystal Cave was directly beneath the Collins house, and that's where Floyd was buried at the time, lying in a casket exposed for all to view, although the cave wasn't open to the public at that time.
>
> I had heard stories of rangers who had sighted Floyd Collins—a man who walked by wearing 1920s overalls and so on. One night I was sitting up reading

and I heard footsteps outside the house. I know it was not my imagination because both of my cats raised their heads and looked at the door. I hadn't heard a car drive up; there was no access to the place. I sat there a few minutes and the footsteps stopped. The next morning I went out and found footprints in the snow around the house and up to the door, but then they disappeared. There were no footsteps going back down the steps, and there was no evidence in the snow of a car having been driven in.

Those were the only things that happened to me, but I heard all kinds of stories. My favorite was the ranger who had been listening to the radio in the Austin house and suddenly heard a broadcast of the Floyd Collins rescue attempts. The next day when he asked about it no one was aware of any such radio broadcast at that time.

Dr. Arthur Palmer, a professor in the department of earth science at New York State University at Oneonta, is a longtime member of CRF. "I'm a scientist," he told me, "and I'm not susceptible to this sort of thing. We weren't looking for ghosts. But some of these accounts are fairly well documented, as documentable as these things can get."

He told me of an incident that happened when he and his wife, Peggy, were in Crystal Cave.

Collins's body at the time was in a casket in the entrance room. We had to walk past it. We were in a part of the cave that nobody for hundreds of miles knew how to get to, a totally uninhabited part of the park. Access was strictly controlled, so there was no possibility of anybody else being in the cave at that time.

I was setting up to take a photograph of some geologic features, and I heard, coming down the passage, the sound of banging. It was a very rhythmic,

banging noise, as though somebody were taking a
hammer and was pounding very hard on a slab of rock.
It was the kind of noise we were familiar with, because
we sometimes do that as geologists. It came about once
a second, not random at all, a very insistent, continu-
ous pounding. It was not a shifting of rocks, which
would be a random clattering.

We decided to beat a hasty retreat. It was not until
a couple of years later that it occurred to me that that
noise was coming from the place where Floyd Collins
used to come down and eat, and he would probably
flatten his bean cans with a rock. Some of those flat-
tened cans are still down there.

Probably the most dramatic thing that I can recall
happened in August 1969. The previous story happened later, in July 1973. My wife and I were down at
the same cave, with a park service person. He went
down the entrance to where the Floyd Collins casket
was and he was taking pictures of it, and we were up at
the entrance taking pictures. There seems to be some
kind of association here with photography. He came
running up and said, "Did you hear that noise?" We
hadn't, so we went down with him and listened.

It sounded as though a huge bird was flapping
back and forth across the ceiling, perhaps one hundred
feet back and forth over our heads. We shined lights up
there, but there was nothing there. It sounded like
heavy wings beating. But there was no way for a big
bird to get in there. Also, there were no feathers or bird
droppings. We never found any evidence of what could
have been causing this noise.

I would like to close this part of the chapter with an
old standby—the phone call from the dead. As a writer on
parapsychology, it heartens me when the same sort of
experiences keep cropping up—pictures falling off walls,
faucets going on and off, doors opening and closing with-

out live human help, dogs frightened by something un-seen. Farther on in this book (Chapter 19), you will hear of an ancient, crank-type phone, hanging on the wall of a restaurant as a decoration and disconnected for many de-cades, that suddenly rang late one night. Nobody had the nerve to answer it. But in this Mammoth Cave park story, somebody answered!

And that man was Dr. Will White, a CRF member and a professor of geochemistry at Pennsylvania State Univer-sity. This also happened in Crystal Cave, where Floyd Collins's body was on display in the entranceway. Dr. White told me:

> Back in the old days, when it was a commercial cave and they had tourists, there was an old army field telephone down in the cave. I guess they used it to call the guides that some people were coming, tell them to wake up. I was with a fellow CRF member, George Deike. As we were going by the phone, it rang. We looked at each other, wondering what was going on, but we continued walking. When we got about two hun-dred feet farther on, the phone rings yet again. So we ran back. I picked it up and answered. It was one of those old-fashioned army phones with a sort of butter-fly switch on it. What I heard sounded like a phone sounds when it's off the hook and there are people in the room. You hear the sound of voices but you can't tell what they are saying. I said hello or something like that. And on the other end there's a startled gasp. And that was all. No one responded. The line was now dead.
>
> We went on about our business down the passage-way, but on the way out we traced the phone line out of the cave all the way to a guide shack, the old ticket office, but the line was disconnected.

History: The age of Mammoth Cave has been estimated at 340 million years. Recorded evidence of the cave dates from 1798, when tradition has it that a hunter chasing a bear stumbled across the mouth of the cave. Evidence of early human habitation has been found in the mummified body of an Indian man, estimated to be more than two thousand years old. Further evidence of Indian use has been established through pottery, partially burned torches, wooden bowls, and sandals.

The cave gained wide public awareness during the War of 1812, when saltpeter mined there by slaves was used in making gunpowder. By that war's end, Mammoth Cave was famous, and visitors began pouring in by stage-coach and train.

Aside from tourism, the cave has been the site of an occasional offbeat use. In 1842 it was owned by a physi-cian, Dr. John Croghan. He got the idea that the constant temperature and humidity of the cave would prove benefi-cial for sufferers from tuberculosis, so he established there the world's first hospital exclusively for tuberculosis pa-tients. But once they were in the cave, the condition of the first eleven patients worsened, so the hospital closed in ten months.

In 1881 a more likely enterprise was established in the cave—a mushroom farm. This didn't work out either, how-ever, because of difficulty in obtaining water, distance from markets, and inept financial management.

But tourism continued to flower, under individual ownerships of Mammoth Cave and the dozens of smaller caves that occupy the area that is now the national park. The movement to convert the area into a national park began in Congress soon after the turn of the twentieth century, and gradually gathered steam until the park was established in 1941.

The trapping of Floyd Collins, a spectacular media event, occurred in 1925. Collins lived about five miles from Mammoth Cave, but within what is now the park area. He had in 1917 discovered and at the time of his death owned Crystal Cave. He had in 1925 found nearby Sand Cave and was exploring it when he met his final adventure in this life. For some time, his body was displayed in the entrance of Crystal Cave as a tourist attraction.

Identities of Ghosts: A primary candidate would certainly be Floyd Collins. Other possibilities might be Melissa, the bitter Southern belle, and Stephen Bishop, the early slave guide who became so identified with Mammoth Cave.

But there are many anonymous spectres and other happenings attributed to spirits. Examples are the man formally dressed, complete with cummerbund, a fashionable costume for tourists at one time; and whoever it was who gave guide Joy Lyons a playful shove; and the coughing lady, whom some say is Melissa. And what of the eleven tuberculosis patients who spent ten months in the ill-fated hospital in the cave? There must have been a lot of coughing down there.

And how about the lady people hear calling for someone, again attributed to Melissa? Although, of course, it could have been the spirit of some distracted mother looking for a lost kid. Or, some spoilsports might say, a live mother, a current tourist a bit off the beaten track.

Don't forget those two pairs of disembodied legs in overalls and work boots, tramping blithely down the hill near the main tourist center.

And who is leaving incomplete footprints around the Collins house, and banging what sounds like cans down in Crystal Cave, and knocking that whiskey bottle off the shelf, and stimulating the candles when it's time for guides to move on? Well, if that's not Floyd Collins, this is not a well-ordered world, and that includes the next one.

And finally, my favorite, how about that mysterious phone call with what sounded like a cocktail party on the other end, complete with ghostly gasp?

Mammoth Cave and its surrounding caves certainly seem well worth a trip to Kentucky, above or below ground, in more ways than the National Park Service's handouts admit.

Personalities of Ghosts: None seem unfriendly.

Witnesses: Joy Lyons, guide; Lewis Cutliss, guide supervisor; Chris Handly, air monitor; Larry Purcell, former guide; Albert (Shorty) Coates, former guide; McNeill van Meter, former guide; Gary Bremen, former guide; Laura Appler, former guide; Charlie Hanion, former guide; Roger Brucker, CRF; Arthur N. Palmer, CRF; Will White, CRF; Greer Price, formerly CRF and park employee; George Deike, CRF.

Best Time to Witness: Time does not seem to be a factor.

Still Haunted?: If it ever was, it presumably still is.

Investigations: It would seem that during the caves' two-hundred-year modern history, a few psychics, more likely quite a few, would have stumbled around among the rocks and passages. However, the only professed psychic I heard of during my inquiries was the lady who asked "who's that standing over there?" when nobody corporeal was, and who then insisted that she was not rung in by the other staff to josh the guides who had reported such a figure the week before but was a genuine tourist who just happened to be psychic.

Data Submitted By: The above-named witnesses, plus Lois Winter, park public relations officer; Joe McGown, guide supervisor; Bob Ward, park historian; Bill Ritter, guide; Jim Norris, guide; Jeff Foster, guide; Mel Park, CRF.

Also material from the National Park Service; an account in the *Encyclopedia Americana*; *Trapped!*, a book about Floyd Collins by Robert K. Murray and Roger W. Brucker; original copy of the Melissa story from *The Knickerbocker* magazine; written account by George Wood of hearing Collins's voice calling for help.

9
A Haunted Inn on the Coast of Maine
Is the Chief Ghost a Woman Who Was Killed Violently?

Location: The East Wind Inn is in Tenants Harbor, Maine, about two hours northeast of Portland. You can go north on Route 95 about twenty miles past Portland, then swing east onto Route 1. At Thomaston, turn south on Route 131, go about nine miles, and at the post office in Tenants Harbor bear left and go down the hill to the inn, on the water.

Description of Place: The inn is a large, three-story, white frame building with a wraparound porch. The building is tastefully furnished throughout, with a grand piano and many books and magazines available. It has nine rooms on the third floor, seven on the second. The first floor contains a lounge and a restaurant that serves breakfast, lunch, and dinner to guests of the inn and also to the public. The kitchen and offices also occupy the first floor. Tim Watts, owner, lives in an apartment in the basement.

The official name of the enterprise is the East Wind

Tim Watts, owner
of the East Wind Inn.

Art Myers

Inn & Meeting House. In 1974, Watts bought the inn
building, which had been standing empty for about two
decades, and restored it. In 1984, he purchased a nearby
old sea captain's home and restored it with rooms, suites,
an apartment, and meeting facilities. Both buildings are
open year-round.

Tenants Harbor is a small coastal village with an
active deep water anchorage. In the 1800s it was something of a shipping and shipbuilding center.

Ghostly Manifestations: I first heard of the haunting of
East Wind Inn when some friends of mine, two couples,
stayed there. Something happened to one member of the
party, Sheila Coote, that was so typical of hauntings that I
felt immediately the place was haunted, whether or not
management would admit it. It turned out that owner Tim
Watts not only admitted it, he urged me to import a com-
petent medium so he could get some indication as to what
on earth was going on there.

Sheila told me this:

I was fast asleep. I woke up and I was absolutely freezing cold, and I couldn't turn over. There was a menacing shadow over me. First, I tried to call John [her husband] but I couldn't do anything. I couldn't move and I was absolutely petrified. Sort of inside myself, I said to this shadow leaning over me, "You are not wanted here, please leave." And the second time I said it, it lifted and went.

It was so cold that I thought I must have left the window open, but when I got up it was closed, and the room was quite warm. After that, I wouldn't go into the room by myself.

As Barbara [Boviard] and I were coming downstairs for breakfast the next morning I told her what had happened, and she said to the woman who was on the reception desk, "This is an old place, are there any ghosts here?" And the woman said, "Nothing to talk about," and walked away. But when we were talking about it at breakfast, the waitress said, "Yes, we do have a ghost here, up on the top floor." It was in the area where we were. She said her husband would not go up to that floor.

I called Tim Watts and told him of Sheila's account, and he said, "That's not the first time that's happened. Other people have had the experience of being held down in bed and sensing an extreme cold. Generally it happens in Rooms 12 and 14, but not always, sometimes in other rooms on the top floor."

He told me of a guest named Terry Wentworth who seemed to inspire something to break windows. "We put her in two rooms," Watts said, "and in both rooms windows broke. The first window had a stick under it, which flew out and the window smashed. The other one, we have no idea what happened to it. There was a screen on the outside so there was no way it could have been hit, yet it shattered. In the first instance, Terry and a friend had

adjoining rooms and they were in the friend's room playing
cards when the window in Terry's room broke.

"I've often sensed a presence in this building. I've
heard noises, and physical things happen like doors slamming and the dining room doors swinging."

Tim Watts, I realized as we spoke, is a natural psychic,
marooned on his own special island, as such folks usually
are, in a sea of tuned-out people. His forebears were
settlers of Tenants Harbor. His father is a sea captain.
"Nobody in my family is psychic," he told me. "They won't
even talk about it."

As I spoke with him, I wondered if his openness might
have stimulated the unseen occupants of the building.
Nancy Wilson, curator of an extremely haunted museum
in Oregon City (Chapter 20), told me that her museum had
never had a reputation for being haunted until she came
there fifteen years before, yet now scores of people are
turned on or off, according to their proclivities, by the
goings-on there.

As I spoke with Tim, he really warmed up. He told of
viewing his grandfather's death, "as though on a TV
screen," five years before it happened. And he thinks he
has seen him since he died. He told me of playing the
piano in the inn the night after a close friend was buried.
He had often played piano-organ duets with this person.
"The night she was buried," Tim said, "I awakened about
two or three in the morning and for some reason I went
down to play the piano, and I heard my organ start to play.
For about thirty seconds, she was playing the organ along
with me."

He spoke of sometimes being seen in places he was
not, and I hope I cheered him up by telling him of a fellow
I used to know, a quite substantial citizen, head of the
arts department of the local college, who had a habit of
appearing in his home in Massachusetts when he was

actually spending the weekend in New York. Both my friend and Tim professed complete unawareness of what was going on.

"Twice," he said, "I've been pushed in the attic. For quite some time I didn't cherish going up there."

Several times, Watts said, guests on the third floor have told him that presences have shown themselves. When a friend of mine, Ginny Cutler, and I stayed on the third floor, she told me the next day that she had heard a faint wailing at three in the morning. It went on for about half a minute, she said, and she got up to look out the window to see if there was a wind. There seemed to be no wind, nor did the wail seem to be coming from outdoors. "It was a very sad wail," Ginny said, "a pathetic sound."

Watts told me that other people have heard this sound.

Art Myers

He mentioned that he has had two dogs over the years, and both seemed to sense other-worldly presences. They would growl, show their teeth, stare around the room, their hair would stand up. You can always trust a dog in these things, I say.

In fact, Ann Goldsmith, a friend of Watts's who runs a retreat center in Tenants Harbor, told me of house-sitting the inn one winter, staying in Watts's apartment when he was away. She had a dog named Mother Jones, and both she and Mother Jones would hear footsteps overhead in the dining room and kitchen area. They'd go up, but no one would be there.

John Thomas, a onetime chef, now a high school teacher in Bangor, used to house-sit for Watts in the winter and he also told me of experiences. "In the pantry, out of the corner of your eye, you'd see a figure," he said. "This would happen often, many times while I was putting away produce in the evening. I felt I was never alone. I'd call up people and ask them to come and stay with me, but they wouldn't."

Watts told me that Thomas got into the habit of sleeping all night in the lobby, with the lights on.

"Either there's something here," Watts told me, "or a bunch of us are just a little nuts."

The first people I met at the inn were a French-Canadian woman from Montreal and her lawyer husband and two grown sons. She was delighted to know I wrote books about hauntings, and said she had felt something when they arrived at the inn, a couple of hours before. I wanted to interview her after a night there, but she eluded me. So I phoned her at home.

"I was afraid to tell you about it," she said, "because I was so afraid my experience was subjective. I was afraid my imagination had gone wild. We were on the second floor, I believe we were right under the rooms that are said to be haunted. I woke up about four in the morning and on the ceiling, in the corner, I heard two strokes—a long one and a short one. I woke up because I was pushed off my bed. But it was such a small bed that it could have been my husband. And it could be in my little head. But then I heard the noise near the ceiling. I vibe a lot because I'm sensitive, I'm like that. It's a sad house, that would be my feeling, there's a feeling of sadness there. Ghosts are usually people who are unhappy or don't want to leave or who are afraid to go elsewhere."

History: According to John Falla, the town manager, who has an interest in local history, the East Wind Inn building was built by a local businessman, John Fuller, around 1860. Falla said the building does not appear on an 1857 map of the area, but that in 1860 the local Masons contracted to occupy the top floor of the building, which they continued to use until 1894. Fuller's sons had a tin shop in the basement of the building. The second floor was a sail loft, a large room in which sails are laid out and sewn together. Later the second floor was used as a community meeting place. The first floor was used by John Fuller as a general store.

The building was renovated in 1921 by Charles Rawley for use as an inn, which he called the Wan-e-set Inn. From 1941 to 1974 it was owned by Frank Scrutin. When Tim Watts bought the building in 1974, it had been empty for about twenty years.

Identities of Ghosts: Psychic Annika Hurwitt visited the inn a few weeks after I had been there, and gave me this report:

> The first experience I had was when I walked into the room (Room 12 or 14) with Tim and within a couple of

Annika Hurwitt.

minutes I felt my whole chest just seething up. It was hard to breathe. When we went downstairs I told Tim that I felt really, really sad. He said he was glad I had said that because there were a lot of times when that sadness would just kind of overcome him out of the blue when he'd been up there.

So I went in there that night and meditated, and the story I got is that it was a woman. This was in the late 1800s. I think she had been married to this guy, or else he was her lover. He was involved with another woman and he killed her (the ghost) by stabbing her through the heart. Whenever I tuned in to her I would feel a lot of anger, and that she was haunting people in order to feel empowered. She wakes people up, they feel cold, they try to get up to get a blanket and they can't because someone's holding them down. Then they try to scream and they can't. I feel that's how she's getting out her revenge, because that's what happened to her—she was held down on a bed and stabbed. The sadness is because underneath all that anger she's really, really hurt.

Either her husband or her father were like shipping merchants—or both of them might have been. The husband had her killed to be able to carry on with his lover. I think this was done secretly.

I didn't want to stay in the room with the ghost, but a friend of mine came up one night and he slept there. He's not psychic, and he is a really deep sleeper. He felt something wake him up. He felt the pressure in his chest, and he felt a lot of constriction around his throat.

There are some other ghosts there. Down in Tim's apartment there are some really benign ghosts who are just hanging around. Tim felt a presence in his living room, and I got an older sort of sea captain who was just smoking his pipe and looking out at the water and feeling annoyed at this crazy, vengeful woman, of whom he was aware.

I also had a sense of a group of men who sort of hung around like a club and played cards. I asked Tim about it and he said there used to be a Masonic club in the building.

[Also, people might have used the town meeting room to play cards, or perhaps the Fuller brothers might have had some card-playing cronies down in their tin shop, where Watts's apartment is now.]

Annika also said that Tim told her that the room in which she had tuned in to the woman had its roof blown open several years ago—the damage was only over that room. Also the mattress in that room was sliced in half.

Personalities of Ghosts: The old sea captain and the men playing cards are obviously bit players in this account. The star is the lady who is raising various kinds of rumpus on the top floor. I made efforts to get a clue as to who she might have been. No one I interviewed had ever heard of a murder in the East Wind building. However, Annika did suggest that it might have been done secretly.

The history-minded people I spoke with said that murders tend to be rare in small coastal Maine towns, but they all cited the killing of Sarah Meservey in 1878. She was strangled in her house, not far from the East Wind building. Her body was found there about a month after the killing. A man was arrested and convicted, but there was considerable question whether he was guilty. Sarah was in the house alone, her husband was off at sea. Reports say she was strangled with a scarf, possibly during a robbery, but one informant thought she might have also been stabbed.

I have known of ghosts who inhabit houses they had no known connection with during their lives. An example, from *The Ghostly Register*, is a town drunk who burned himself up in his shack at one end of Provincetown, on Cape Cod, but is haunting a house, now a bed and breakfast, at the other end of town. No one seems to know why he would be there, and the ghost himself has a noticeably confused air about him.

Could Sarah Meservey have moved over to the East Wind? Annika also said she sensed the name Caroline in connection with the obstreperous ghost. One historian said that a Caroline Jackson seemed to have disappeared between 1870 and 1880, and she lived quite near the East Wind. This buoyed my spirits considerably, but later my informant told me that further investigation indicated that this Caroline had divorced her husband, Robert Rawley, and moved to Canada with a new mate.

Witnesses: Tim Watts, owner; Annika Hurwitt, psychic; Sheila Coote, guest; Ann Goldsmith, house sitter; John Thomas, chef and house sitter; Ginny Cutler, guest; a French-Canadian woman, guest. Various other guests and staff members.

Best Time to Witness: Incidents seem to take place at night.

Art Myers

The East Wind Inn.

Still Haunted?: There would seem no reason to think it's not. I asked Annika if Tim had suggested that she attempt a soul rescue, exorcism, or whatever. She replied, "I asked Tim if he'd like me to contact her more closely and maybe find out more about her, but he didn't want me to possibly release her."

I asked Annika why he would feel that way, and she said, "After my experiences in the restaurant in New Hampshire (see *The Ghostly Gazetteer*) I realized that people get very attached to their ghosts. I feel the reason is that it's the only tangible experience they have of another world. They're not people on a spiritual path, they don't have the sense of being in contact with another reality, and this ghost is such an exciting proof that there is another reality."

Investigations: Annika's visit seems to be the only formal, scheduled inquiry. However, in a public hostelry of this nature, some of the guests and other people frequenting the place are bound to be psychic—for example, the French-Canadian woman I met there who, when she realized I offered a sympathetic ear, shyly confided her sensitivities. As another example, Sheila Coote is English and has had psychic experiences in her spirit-rich native land. And owner Tim Watts, who lives there permanently, is a sensitive.

Data Submitted By: Above-named witnesses, as well as John Falla, town manager and historian; James Skoglund, member of the Maine legislature and historian; Everett Watts, historian; Betsy Scott (nee Hunter) of New York City, descendent of Tenants Harbor businessmen, owner of sail loft in Tenants Harbor; Sheryl Parker, waitress.

10
A Couple of Happy Ghosts
Traipsing About in Boston
Public Gardens

Location: Boston Public Gardens are in central Boston, Massachusetts, an extensive area devoted to trees, flowers, fun, and rest from the surrounding city. The gardens are contiguous with Boston Common.

Description of Place: Nice.

Ghostly Manifestations: This account was first given me several years ago by Lorraine Lauzon of Pittsfield, Massachusetts. At the time I was the editor of a regional magazine there, and she often wrote for me. When she told me this story, I told her to write it, and I published it. Every now and then, in a book of this nature, I like a short, sweet chapter, and this certainly is that. So I recently called Lorraine, and she told me the story again, in exactly the same way, which always impresses me.

She and her husband, Paul, and their three small children had, in the 1960s, gone from Pittsfield to Boston, about 140 miles away, to see an annual arts festival in Boston Gardens. Lorraine is also an artist.

> They had this marvelous festival every year with paintings, sculpture, ballet, poetry readings. It went on for about a week, and they had it for about ten years. Paul was off looking at something, and I was with the kids. One was in a baby carriage, and the other two, who were five and seven, were running around the place.
>
> Out of the corner of my eye I saw these two women coming across the street into the Gardens. I had the impression they were coming from the Ritz Carlton. I didn't actually see them coming out of the Ritz Carlton, I guess I just assumed that's where they were coming from, since they seemed very much moneyed people who would be staying in a hotel like that.
>
> Anyway, I took my eyes off them for a moment and the next thing I knew they were in the Gardens and coming toward me. They were elderly women, very thin, holding onto each others' arms. They were completely in white, beautifully dressed, in clothing of the 1930s. They were very noticeable because of the white—although their faces were pinkish. They were walking very slowly, gracefully, very ladylike. I can still see their faces.
>
> Nobody else around me seemed to be seeing them, and I remember being slightly surprised at that, because they were certainly very unusual in those old-fashioned dresses, and very noticeable. They sat down on a bench about ten or fifteen feet away from where I was sitting. We caught each others' eyes for a moment, and they smiled at me—very bright, sweet smiles.
>
> I wanted to check on the kids, and I took my eyes off them for just a moment, and when I looked back they had disappeared. I was amazed. I couldn't believe they could have left in the instant I had looked away. I gathered the kids and went running all over the place trying to spot them again. But I couldn't.

Art Myers

The Boston Public Gardens, with the Ritz Carlton Hotel in the background. The lady just happened to be sitting there.

Identities of Ghosts: Lorraine thinks they were the spirits of two women who probably stayed at the Ritz Carlton when they came to Boston, and were used to coming across the street into the Gardens, especially if something lively like an arts festival was going on.

Personalities of Ghosts: Very friendly. Seemingly having a good time.

(I wondered if they could have been the type of spirits that have been called place memories, energy once implanted in the atmosphere that is sometimes visible in a sort of time warp situation. But such apparitions are not aware; they are more like a TV picture. They do not interreact with living people.)

"They probably were real spirits," Lorraine says, "since they smiled at me."

Witnesses: Apparently just Lorraine, who describes herself as intuitive, attuned to other worlds. She asked her children if they had seen anything, but they said they hadn't. "Of course," she says, "they were running around."

Best Time to Witness: "This was a gorgeous, sunny day," Lorraine says. "You usually think of people seeing ghosts at night, or on a dark, stormy day, but this afternoon was anything but. Who says there aren't happy ghosts?"

Still Haunted?: Lorraine is the only person I've heard of who has seen these delightful apparitions, although Boston may be filled with people who have seen them at one time or another and who just haven't gotten around to telling me.

Data Submitted By: Lorraine Lauzon.

11
The Ghost in the YMCA
Locker Room
Hanging Out in the Men's Health Club

Location: The Cambridge YMCA is at 820 Massachusetts Avenue, about a block from an area known as Central Square. Cambridge, Massachusetts, is across the Charles River from Boston, and is the home of Harvard University and Massachusetts Institute of Technology. Both of these august institutions are on Massachusetts Avenue, and the YMCA is about halfway between them.

Description of Place: The Y is a five-story, red brick building. It goes back to the turn of the century, and looks it. The Men's Health Club quarters are either in the basement of the building or the ground floor. (The huge building sits on a slanting terrain and it's hard to tell what floor you're on.)

Ghostly Manifestations: I heard about this haunting in a bookstore in Cambridge. Authors don't usually admit this, but sometimes they go into bookstores to see if their

Art Myers

The YMCA.

books are there. I hastened to the occult section and found
that this excellent bookstore had a couple of copies of my
latest book. A friend was accompanying me, and she was
thrilled, almost as much as I was. Pointing to me, she said
to a young man standing nearby, "He wrote this!" This was
slightly embarrassing, but it led to the production of this
chapter as well as the next one.

Three young men are witnesses to this haunting, but
they are so sheepish about the whole thing, so uneasy
about ghosts in general, that they might well be chagrined
to have their real names in public print involving this. So
let's call them Larry, Curly, and Moe.

The young man in the bookstore, Larry, was tall and
athletic. He made a living as a security guard. He was in
the store to peruse books about the mystical, primarily, I

gathered, because he had recently had a shaking experience. He had seen what seemed to be a ghost in the YMCA
Men's Health Club locker room. He told me:

> I saw something there. My reaction to it was negative,
> because of my beliefs. The first time I saw it it scared
> me because I'd never seen anything like that, but after
> that I calmed down. I don't know if I'd call it a ghost or
> what, but there's something there.
>
> It was dark, like a shadow. It was up against the
> lockers, and we just looked at it. It was maybe five feet
> away. It didn't move, it just sort of hung out in one spot.

Larry had gone there late at night with Moe, who had
been an attendant at the Y. Larry said:

> I've seen it several times when I go down there with
> Moe. We don't go to see it, we go to play basketball or
> whatever. When we go in, there are no lights on, and
> that's when you see it. If there are lights on, you don't
> see it. Moe was really into like checking it out. I don't
> really care for that kind of stuff. A couple of times we
> brought friends down to see it.
>
> It's like energy or something. It's like a gray, shad-
> owy substance and it moves. It's just something that
> hangs out, it's just there. You can see like different
> colored rings, and the rings move. Moe is like more
> interested. Me, it's like I saw it, fine, life goes on, I don't
> really want to get into it.

I called Moe, but he wasn't in so I spoke with his
brother, Curly. Curly works in real estate and also sells an
organic product that is designed to boost the immune
system. He said:

> There was something there. I wasn't quite sure. I don't
> know what a ghost is or what a ghost isn't, but it
> definitely seems like something.

It had a kind of greenish look to it. It was pitch
dark in the locker room and there was this kind of
greenish aura in this specific area. I did see that, but
I'm very skeptical. It could be just the reflection of
something.

My brother's seen it quite a bit. The time I saw it,
he said it really wasn't that strong. But there's definitely
something.

The key witness here is obviously Moe. As I spoke
with him, it became clear that he is a natural psychic, and
it's something he'd rather not be. He doesn't understand it,
and it frightens him. I asked if he has a tendency to see
things that most people don't see. He reluctantly replied:

Yeah, I've got something like that. I don't know exactly
what it means. If you really want to you can become
immersed in it, and it becomes a part of your life. And
then when you don't want it in your life, when you try
to have a normal life, it's not something for you. I'm not
sure how I fit into this spiritual thing. One thing is for
sure, I don't want to get into spirits and ghosts and so
forth in my life, and I try to keep them out.

Moe spoke of the first time he had seen the apparition
at the Y:

I was there late at night working out, after hours. I went
into the locker room with the lights off. I looked across
and I saw something was there. I didn't *see* it, exactly. It
was across from the chin-up bar.

I asked, what is it I really see? I stared really hard,
to get away from something I'll be building up in my
head. I didn't want my mind playing tricks on me.
Usually when I do that I can clear things away. But the
deeper I looked, the more form it took. There was
something outlining. It was closer than ten feet, up

against the lockers. The only time it started to change shape was when I started bringing people in. Originally it looked like a diamond. Sometimes it would go up to the ceiling, sometimes up to about five feet.

Moe brought in Larry and Curly, and from time to time other young men. One friend saw it but passed it off as an optical illusion. Another denied seeing anything. "Another guy," Moe said, "tried to feed it energy, and that left a white spot on it. The only time it seems noticeable is at night when you're there alone. When the lights are on and everybody's there the presence is very light, I can't see it. Since I've been bringing a lot of people down it isn't the same. Maybe it's something that doesn't need to be bothered."

Moe thought it would be a great idea if I brought in a professional psychic, so I made some moves to do that.

Investigation: The membership director of the Y, David Alves, said a ghost in the basement was news to him, but he invited me to look the place over if I wished. Moe said he was eager to accompany me, but didn't show up. I saw nothing, but I didn't expect to, since I am not particularly psychic. I found the men who were dressing, undressing, and working out in the club were very interested.

"I'm a new member here," one said, "but I'd be intrigued by it. I love that stuff."

Another said he hadn't seen anything in the twenty-five years he'd been there. Another said, "Now you've got me worried."

After this preliminary look, I asked Alves if I could bring in a professional medium, and he referred me to a colleague, Ron Lahti, director of residences and counseling at the Y. Lahti was not only interested, he was eager, since he himself is a psychic. On the appointed day, he brought

Erle Myers at a seance
in the locker room.

along two other psychics, John McCooey and Roy Bauer.
McCooey is an advertising copy writer, and Bauer is a
professional shamanic healer and teacher.

My own entry was Dr. Erle Myers, no relation to me.
He is a practicing psychologist and also the pastor of the
Spiritualist Church in nearby Watertown.

We repaired to the Men's Health Club quarters and
located the chin-up bar that Moe had referred to, and used
it as a starting point. The psychics immediately felt cold
spots—presumably psychic cold—in the area. The room
was long and narrow, and although Ron Lahti turned off
the lights there was plenty of daylight from windows at the
far end of the room. A middle-aged man was working hard
on a stationary bicycle. I wondered if he knew what we
were doing. He began whistling, so maybe he did.

The psychics meditated for a few minutes, then began
telling what they had sensed.

Erle Myers said, "I allowed myself to raise my own vibration to move into the energy of the spirit, and I perceived a man who would have been very tall and thin. He probably stood about six four, or perhaps even six five, a wiry type of man. As I perceived him, he would have been in his early to midfifties."

Roy Bauer said that he first perceived the energy as an elongated diamond, saying that often when he encounters spirits they appear to him as geometric shapes. I was struck with the thought that Moe had also seen the spirit as a diamond, one that varied from a height of five feet to up to the ceiling. When I later mentioned that to Roy, he said, "It was a pulsation of energy. The man was tall and thin." He added that since he himself is short and stocky, in his case the diamond would be more of a square shape.

Roy agreed with Erle's assessment of the spirit. "It's a male energy, stretched," he said. "He had either sandy brown or grayish hair. Middle-ageish. It's sort of wandering in the area. It has a lot of curiosity right now as to what we're doing here. There is almost a feeling of anxiety."

Erle felt that the person had had a broken neck. "I'm picking up some energy in the back of my neck," he said. He also was aware of chest pain, and felt that the person might have had a heart attack, fallen to the floor, and injured his neck. Erle felt that the person was taken out on a stretcher.

Ron Lahti felt that the energy was a "fragment." He said, "A certain amount of energy, a thought or very strong emotion, can build up a charge of energy that can be cast out from the soul and that can hang, or wander. That's what I sense here. It's a fragment, like a thought that's been imprinted here."

Roy, Ron, and John are followers of the shamanic traditions, and some of their assessments were new to me, such as the idea of a soul fragmenting. I wondered if a so-called fragment was similar to what I had come to know as a place memory, an apparition or other ghostly manifestation that does not interact with living people, that can be seen sometimes, but is more like a TV picture, there but not really there. I later discussed the matter with Roy Bauer, and he said, "The place memory is like a hologram; it's a static thing. The soul fragment would have life, it would react. But it's stuck in time. An ordinary, full-fledged ghost knows that it's 1991, it will know that times have changed. But the soul fragment is still back in the 1920s, it's frozen in time, it doesn't know that things have changed around it."

This certainly is a description of many of the ghosts I have written about. They seem to be attached to a space, but don't seem aware of the changes that have occurred in that space.

As the seance proceeded, there seemed general agreement that the spirit was not an unaware place memory, but—even if it was only a part of the person's original soul—was aware of what was going on around it.

The group meditated further, and Erle said, "The name Murray [I've changed it slightly] came in, and I also received the feeling that he was a teacher. There are younger people around him. He was not a very happy man. There is a sense of weighty sadness. He did not know how to connect with people around him. He used his teaching as a way of building up a network of support around him."

Roy Bauer said, "I agree that the neck injury is secondary to something else. I think it happened over by the chinning bar. I also sense his being carried out on a stretcher, but it was from a cardiac.

"He had a German shepherd, to which he was very attached. I think he was single—either single or in a sterile, barren marriage. He has children, but not his own."

Both Erle and Roy felt that the man had died in the 1920s or 1930s. Roy mentioned that his assessment was based on the way the person was dressed. Roy felt that he had not died in this room, but that he had lost consciousness—"lost connection to this world"—here.

There was a discussion between Erle and Roy as to whether to urge the soul to move on.

Erle said, "We [followers of the spiritualist tradition] feel that sometimes a spirit can get earthbound, and often the spirit is not basically happy. So we do what we call rescue work, we bring the person to the light."

Roy said, "Sometimes the person doesn't know he's dead, or is afraid to move on for any one of several reasons. But I don't feel he's unhappy here."

Erle said, "I feel he can be made a much more productive kind of energy than to allow him to stay here. He may not know there is a place he can move on to."

The mediums decided to ask the spirit if he wanted to move on. Roy told me later, "Erle and I agreed that you shouldn't send a spirit away unless it agrees. Neither of us believed one should twist the arm of a ghost to get him to go, although that often is done."

At this point, John McCooey made a point that the other mediums had apparently been aware of but had been reluctant to state.

"The first thought that came to my mind when I came down here," John said, "was that there was a lot of sexualization in the energy. I think this man abused boys."

There seemed a relief among the psychics that somebody had finally said it. "I'm very glad you made that point," Erle said, and Roy said he had also felt this.

Roy said, "The only joy he had in this life was the teenage boys around him. Whether he actually physically abused them . . ." He shrugged. "But he enjoys hanging out here. The men are a little too old for him, but . . ."

Erle said, "I would like to ask him about leaving, and to draw him to the light. I don't think it's any help for him to stay here." The others agreed, and Erle sat on a stool in the corner and spoke, addressing the spirit:

> You will be able to understand, you will be able to communicate, and you will learn how to feel enriched by the network of other spirits that will work closely with you. If you are willing, please take my hand, and you have the support of the other people here. And let us walk down the long corridor to the glowing white light at the end.
>
> You have a choice as to whether you go or whether you stay, but you must learn that there is another dimension, where there can be support and love. I will walk with you to the portal through which you will pass into another wonderfully growthful life, with many people to care and help you to grow and enable you to overcome the pains of your earth life.

After a pause, Erle spoke to the rest of us, saying, "There was a lot of reluctance. The energy would go and then come back, and go and come back. At the very end, it stopped at the portal, waited, and all of a sudden it turned to me and hugged me, and walked through into the light."

I spoke with Roy Bauer later and he told me, "The spirit was very concerned. I heard him say, 'Do you want me to leave?' He wanted to stay there, but if we wanted him to leave he was willing.

"He had stayed there because he was a voyeur. He was like a Peeping Tom. This place for him was paradise. But the spirit of this man could not be at rest while separated. He was gone before we left."

History: The YMCA building was constructed in three phases, the first in 1896, the second in 1912, the third in 1958. Ron Lahti told me, "The room we were in was part of the 1958 expansion. But where we saw the manifestation is against a 1912 wall."

In any case, Lahti pointed out, it did not seem that the man had actually died in this room, although, as Roy Bauer said, he may have had a coronary attack and "lost connection to this world" there.

Lahti said there was no record of anyone dying in that area during the 1920s or 1930s. A man had died there about eight years ago, but this man did not "fit the picture."

Identity of Ghost: According to mediums at the seance I attended, it was a man who had had a heart attack in the room and died soon afterward in the 1920s or 1930s.

Personality of Ghost: Agreement of the mediums was that he was a man who was isolated and withdrawn, and who had a homosexual orientation.

Witnesses: Larry, Curly, and Moe (the three young men I interviewed) and some of their friends. The mediums at the seance were Erle Myers, Roy Bauer, Ron Lahti, and John McCooey.

Best Time to Witness: The energy was best seen with physical eyes when the place was pitch dark. When it was light, apparently only psychically sensitive people could be aware of anything there. Ron Lahti told me that Moe and his friends, particularly Moe, were probably the only people to have seen it visually, since very few people go down into that area at night.

Still Haunted?: The mediums believed that the spirit had left. However, spirits sometimes return. Lahti said he planned to go down there some night when the lights are out and try to ascertain if the spirit has truly gone.

Data Submitted By: Larry, Curly, and Moe; Erle Myers; Roy Bauer; Ron Lahti; John McCooey.

12
Spirits in an Old Church's Burial Chamber
They Seemed to Be Expressing Resentment

Location: The church did not wish to disclose its identity. Suffice it to say that it is a very old church in eastern Massachusetts. I found this story so intriguing that I decided to include it in this book even though it cannot be readily visited by the reader.

Description of Place: The church has a burial chamber in its basement with about forty tombs, each of which has multiple interments. There are between eight hundred and one thousand individual graves, going back to the 1700s and the early 1800s.

Ghostly Manifestations: I ran across this account while working on the previous chapter. Four psychics were scheduled that morning to explore the reportedly haunted locker room of the YMCA Men's Health Club, but only three had arrived. The fourth, Dr. Erle Myers, a psychologist, had been delayed.

We were waiting for him in the office of Ron Lahti, the director of residences and counseling at the Y. Lahti, a psychic, is also a psychologist. Also present was Roy Bauer, a professional shamanic healer and teacher. While waiting for Dr. Myers, they began to discuss an experience they had had a few days before.

They had been hired by the owner of a construction company that was doing extensive renovations at an old church.

"The only manifestation that the site boss had noticed," Bauer said, "was an uneasiness on the part of the workers. The ambience was uncomfortable."

"There was a general anxiety among his workers," Lahti added. "They wanted to be out, away."

"And also," Bauer said, "when the priests of the church went through they didn't dally at all, they just didn't want to be around the area.

"The main concern of the construction person who hired us," Bauer said, "was that he feared they might be desecrating graves."

Investigation: Bauer and Lahti related that they went to the church and made contact with the spirits buried there.

"The problem," Bauer said, "was not the new construction, it was the way the tombs had been treated by the church. There were things stored in front of—and right in—the tombs. It wasn't done disrespectfully. The things there were just things that would be stored in the basement of any church, but because the tombs were so old they were just considered commonplace."

Some of the spirits there had apparently taken umbrage. Lahti said, "We spoke to them and explained to them what was going on, that no one meant any disrespect. Roy invited the spirits to help the workmen and make sure they didn't get hurt, and that would make the place a more celebrated space. And that seemed to bring a great deal of peace to them. In psychotherapeutic terms, it engaged these spirits into the process going on around them."

During the session, Bauer and Lahti related, an apparition of a woman in the dress of prior times appeared. "When the woman appeared," Bauer said, "I had started a shamanic ritual, and Ron saw her first. When I turned, I was annoyed because I thought it was a woman from the church's bookstore/museum/gift shop dressed in period costume, and there was supposed to be nobody with us when we were doing that.

"There were other things that manifested while we were doing this. We made offers of corn and tobacco and salt and sage, and during this there were flashes of light, almost like strobe lights. It's a common occurrence in heavy spiritual workings. We went from tomb to tomb addressing spirits who were there. We could also see the spirits of cows and horses who were also buried there."

I asked Bauer if he meant actual apparitions or a visual sense in one's mind, and he replied, "A vision you see with your eyes open. A normal spiritual manifestation you see with your eyes closed, when you are in an altered state. But some of this you could see as clearly as I can see now, as a vision."

Lahti said he felt the current vibrations at the church were caused more by curiosity on the part of the spirits than any hostility, and this was conveyed to the workmen.

"When we left," Bauer said, "the spirits were at peace, and the construction company is going to do what they can to see that the area is cleaned up."

History: A Massachusetts church dating from the 1700s, with tombs in its basement.

Identities of Ghosts: Presumably the spirits of people buried there.

Personalities of Ghosts: Resentful that their tombs have been used as a routine storage area. Curiosity about the new construction work.

Best Time to Witness: Anytime, it would seem.

Still Haunted?: Presumably. However, according to Bauer and Lahti the spirits are now more at ease, and the living people in the basement area should be too.

(Having now published several books on the subject of parapsychology, including close to two hundred cases of hauntings, I am constantly aware of interesting similarities. This case reminds me in a couple of ways of a case in my book *Ghosts of the Rich and Famous* involving the Eisenhower cottage in Gettysburg, Pennsylvania. The site is now administered by the National Park Service. Park rangers were being disturbed by constant parapsychological manifestations, including slamming doors, lights flicking on and off for no apparent reason, music coming from empty rooms. At least one ranger reported seeing an apparition of Mamie Eisenhower. Several of the rangers were threatening to quit.

To deal with this, the National Park Service engaged a well-known medium from the Washington area, Anne Gehman, to go to Gettysburg and check out the cottage. Gehman reported that she contacted Mamie and Ike, as well as some of their retinue, and also Indians who predated the modern era. Many of the poltergeist happenings, Gehman said, were being caused by the spirit of Mamie's maid, who had loved the place and wanted people to know she was there. Anne suggested to the maid that she cool it, that she was upsetting the living people there, and the place seemed to quiet down.

While writing this chapter, I was reminded of the

Eisenhower case for two reasons: one, because of mediums mediating between the living and the dead, but also because of two ordinarily most mundane human agencies, a construction company and the U.S. government, employing psychics to ease a spiritual problem. It makes one suspect that we may be living in changing times.)

Data Submitted By: Roy Bauer and Ron Lahti.

Some former guests of the Vokes Theater were Katherine Cornell, Ellen Terry, George Arliss, Ethel Barrymore, and John Drew.

13
A Beautiful Little Theater
That May Have an
Unseen Resident
Legend Has It that
Its Founder Has Never Left

Location: The Vokes Theatre is on Route 20—Boston Post Road—in Wayland, Massachusetts, about fifteen miles west of Boston.

Description of Place: This miniature theater, built in 1904 and enlarged and renovated over the years, is a show in itself, done up with boxes, a balcony, and the gilded decorations of days gone by. It was originally built by Beatrice Herford, an English actress who settled in Wayland, as a place to entertain her friends, many of them famous theatrical figures. Among her guests were Katherine Cornell, Ellen Terry, Lotte Crabtree, George Arliss, Nora Bayes, Ethel Barrymore, and John Drew. Their photographs, many inscribed to Beatrice Herford, line the walls.

In 1937, use of the theater was given by Miss Herford to a local amateur group. The organization has prospered. Their productions are almost all sellouts, and the Vokes Players have developed into possibly the most professional of community theaters in the Boston area.

Ghostly Manifestations: When it comes to attitudes toward the supernatural, working on this chapter was like dealing with a microcosm of mass American opinion. I interviewed about eighty people who have been involved with the Vokes, most of them members, others non-members who have been in plays there. The legend that Beatrice Herford haunts the theater is widespread, but I ran across people who had never heard of it. Others had heard of it but didn't believe it. Others believed it but had no personal experience of it. And I found a dozen pay dirt types—people who told me they had had direct experiences and who were willing to talk about them.

I also ran across people who told me of having experiences but who didn't believe in them, and others who denied having experiences but who I was told had had a few. Some people seemed indignant at the very idea that rumors of haunting could be taken seriously. A cross-section of America.

Here are a few quotes for starters:

"You get a hundred-year-old theater and somebody's going to think they heard something."

"It's sort of a myth that's been carried on; it's a cute story, but I don't think anybody really believes it."

"In forty years I've never heard about ghosts. I think they're drinking too much booze down there."

My first interviewee to own up to a strange experience, Mike Willhoite, led off, "I don't believe in ghosts or spirits or anything in the supernatural. It was really quite funny. I was in a show, and it was between scenes. I was lying on a bench in a little hallway where we do makeup, and I was reading. I was completely alone. And I heard someone distinctly whisper in my ear, behind me, on my left side—'Michael.' I turned around and said, 'Yeah?' And nobody was there. I felt it was an interesting phenomenon,

Art Myers

The Vokes Theatre.

that's all. I walked into the next room and told people, and everybody exchanged looks and they said, 'Oh, he heard Beatrice.' I don't believe that, not for a minute."

A few nights later he was in the same place and he heard it again. "It was so distinct, it was not my imagination," he told me. "I couldn't tell if it was a man's or a woman's voice. They tell me it was Beatrice, but I think they were just razzing me. I'm a complete rationalist. I've never had anything like this happen before or since. I still do not believe in ghosts."

I went on to interview other people, and had several strike-outs, hit a few pop flies, a few easy grounders. It was very hard to get to first base. If someone told me they felt a presence in the theater, I gratefully chalked it up as a base on balls. But if Willhoite's account was a scratch single, I had my first solid hit when I spoke with Mike

Hirsh, who had been president of the Vokes for a number of years and who came on very much as a no-nonsense type.

"Well, it's a strange old theater," he said. "I've felt uncomfortable there at times." He hesitated, then went on, "Well, I'll tell you the truth. A long time ago, I had an afternoon there when two things happened. I was upstairs in the theater and the front door opened and slammed shut. I waited a minute to see who was going to come in. I didn't hear anything so I went down and checked the door, and it was securely closed. And the same afternoon I heard the water go on in the kitchen down below and run for a bit, and then it went off. I went down and looked around and I was still the only one in the building."

When somebody tells me about a faucet going on, it's almost as good a sign to me as a dog's being scared, which comes later in this chapter. As I worked my way through the membership list of the Vokes, I gradually began piling up symptoms of an authentically haunted building.

I visited the theater during a rehearsal, and the show's stage manager, Derby Swanson, told me, "A couple of summers ago we were dancing on stage and we had some lights on and were sort of hanging out. All of a sudden, of those little lights up along the balcony, one of the bulbs went out. Someone walked up into the balcony and found it had come unscrewed. So some said it was Beatrice, because it was late and we were being loud, and she wanted us to close up."

Vokes member David Wood told me "Lights would go on and off. Sometimes when people were going downstairs the lights would go on, as though Beatrice was helping them out."

Tara Stepanion, the producer for the show that was rehearsing, told me, "At a party one time, stage lights kept going on and off for no reason at all. You can't assume it was Beatrice doing it because it could have been a short in the wire. It could have been anything. And yet it kept happening repeatedly, and it didn't happen during the show that we had done that night."

Bobsie Mitton, who was to tell me the dog story that I consider the piece de resistance of this chapter, told me, concerning lights, "I had heard these tales, but I didn't put much credence in them. I figured everybody says theaters are haunted. Every once in a while something funny would happen with the lights and everybody'd say, 'Oh, that's Beatrice!' I'd say, 'Yeah, yeah, yeah, it's Boston Edison, don't kid mc. Or, somebody's up there fiddling with the board, I know.' "

Judi von Dohlen told me of another syndrome dear to the hearts of parapsychological researchers. "I've lost things," she said. "Jewelry and things like that have just disappeared. A lot of times, especially when the theater is empty, you feel a presence. And we all kind of believe it's Beatrice."

Judi came up with a fascinating new twist. "Certain plays that we've done," she said, "there have been a lot of strange things that have happened. We did this show called *Dark of the Moon*, which is filled with all kinds of magical types of things, and we had some experiences on that show, some weird things happened."

The plot thickened as I talked with Bob Jacobs and he spoke of a strange thing that had happened while they were doing *A Midsummer Night's Dream*, Shakespeare's story of mysticism and enchantment. Putting together *Dark of the Moon* and *A Midsummer Night's Dream*, I remembered a theater in Albuquerque, New Mexico, which comprises a chapter in my book *The Ghostly Register*. The stage manager, to her dismay, had seen a ghost on stage during an intermission. The play was *Blithe Spirit*, in which a man's dead wife comes back to haunt him. Could there be something about working on such material that opens people to other realities? I know that when I am writing these books about hauntings some strange things—comparable to those the Vokes people have encountered—occur in my workroom.

Bob Jacobs's *A Midsummer Night's Dream* story is as follows:

> We were having a cast party after the show. We were playing Stevie Wonder tapes, and no matter what tape we played the music always would be turned off in the middle of the tape. Nobody was upstairs in the booth. Anything besides Stevie Wonder would play to the end of the tape, no problem. It was weird.
>
> Most of the time, it's just a strong presence in the theater. My strongest experience was when I was on stage one night during a rehearsal. I looked up and saw somebody sitting in a seat up in the balcony. I saw it out of the corner of my eye. I looked again to fine focus, and there was no one there. I know it was a woman figure. I stopped and came offstage and asked people, "Was anybody up there?" But nobody was.
>
> I've had a few other experiences, such as hearing whisperings. I never could make out what was being said.

The balcony seems a favorite haunt of whoever the spirit may be. Mike Wresinski told me of this happening:

> My first wife and I were doing a show at the Vokes around 1975. We were involved in the last stages of putting it together, and we stayed late to finish a set. It must have been about three in the morning. We were both exhausted, and we sat in the center of the stage looking at our work. We were the only two people in the theater. We heard footsteps going up the back stairs

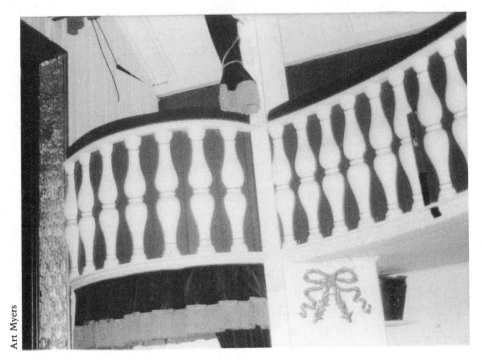

Art Myers

Beatrice Herford's reserved box.

into the balcony, and we wondered who was there at that hour. Then we heard footsteps coming into the balcony area. From the stage, you could clearly see the balcony, and there was nobody accompanying the footsteps. Other people have had similar experiences— hearing footsteps late at night.

Laurie Wayne provides a similar instance:

Yeah, there's definitely somebody there. One time I was sitting down in the basement by myself, and I heard a door slam and feet walking. I called, 'Hi, hi, hi,' and went upstairs and there wasn't a soul there. It wasn't creepy or anything. I know there's something there, but it's completely friendly, it's very happy with whatever's going on.

Whatever's there likes to play. It hides things and then they reappear—just in the nick of time, sometimes. Props disappear. Well, you think, somebody may have moved them. But you'll look in a spot and it's not there, and you'll look again ten minutes later and it's in that spot. It's there and it isn't there, and then it's there again. You find things in different places from where they were.

Many people speak of a "presence." Mary Ellen Pastor told me, "I remember the presence upstairs in the old costume room. Nobody had told me that the costume room was a strong room. I went up there for something, got into the room, and the presence in the room was so overwhelming that it enveloped me. It was, for want of a better word, a *palpable* presence. It was in the back of my throat, it was warm all over my body. It had intelligence. It was a loving kind of feeling. But I had to get out of the room because it was simply more than my human body could manage."

Perhaps what Mary Ellen then said had something to do with her experience. "I know that for myself as an actress, before I went out on stage every night I would stand on the stage by myself. I would meditate, and I would talk to Beatrice. I would say, 'Beatrice, I know that this is your stage. I want to be the best performer I can for you. I want to honor your stage.' I always felt protected and loved by her. She didn't have any problems with me."

I heard from the beginning of my inquiries a rumor that someone had recently seen an image looking out a window of the building, and eventually I found out who it was. It was a law student, Mike Meyer, who had acted in William Gibson's play, *A Cry of Players*, about Shakespeare and his entourage. Mike told me:

After a show I drove over with friends to Hillary's [a nearby restaurant], leaving my truck at the theater. I stayed at Hillary's till it closed, probably around midnight. I then walked back to the theater. There was one other car besides my truck in the parking lot. I got into my truck, which was to the left of the theater, and backed it up, preparing to pull into the main part of the parking lot. As I started forward I saw a figure that I thought was either dressed in white or some bright color looking out the window that is the kitchen window.

Now there was one other car in the parking lot. I told people about this the next day, and I don't think anyone owned up to being there late at night. But there *was* a car there. To put this in context, this was very recently after I had read a newspaper article about the ghost of Beatrice that was hung up on a wall in the theater, so it may have been that the thought was in my mind. But I'm quite sure I did see something, and at the time I was terrified and I drove away very quickly. It may have been someone who was staying afterwards to clean up, but usually that person is Sarah Clawson and it wasn't Sarah, nor was it her son.

What really scared me to death was that it looked like someone in a dress, not a T-shirt or something like that. I don't remember much about the face. It seemed to be looking out the window, not putzing around in the kitchen, and I remember seeing no lights in the kitchen.

Bob Zawitowski told me something that makes a nice lead-in to the final note in this section. He said, "I've never had any experiences, but a few years ago I was stage managing a show and I'd be the last to leave at night. And as I went by the lobby I'd always turn to Beatrice's portrait and say, 'Good night, Beatrice.' I figured if she *was* here it would be a good idea to keep her on your side."

As far as I am concerned, dogs are not only man's best friend but also the most reliable witnesses to hauntings. Dogs never lie. When I interviewed Bobsie Mitton, I was coming off a run of about twenty people who had seen, heard, or felt nothing suspicious in the Vokes, and I needed a lift. Bobsie gave it to me, and I made her my last interview. With Mike Hirsh and his running faucet at the start and Bobsie at the end, I felt the investigation was nicely bracketed. Bobsie said:

> This happened in the late seventies. You know the portrait of Beatrice Herford that's hung in the lobby? I had a very big German shepherd named Jeffie who was just a kind of easygoing critter, and he was over there with me one evening when I was going to a rehearsal. I walked in the door and he came in behind me, turned right, and he came to a screeching halt. He stared at the picture, backed up, turned around, went flipping out the door, and I couldn't get him to go back in the theater.
>
> This was a serious kind of dog. He'd sit around the yard kind of mellow, complacent. He looked like he wanted to become a lawyer. But this night I had to put him in the car. He was transfixed.

History: The little theater was built in the summer of 1904 by Beatrice Herford, an English actress who married an American and came to Wayland to live. The theater was tucked into a corner of their estate. It was named after Rosina Vokes, a well-known English comedienne of the time, whom Miss Herford admired. Miss Herford used the theater for the amusement of herself and her friends. Dances and parties were held there as well as theatricals.

In 1937, she gave a local amateur group permission to use the theater, and in 1946 she gave the theater to this organization, the Vokes Players. She died in 1952.

Art Myers

Portrait of Beatrice Herford that hangs in the lobby.

In observance of Miss Herford's generosity, the box that she used is roped off and unoccupied on opening nights.

In 1973, a portrait of Beatrice Herford that had been painted in 1937 was purchased by the Vokes Players, and it now hangs in the lobby of the theater.

Identity of Ghost: If it isn't Beatrice Herford, a lot of people are going to be bitterly disappointed.

Personality of Ghost: Warm, loving, seemingly watching over the theater and the people in it. Occasionally prankish. Nothing unpleasant has ever been reported.

Witnesses: These are the people who gave me reports of definite phenomena: Mike Willhoite, Mike Hirsh, Derby Swanson, David Wood, Judi von Dohlen, Mike Wresinski, Bob Jacobs, Mary Ellen Pastor, Laurie Wayne, Tara Stepanion, Mike Meyer, Bobsie Mitton.

And by all means, let us not forget Jeffie, the German shepherd.

Other people spoke of feeling a presence. For example, Maureen Connors said, "I've been alone there a couple of times and felt like I wasn't."

Others said they certainly hoped the place had a ghost, although they'd never experienced one. Kippi Goldfarb said, "Actually, I always wanted there to be something like that and I just never ran into it. It's frustrating."

Best Time to Witness: Phenomena were reported at various times of the day or night. They seem to be more noticeable when the place is almost empty.

Still Haunted?: It seems to be.

Investigations: No formal psychic inquiries were reported. However, Mike Wresinski has had some experience in psychic investigations. He told me:

> Not necessarily at the Vokes, but I used to do a lot of parapsychological work. I gave it up because things would follow me, I couldn't get a good night's sleep. This was in my late college years and my early twenties. There would be footsteps in my dorm room. The dormitory had originally been a hotel. My room-

mate and I would hear footsteps going back and forth across the room at night. I experienced tappings on the shoulder, rapping on walls, moving of books and papers. So I was pretty attuned to it. I stopped doing any psychic work because I wanted some peace.

Data Submitted By: About eighty members of the Vokes Players and other people who have been associated with plays there.

The Ashley House.

14
The Restaurant Owner Who Won't Let Go
Vincent's Steak House Has Changed Owners and Names, but Vincent Still Seems to Hang in There

Location: The restaurant, now called the Ashley House, is situated on Riverdale Road (Route 5), a broad and busy highway in the town of West Springfield, just west, as the name implies, of Springfield, Massachusetts. It is probably most easily reached by taking Exit 4 off the Massachusetts Turnpike and going south for half a mile.

Description of Place: The place, a large, commodious, and, as the current phrase has it, upscale restaurant, is housed in a sprawling building that is a combination of old and new. The central part of the building, as noted on a plaque at the entrance, was built in 1829 by Charles Ashley and was, according to material provided by the Massachusetts Historical Commission, "originally the farm house of a substantial homestead that included barns, ice house, aqueduct, and other buildings. Alterations began in the 1930s and 1940s to convert the private dwelling into commercial property. The house apparently began as a standard Greek Revival side hall plan with arched gable windows. Some of the Greek mouldings are still intact."

The place seems to have grown like Topsy, as the no-longer current phrase has it—something here, something there. The original farm holdings are now an extensive parking lot, and nearby, under the same ownership, looms a sizeable motel. The place is something of a melange of the 1820s, the 1990s, and various points between. The building is two stories high, with the dining and drinking rooms on the first floor, offices on the second, and a basement. A large area in the basement is currently used as a banquet hall.

Ceil Lewonchuk.

Art Myers

Ghostly Manifestations: I first heard of the Ashley House and the phenomena reported therein through a psychic and medium I know named Ceil Lewonchuk, who lives in Springfield. Ceil has a call-in show on radio station WRED in nearby Holyoke. David Colson, owner of the Ashley House, began to advertise on the station, and one evening station staffers went to have dinner there. They got an added dividend—restaurant employees regaled them with accounts of ghosts.

Ah, thought the radio people, this is a job for Ceil Lewonchuk! And before long they had Ceil touring the place to see what she might pick up. In the basement she saw an elderly couple, antiquely dressed, sitting before a fireplace, and heard indistinguishable sounds of men talking in a large adjacent room. (Many other people have heard these vague crowd sounds.) These manifestations may be place memories—sounds and sights imprinted on the space, rather than the actual spirits of these long-gone people. Ceil thinks the elderly couple, whom she could hear speaking, were real spirits, probably members of the Ashley family. But the manifestations that the live occupants of the building were most interested in were not such *incidental* former inhabitants, but one in particular— Vincent Lanzarotto.

Vincent—usually called Mr. Vincent—was the co-owner during the restaurant's palmiest days, when it was called Vincent's Steak House. Vincent *was* Vincent's Steak House. From the establishment of that restaurant in 1951 until his death in 1978, he was the kingpin. "For thirty years," says David Colson, "he was the king of all the restaurants in western Massachusetts. He was a famous restaurateur. Ever since he died no one has been successful here."

Colson, and almost everyone else at the restaurant, is reasonably certain it is Vincent who is creating the most noticeable unorthodox happenings in the place. "He was so much a part of this building," Colson says, "and such a strong personality that we have the feeling he would not want to give up. He feels it is *his* restaurant."

The ghostly manifestations are many and varied, but the most unusual is an occasional and very localized odor, usually characterized as vile, although one waitress thought it smelled like perfumed pipe tobacco. However, she was the only person I interviewed who had a good

David Colson.

Art Myers

word for the smell. (I interviewed two waitresses who had
known Vincent, and neither could recall his smoking a
pipe.)

When Colson first bought the restaurant, he was irritated with constant offbeat reports from his employees.
"I'd tell them it was their imaginations," he told me, "get
back to work. The thing that made me a believer was the
odor. I finally had an experience with it. It was a stench, an
awful, dead smell. It was like rotten eggs."

Sandy Cormier, dining room manager, told me, "The
smell was indescribable. You'd be standing in a four-foot
square. You'd step away, and you couldn't smell it, but if
you'd step back in it would be there. It was usually in the
foyer area, where I'm told Mr. Vincent used to greet the
guests."

Mimi Lariviere, a waitress, told me, "Both Sandy and I
have had the experience with the smell. The others have
smelled a real rotgut smell, but I think it smells like sweet
tobacco. One time Sandy called me into the entranceway,
the foyer. There was a four-foot square where you could
smell this very strongly, but if you stepped out of it you

couldn't smell anything. I was stepping back and forth, back and forth. They don't allow pipes or cigars in there, so maybe it's not a pipe smell, but that's what it smells like to me."

Sharon Colson, David's wife, was more downbeat about the odor. "It smells like sewerage," she told me.

While writing about hauntings I have many times run across unexplained odors. However, I can't recall their ever being unpleasant. They ranged from flowers to perfume to newly-baked bread to cigars to chocolate. But in all my investigations, this was the first vile smell that I can remember. For an opinion, I called Enid Hoffman, a psychic and medium I know who has written several books on parapsychology. Enid said:

> All of us have an essence, and that essence has an odor. In living people it comes out in perspiration. A fearful person will emit a strong acrid odor. When people die they can die with very strong feelings. The spirit of an evolved guru emits a beautiful fragrance, but the opposite can be true. Suicides, or people who died in a state of rage or guilt, can emit a very repellent odor. The most common smell of that sort is a sulfuric smell, like rotten eggs.

Vincent Lanzarotto, from all reports, was a very concentrated man. He had started as a waiter in many restaurants and had worked his way up. There seems no question that he watched his employees intently, that he sometimes worked himself into a state of exhaustion and depression. Some people who knew him characterized him with such words as "different," "difficult," "eccentric," "terse."

I spoke with Colleen Nickerson, who had worked in the restaurant as a teenager. She lasted two weeks. "He was very quiet," she told me. "He sat up in the balcony, watching people as though he was afraid they were going to steal from him. He never said anything, he was always just there and staring. The place felt so awful I just couldn't work there."

Yet opinions of this complicated man differ drastically. In fact, ambivalence is quite apparent in many people who knew him.

Kathleen Harrison worked there as a teenager and liked Vincent very much. "He liked me and I liked him," she told me. "He was a businessman. I think if you did good work he would treat you fairly. There were kids who were goofing off, but he was very friendly to us. At the end of a busy Saturday night he would go to McDonald's and buy fifty hamburgers, and we'd all have hamburgers. He was there all the time. He lived there, practically."

Kathleen's mother, Kathleen Hamel, also had a good word for Vincent. "He was very nice," she told me. "He'd give candy to the girls on Valentine's Day. But he wanted things his way, and he had very high standards."

Toward the end of his life, Vincent had an unpleasant experience that must have affected him drastically. He went off on his own and started an additional restaurant, and it failed. I spoke with Bob Dupont, a businessman who had gotten Vincent started at the Steak House, and who was his partner.

"He opened this place downtown," Dupont told me, "but it was very unsuccessful. It folded after one year. He lost a lot of money on it. It was a real bonehead deal, but he wouldn't listen to anyone who was smart."

I was able to interview only one person who said he had seen an apparition of Vincent, although I also heard of a now-deceased waitress who said she had. The person I interviewed was Bernie Pietrewski, a chef who worked for Vincent and who has also worked part-time at the restaurant since Vincent's death.

"I saw him early one morning," Pietrewski told me. "It was about four-thirty or five, and I was fixing lunch. I saw him in the dining room. He was right there."

I interviewed Pietrewski by phone from my home in Wellesley, about eighty miles away, and taped the interview. When I played the tape back I found that, except for this opening, the entire interview was backward. And as I recall, Pietrewski spoke well of Vincent.

(Getting backward or blank interviews while doing these books on the paranormal is nothing new to me. It has happened many times. Two times that stand out in my memory involve a restaurant in Nashua in *The Ghostly Gazetteer* and an interview with the lover of a dead South American dancer in *Ghosts of the Rich and Famous*. In the former, all sorts of untoward things happened while I was taping interviews, both at the restaurant and by phone to various people's homes. The tape would be blank, faint, too slow, or too fast. Sometimes the tape recorder would jam altogether. In the latter interview, whenever I asked a question about the dancer, the response from his friend was missing from the tape. There would be my question, silence, and then my next question, and more silence. When we talked about dancing in general, her responses were quite clear on the tape.

When I asked Enid Hoffman about smells, she mentioned in passing, "Electrical fields can be influenced by people who are disembodied." That she didn't have to tell me.)

Although Bernie Pietrewski's experience was the only full-fledged apparition I heard of, other people came close. "One time," Sandy Cormier told me, "I saw a white wisp going through the dining room. Another night there was this noise that sounded like an ashtray falling on a table. And late one night I heard a man's voice calling my name, someone calling, 'Sandy, Sandy.' I looked through the res-

Sandy Cormier.

Art Myers

taurant but there was no one there. I was completely alone."

Mimi Lariviere reports a similar experience in the basement. "I'm not so sure I believe in ghosts," she told me, "but I know there's something around. I went downstairs one time for a smoke. There's a smoking room in the basement. There's a door from that room into a place that's just cellar, with electrical wiring and so on. I happened to look through the door into that cellar part, and I saw mist or whatever rising. I thought—my cigarette smoke? But I haven't even lit up yet. And there was way too much for that."

Poltergeist activity—things moving around, flying objects—don't seem so prevalent here as in many of the haunted restaurants I've checked out, but they're there. "I saw a glass go flying," Mimi told me. "It was on a shelf in the bar. It didn't fall off, it went four or five feet. There was another waitress just on her way into the room, so she didn't actually see it. But I saw it, it came over my head. I was alone in the room when it happened, the bartender had just gone out the other way. It got my attention."

Many people have heard what sounds like place-memory noises. For many years, the building was the Ashley family homestead, but in this century it has been a public place most of the time, and it has been rumored that sometimes the activity there was rather sporty. I was told that there are elderly people in the neighborhood who remember when the building housed a tavern that respectable women would not enter. It was said that upstairs there were women who were paid to play. What's even more exotic is that I was told that at some period in history the basement was host to cock fights, with their raucous attendants. They must have made a lot of noise, and it may be reverberating down the years.

A specific account of such off-stage noises comes from Sandy Cormier. "One time I was standing at the cash register, where my desk is," she told me. "It was New Year's Day, in the morning, and there was just the chef and myself in the building. And I could hear like people talking very faintly. I went into the kitchen and asked the chef if he was calling me, and he said no. He said he heard that too, and had at other times, especially like Sunday mornings when he was alone. I went back out to the restaurant. I was standing with my back toward the wall and I felt a tug on my shirt—and there was nobody there."

In recent years, there was a caretaking couple who had an apartment on the second floor. David Colson told me they would constantly hear footsteps downstairs. The building has a Sonitrol alarm system, which is based on sound. "This couple," Colson said, "would hear the noises downstairs, but the Sonitrol wouldn't have any record of it. There wouldn't be anything on the tape. And when they'd go downstairs to check there wouldn't be anyone there."

A person who seemed to attract poltergeist activity was Cindy Paul, a bartender. Several people told me of an adventure of Cindy's with the dish-washing machine, and when I caught up to her she verified it. "I was walking through the kitchen," she said, "and the dishwasher turned on and soaked me from head to toe. The cover was up, and it just went off by itself and soaked me, and then it shut off by itself.

"And the faucets would turn on and the lights would flicker on and off. Things would be rearranged sometimes on me. I would come into the bar and things would be changed a little from the way I had left them. I was closing and opening, so I knew it couldn't be anyone else. Silverware would be pushed forward a little bit, or whatever. It was starting to make me think I had Alzheimer's, and I'm only twenty-five."

Mysterious rearrangements were not restricted to the bar. Rita Tassone, a bookkeeper, had her share of them on the second floor. She told me:

My office was at the top of the stairs, to the left. I shared the office with Pam Clapp, who was the banquet manager. We heard a lot of walking around, constant footsteps. I was kind of a jokester, so people would kid around and try to scare me. The steps coming up to the second floor are wood, so if someone was coming up you could hear them. A lot of times we would hear someone coming up who never turned the corner. In the beginning, I thought it was someone trying to scare me. I would tiptoe over to the staircase to scare *them*, and when I turned the corner there was nobody there! That happened quite a bit. We'd be sitting there and we'd hear the door at the bottom of the staircase open, and nobody would come up.

And there was the business with the adding machine. Everybody would say it was a surge of electricity. [Which reminded me of the explanation that UFOs are marsh gas.—author] But the adding machine would periodically go on by itself. Numbers would come out, but Pam and I couldn't see any significance to them.

I'd often put things down and find them in different places—papers, invoices—they'd be on a different part of the desk. Or instead of being on the desk they'd be on the counter.

Pam Clapp told me:

I had bizarre experiences. I would be standing in the office using the Xerox machine and I could feel somebody there with me. It would walk by and bump into me. It was as though something was rubbing up against me, as though somebody was standing looking over my shoulder. It was the weirdest thing.

I was pregnant, and I was really getting spooked. It's not that anyone was ever harmed, but I was so fearful of going up there alone, and I used to have to go up there every Saturday morning by myself.

This was in the early 1980s, and at the time a family named Zurlino owned the restaurant. "They had their son, Robert, work here awhile as manager," Rita said. "He was an unbeliever from the word go. He'd be trying to scare me all the time. But one time he went into his room at the end of the hall and he felt something grab him. He ran, and he came down those stairs and missed every one of them. He rolled down. I was standing at the bottom, and he hit every step. He was petrified."

I called Robert Zurlino in Boca Raton, Florida, where he now lives, and he made no bones about his experience. "I felt like there was a presence in the room," he told me. "I was sitting at my desk and I sensed somebody walking up behind me. It was a room that Vincent had used. I felt like someone was touching my shoulder. I flew out of the room.

It scared the living daylights out of me. I ran down the stairs and I tripped. I never felt comfortable again going in there by myself, I'll tell you that much."

In fact, he gave his successor in the job, Paul Teehan, some advice. Teehan is now a high school teacher in Moncks Corner, South Carolina, but he still remembers his first day at the restaurant. "When Zurlino showed me around," Teehan told me, "he said, 'Do not go in this room alone.' I did try going in the room a few times. I don't know if it was the power of suggestion, but I didn't like being in that room."

History: The original part of the building was erected by Charles Ashley in 1829. The Ashleys were a prominent family, and this was their homestead until the final Ashley to live there sold it around 1920. David Colson, who did some research on the place, is not sure what the building was used for during the next twenty-five years. It was probably during this period that it was the tavern with the special accommodations upstairs.

Colson says that at the end of World War II it became Matteoli's Spaghetti House, and in 1951 Vincent and Bob Dupont began their very successful steak house there. On Vincent's death in 1978 the place was taken over by his lawyer and accountant, who Colson says ended up with it "by default." Not long afterward it was sold to the Zurlinos. More recently it was purchased by a restaurant group called the Steak Club, which for a time owned eleven restaurants. "Last March [1991] we dissolved the Steak Club," Colson told me, "and I ended up with this restaurant and the motel."

Identities of Ghosts: If the most evident spirit isn't Vincent Lanzarotto, the folks at the Ashley House are under a serious misapprehension. The crowd noises that emanate from downstairs might indicate some leftover energy from groups who congregated there during the past century and a half.

Ceil Lewonchuk says that on her first tour of the basement she heard the apparition of the old woman say to the old man, "We have to go across the river and get the minister for the wedding." She feels these two are real spirits, probably Ashleys.

Personalities of Ghosts: Assuming that the most prominent spirit is indeed Mr. Vincent, he seems to be keeping a close eye on the way the place is being run.

Witnesses: Ceil Lewonchuk, psychic; David Colson, owner; Sharon Colson, wife of owner; Rod Lewonchuk, onetime Vincent's Steak House busboy, currently an airline pilot; Colleen Nickerson, former waitress; Robert Zurlino, former manager; Georgia Zurlino, former co-owner; Effie Johnson, waitress; Sandy Cormier, dining room manager; Mimi Lariviere, waitress; Bernie Pietrewski, chef; Nora Lafond, waitress; Cindy Paul, former bartender; Rita Tassone, former office manager; Pam Clapp, former banquet manager; Kathleen Harrison, former waitress; Clark Bertera, former employee; Paul Teehan, former manager; Mike Lecca, former employee.

Best Time to Witness: Phenomena have been reported pretty much around the clock.

Still Haunted?: Ceil Lewonchuk, at this writing, had paid three visits to the restaurant. On the second visit, she "smudged" the building with a stick of sage; sage is believed to quiet spirits.

"I did not have contact with Vincent," she told me, "I just felt his presence. I told him to go to the light." By that, she meant she urged him to change his earthbound status and go on to higher spiritual planes. But she added, "I don't know if I got rid of him." However, this would presumably have no effect on the other psychic manifestations in the building.

On Ceil's tours, she observed a second-floor storage room that the employees call the spook room. She said her throat felt tight and her stomach hurt in that room. "In there," she told me, "David has a lot of stuff left from Vincent—awards given to him for serving so many Hiram Walker drinks; a sign, "Vincent's Steak House"; napkin rings from the old restaurant. I felt that David should get rid of all that stuff that belonged to Vincent, it would help get rid of his spirit."

Investigations: Aside from those of Ceil Lewonchuk, no mention was made of any other formal inquiries.

Data Submitted By: The above-named witnesses. Enid Hoffman, psychic; Bob Dupont, former co-owner; Kathleen Hamel, mother of Kathleen Harrison. Material from the Massachusetts Historical Commission and the West Springfield Historical Commission.

15
A Nice Little Ghost Town—
In More Ways Than One
On the Shores of Lake Superior, the Spirits Gambol

Location: The village of Sheldrake, Michigan, is no longer on the map, but it's four miles north of Paradise, which is—barely. Paradise is sixty miles north and west of Sault Sainte Marie, the largest town on Michigan's Upper Peninsula. It can be reached by going west on Route 28 through Hiawatha National Forest, turning north on Route 123. Or the scenic route can be taken along the shores of Lake Superior. From Paradise, Sheldrake can be reached by taking the Whitefish Point Road north.

Description of Place: Sheldrake is an old logging village that once numbered some fifteen hundred people and about 150 buildings. Only a few buildings were left after a fire in the 1920s and only about a dozen houses are currently standing. They are owned by Brent Biehl, an entrepreneur from Detroit who moved his family here in the 1960s and who has developed a small manufacturing plant for wood products that employs a dozen people.

Biehl, his wife, and their six now-grown children have been for the most part the only year-round residents of the place, although they have renovated some of the wooden houses and do summer rentals.

The Biehls collect artifacts of the old Sheldrake, and hope eventually to turn one of the houses into a little museum, a memorial to the logging village that once existed.

The place is on Whitefish Bay, part of Lake Superior, and is a timbered retreat far from the madding crowd. "You can see the mountains of Canada across the Bay," Biehl says.

Ghostly Manifestations: When Brent Biehl arrived from Detroit some twenty-five years ago he was a go-getting young businessman who wanted to get away from city life. Ghosts were far from his thoughts. So when he heard about a sea captain who was wont to appear and disappear on one of the village's dilapidated docks, he chalked it up to tradition. But before long he and his family began to have strange experiences, and so did some of the people to whom he rented summer homes.

"These are people in responsible positions," Biehl told me. "They're not people who are given to hallucinations or exaggerations. Whether they would want to talk for publication I don't know."

What attracted me to this story was that Biehl himself was undecided whether or not to talk for publication. He said he wanted time to think about it and discuss it with his family. I found this reluctance most refreshing, since I had just spent considerable time and money researching a bed and breakfast, the owners of which, I began to strongly suspect, were inventing quite a bit just to get into these pages. I had scratched that mission, and was not in the mood for another like it.

But Sheldrake is on the Michigan Historic Register, with a state marker just across the street from the Biehls' house, so they decided that a few tourists wouldn't be too troublesome, and maybe they were entitled.

Regarding the sea captain, Biehl told me, "Back in the early 1900s, the story is that people approaching from he lake could see this sea captain standing on the dock. He had a cap and a pipe and a cape. People would see him from about half a mile out, and as they came closer he would disappear. This was reported by a number of people."

Before long, the Biehls began to have experiences of their own.

> Next door to us there's a house that at one time was a stagecoach stop. It was the only post office in the area, and it also served for a visiting doctor. We began to acquire stuff from people who had lived around here, and we put it in this house. The next day I noticed that the door was open. I shut it again and locked it, and a few days later it was open again. Every once in a while this door would be open. I didn't believe in ghosts, but after it happened a few times it began to dawn on me that maybe I was supposed to leave this door open, so that's what I did. I told myself there had to be a logical explanation.
>
> There's a two-story house that we call the Palmer House. It was a company house originally, with a little porch and two front windows. One of the last regular residents was a retired city engineer from Detroit. He liked to sail, and he would sit on a chair on the porch and watch the bay out there. He died and left the house to some nephews. They put up two shades across the front windows. The first time they left, within twenty-four hours one shade was down on the right-hand side in front of the chair where this engineer always rocked. The next time they came they put the shade up, stayed

a couple of days, and left. The next morning we noticed that the shade was down again.

This went on for about two years. One time I was going by the house and I could see the shade shaking. My wife was working in our garden and I called her over. We both stood there and watched the shade shake until it came down. It was really an eerie feeling. Finally my wife told the people what was happening and they took the shades down.

We used to see a light in the house, in the winter when there's nobody here. The house was locked, and there was four feet of snow on the ground, with no tracks in it.

Back in the early seventies, I had a general manager named Gordon Huntwork. He was an Indian and came from the area. One day I asked him if he had had any strange experiences around here. At first he said no, but then he said, well yes, he had. He told me, "One time about two in the morning I was up and reading the Bible and I got to wondering if God really existed. I said out loud, 'God, give me a sign.' I just got the word *sign* out of my mouth when the television came on. It scared the living daylights out of me."

I asked Biehl what program had come on, but he said at that hour it must have just been snow and static.

Biehl told me about the Hopkins House, where an elderly couple had lived. The man was a government trapper, and he also carved birds. "After he died," Biehl told me, "we bought the house from his wife and rented it to some people. I'll see if they will talk to you."

A few days later I did an interview with the woman who had lived there—the live woman, that is. I have interviewed several hundred people concerning various hauntings, and this lady must rank as my most reluctant witness. The psychic experience was hers; her husband worked at night and she was home with two small children.

"I was really angry at my husband for saying to Brent that I would speak to you," she said. "I told him, 'Don't speak for me again.' Most people think that people who see spirits are wackos. I had never seen a spirit before this happened, and I've never seen one since. In fact, I don't know for sure what it was I saw."

She has legitimate cause for reluctance. She is now a top executive in a conservative corporation in a large city. "I can just hear the president [of the company] if he knew about this," she said, "he gives me the raspberries about everything in the world as it is."

I agreed to disguise her identity and she gave this account:

> It was in the middle of the night. I was sleeping, and something made me turn on my side in bed. I saw a form come through the bathroom window. I was going to get up, because we had kids in the house, but I couldn't move. But I had a real peaceful feeling all of a sudden, like something was saying to me not to be frightened.
>
> My interpretation is that whatever came into the house just wanted to check on us, to see if we were good people. I could feel that spirit go through the entire house. It had a form, but it was like an aura more than anything else. When the spirit left it left exactly the same way it had come in, through the bathroom window, and suddenly I could move again. I went to check on the kids and they were all right. They had slept through the whole thing. I went back to bed and fell asleep immediately. It was about six weeks before I told anyone.

Less guarded witnesses are Doug and Paula Smith, who lived in one of the houses while Doug was teaching mathematics and physics at Whitefish Township School. They now live in Marquette, where Doug is coordinator for the Emergency Medical Service of the Upper Peninsula and Paula is a preschool teacher. She told me:

> I was there all the time. I was the one who was raising the kids so I got to run into these things more than Doug. Every once in a while we would have a cold spot, the kind you could just sort of walk through—usually in the living room.
>
> You would hear doors close and latch, but when you went to look they'd be open. You'd hear creaking noises, as though someone was walking across the floor, and you'd turn around and there would be no one there.
>
> We had one of those little mobiles that play music. All of a sudden it started to play and spin around. I looked over at it and said, "Now cut that out!" and it stopped.
>
> One morning at breakfast Doug told me he had had a weird dream. He saw a guy sitting on the couch in the living room and staring through the door into our bedroom. I went, "Oh, I had the same dream!" We started describing the guy to each other and our descriptions were alike. He had a dark, beardish face and a logger-type look about him. We began to see him at night when we were awake in bed. He never went into the new sections of the house. Sometimes he'd be sitting on the couch and sometimes he'd be standing in the doorway. But he never came into the bedroom. It was like having a mysterious person there. We never got up to take a better look at him. In fact, it was about that time that Doug decided I should sleep on the side of the bed that was closest to the door. He said it was so I could get to the babies sooner.

Doug corroborated Paula's account of the mystery guest, adding the detail that he was wearing bib overalls. And he provided this vignette of domestic horseplay.

> One time I was doing the dishes and I thought I heard

Paula sneaking up behind me. I got a bowl full of water ready, figuring she was going to grab me, and I was going to go "Aaghhh!" and dump the water on her. But she never grabbed me, and I turned around and looked and there was no one there. I swear I heard footsteps coming up behind me.

The Biehl family, being among the few people who have lived in Sheldrake year-round in recent years, seems to have had the most experiences.

"In our house," Brent Biehl told me, "a number of people have seen what appears to be a lady in a blue veil. They'd see this person going by them, or standing beside their bed. Everybody saw the same thing—my mother, my wife, our children. We had an old chest of drawers, an antique vanity, that we brought over from the Hawkins House, and it seemed to trigger this thing. We finally took it out of the house and the appearances stopped."

Voices would be heard, pictures would fall off walls, faucets would turn on for no visible reason. "We just sort of lived with it," Brent told me. "If I related everything that happened you probably could write a book, but they are just the garden-variety poltergeist things."

After twenty-five years, one does get blase.

But he still gets a chuckle from the reaction of a group of men who came in to work on one of the houses. "The crew leader was a grizzled old World War II veteran," Biehl relates, "a very tough character. He'd been a prison guard, and he was always getting into fights in bars. He had two of his sons and a couple of other guys working with him and they all began hearing voices, and they could smell food cooking. The sounds and the smells got stronger and stronger, till they all just packed up their tools and left. Of course, they didn't know anything about ghosts and what goes on here. But for this guy to walk off a job because he was frightened was really something."

History: The area was first inhabited by Indians. The French came in the 1600s. They gave the place the name Sheldrake after the diving duck that frequents those parts. The first white settlement developed in the 1800s. "The town existed for some forty years," Biehl says, "before the lumbering gave out. When the lumbering began to run out there were a couple of disastrous fires, the last one being in 1926. There's a suspicion these were set for the insurance, which was almost a common practice in those days. Anyway, the mill burned and the lumbering moved on. They started the little town of Paradise, four miles south."

Identities of Ghosts: They seem to be onetime residents of the town.

Personalities of Ghosts: They have never been known to harm anyone. They merely seem attached to the place and curious about the present residents.

Witnesses: Brent Biehl, his wife Mary, and their children; Doug and Paula Smith; Gordon Huntwork; the frightened workmen; the female executive who testified on the promise of anonymity.

Best Time to Witness: Day or night.

Still Haunted?: Seems to be.

Investigations: As far as Brent Biehl knows, no professional psychics have visited the town. However, we got into a discussion as to why this place would be so seemingly haunted. Places such as Tombstone, Arizona, in this book (Chapter 1) or Skagway, Alaska, and Bodie, California, in *The Ghostly Gazetteer* were rough, tough mining towns with murder, theft, and disappointment saturating the very air. Such negative experiences, parapsychologists surmise, can be very ghost-making. People who suffer sudden, violent deaths or who have had lives fraught with frustration can tend to hold onto the physical plane instead of moving on to spiritual planes. But Sheldrake was a working town, no more depressing than most places on our planet.

I had a suggestion, which I derived from investigating the Spy House, in New Jersey, a spectacularly haunted building (Chapter 18). Two psychics there told me they thought the place was so haunted because it was right on the water, Sandy Hook Bay, the theory being that spirits can manifest more easily, can break through the veil, when there is water involved. "It's a sort of electromagnetic effect," one psychic told me.

It occurred to me that many spirit manifestations seem to take place in lavatories. They seem particularly rife in ladies' rooms, although they probably happen as much in men's rooms but men aren't so prone to talk about it. When I mentioned this to Brent Biehl, he said that their bathroom was the most active room in their house. It was there that the pictures kept falling off the walls and faucets kept coming on by themselves.

Data Submitted By: Brent and Mary Biehl; Doug and Paula Smith; the female executive who wants anonymity.

The Hotel Savoy in its early days.

16
A Ghost Who Turns on the Shower and Closes the Curtain

And Another Who Liked to Chat with His Wife

Location: The Hotel Savoy is at 219 West Ninth Street in downtown Kansas City, Missouri.

Description of Place: This is an old hotel, reputedly the oldest continuously operating hotel west of the Mississippi. In the past couple of years it has gotten a new lease on life. It was built in 1888 and was very fashionable up through World War II. Then, according to the present manager, Sean Byrnes, it degenerated into a flophouse. The present owner, Don Lee, has had it for thirty years, and two years ago took the money he had made from running the place as a low-rent operation and put it into renovating it.

"Now," Byrnes said, "we're bringing it back to a European-style bed and breakfast. For breakfast we have a choice of more than thirty items. You fill out your menu the night before. You can choose things like lobster bisque, scallopini au veal, baked oyster Rockefeller on the half shell, caviar. You don't have to eat breakfast, but the rate is the same."

The now posh hotel will be for the transient trade, but will also have apartments for permanent residents. "We've got fifteen apartments up and running now," Byrnes says. "We expect to have twenty of these, and we'll also have ninety rooms and suites for temporary guests."

Byrnes describes the building as European in design—Italian Renaissance. "The lobby," he says, "has eighteen-foot ceilings, with art nouveau stained-glass windows. There are hand-laid Italian tiles. The outside was once very regal-looking, with a roof garden on top, and antique streetlights done in copper that ran along the side of the building. We're bringing those back.

"It's a six-story structure, done in red brick with a lot of terra-cotta work in front. The entire first floor front is done in stained glass."

Sean Byrnes.

Ghostly Manifestations: This account contains two unrelated ghost stories, from people who currently live and/or work in the building. But the hotel seems to have a reputation for generalized spookiness that goes back in its history. Sean Byrnes has been there only two years but says he has heard stories from the past. Reid Shaylor has been a waiter in the hotel's restaurant for four years, and for the first two, when the room rates were cheap, he lived there. "Before I worked here," he told me, "I'd heard rumors and stories about the place." Byrnes mentioned that current guests have occasionally spoken of the odd incident, particularly images of an elderly man.

But let us now consider the spirit of Larry Freeman's bathroom. Freeman is a young man who works in the marketing department of the Kansas City Chiefs, the professional football team. Larry moved into one of the newly renovated apartments—number 505—in September 1990. His first adventure occurred within a couple of days.

> The bathtub is one you have to step into, and there's a curtain that goes around it. Usually when I get out of the tub I leave the curtain open. I started brushing my teeth after taking a shower and I heard the water running behind me. I turned around and the curtain was closed and the water was running. My first thought was that I had closed the curtain inadvertently, and for some reason the water had come on. So I opened the curtain and turned the faucet off. As soon as I turned back toward the sink the water was running again. And the curtain was closed again. I opened the curtain again and turned the water off, turned around, and the water immediately came back on, and the curtain was closed.
>
> I thought maybe the screw that was holding the faucet was loose, so I got a screwdriver and tried to screw it down as hard as I could. But when I'd turn

around, the shower just kept coming back on. I didn't know what to think.

So I called Sean, and he said the way the system works the screw wouldn't have anything to do with it, that he'd check it out. So I went out to work. Sean called me at work and said there was nothing he could find that was wrong with the shower.

Sean said that later in the day he had gone to his own apartment, which is also on the fifth floor, and about 7:00 P.M. he had gone down to the front desk. "As I was walking past Larry's apartment," he said, "I could hear music playing. I thought, good, we can go out for a beer later. I went down to the desk and Larry walked in. He had his jacket over his shoulder; he was just getting home from work. I told him I had heard music coming from his apartment. He thought maybe he had set his clock radio wrong, for 6:00 P.M. instead of 6:00 A.M. But when we got up there it was not the clock radio that was playing, it was a radio he keeps by his washing machine. He keeps this radio always set to a classic rock-and-roll station. Well, someone had turned the knob over to an all-jazz station and flipped the radio on. Larry told me he had listened to the rock-and-roll station that morning, and he and I are the only ones with keys to the apartment. When I'd been in there to look at the shower the music wasn't on."

Sean told me that the story was that an elderly woman, a longtime resident of Apartment 505, had died in the bathtub some years before. The last person I interviewed for this chapter was Margaret Barber, mother of the hotel's owner, who said she had lived in the place for thirty years. Her recollections involve certain additions and alterations to the information I had received, but nothing essential, aside from her assertion that she doesn't believe in ghosts, and that no ghost has ever darkened the door of the Savoy. Margaret gets her innings later in this account.

Larry Freeman's next adventure occurred a few months later. "The configuration of my apartment," he said, "is one long room, with a sliding door between my living room and bedroom. I normally sleep with that door closed. One night, about 11:30, I heard the door slide open. I opened my eyes, and it was open half way. I sat there about twenty minutes trying to get my cowardice up, to see if there was an intruder there."

(Sean Byrnes told me that the oak door "is tilted, gravity-wise, so that it remains closed.")

(It might also be appropriate to mention that Larry stands six feet two inches tall and weighs 190 pounds. In high school he played offensive guard on the football team and was named all-state. At William Jewell College he played offensive guard and defensive end. He did not go into professional football as a player, he told me, because the injuries had started to mount up. "My playing weight was around 240," he said. "I'm not a small person.")

But who knew what lay beyond that doorway? An intruder with a weapon? A ghost?

"Finally," Larry said, "I just kind of went flying through the doorway, hoping nobody was there. And nobody was. The apartment hadn't been tampered with, and the outer door was still locked. For the next half hour I kept closing the sliding door, trying to see why it would open. But it wouldn't open by itself. This has never happened since, just that one time. I always try to rationalize these things, because when you have these stories people look at you a little cockeyed—unless it's happened to them."

Reid Shaylor, the young waiter who once lived at the hotel, is a psychic person. He is planning to move from his present apartment because he doesn't like the ghosts there.

He had a friend, Kathy O'Dell, who worked on the front desk and who was also psychic. He lived on the third floor and she lived on the fourth. They often did tarot card readings in her apartment. An elderly woman, Mrs. Lightner, lived across the hall from Kathy. Reid told me:

One evening—I think this was in late 1987—Mrs. Lightner came over and asked if she could borrow some sugar. Kathy said, "Sure, I'll bring it over for you." Then Kathy discovered that she didn't have any sugar, so she asked me to run down to the store and get some. So I got some sugar and came back and I knocked on Mrs. Lightner's door. I heard her talking to someone behind the door, but I didn't think anything of that because she did that all the time. So I opened the door and I saw this man standing there right beside her. He was wearing a double-breasted suit like they wore in the 1930s. He was very gray. It was just an outline, but you could see him clearly. Then he disappeared. I asked her who she was talking to, and she said, "Oh, that's my dead husband, Fred." When I turned around, Kathy was at the door, and she said, "I don't believe it, I saw it too."

For about a month after that, in my room a floor down I had several occurrences. I'd come home late at night and cassettes and record albums that I had put away would be laid out on my bed, as though somebody had been selecting something to play. And during the night it would be extremely cold, much more than it should be. And the chifforobe that I had—you could lock it, and I would—every afternoon when I came home it would be unlocked. And nobody had the key but me.

(A chifforobe, Reid told me, is a sort of old-fashioned clothes cabinet.)

Things like that happened several times after I saw Mr. Lightner. Both Kathy and I are Catholics, and we do things like light candles on Sunday. We'd come back from church and the candles would be blown out. Little things like that.

My last interviewee was Mrs. Barber, an elderly and amiable lady who told me she had lived on the fifth floor "for years and years." She said she was raised Catholic and doesn't believe in ghosts. I forebore to mention that two active Catholics I knew of claimed to have had quite a variety of spirited experiences in the building.

But Mrs. Barber, though a doubter, filled in a few chinks in my information. Yes, she said, an elderly woman *had* died in Apartment 505, several years before, but she died in bed, not in the bathtub. "She had a heart condition and lived there alone," Mrs. Barber said. "Her name was Betsy Ward." And, she said, Mrs. Lightner's name was Goldie, and she had died not long before in a hospital.

History: The Hotel Savoy was built in 1888 and was one of the best hotels in Kansas City until the late 1940s, when it degenerated into, as my informants bluntly informed me, a flophouse. It was rescued from this ignominy in 1990, when the owner began converting it back to its former glory.

Sean Byrnes gave me a historical footnote. He said that Harry Houdini, the famed magician and escape artist, was once imprisoned in a phone booth in the lobby, and that it was one of the few times in his life he was unable to escape. Sean said:

> In November 1900 Houdini was traveling through and stopped at the hotel to spend the night. The way you made a phone call then was to give the desk clerk a nickel and the clerk would give you the key to the phone booth. A traveling salesman by the name of B. P. Wilkinson walked by and noticed Houdini in the booth. He was able to get a key and he locked Houdini in. He told everyone about it, and called the press. Houdini had a humongous ego, and he ranted and raved and shook and shook, but he couldn't get out of

the phone booth. They finally had to find a key. By this time Wilkinson saw that it wasn't funny, that Houdini was probably going to kill him, and he got out of there in a hurry.

Identities of Ghosts: According to Margaret Barber, onetime head housekeeper and longtime resident, the spirit in Larry Freeman's apartment may be Betsy Ward, who died there a few years ago. That is, if there were such a thing as ghosts.

The other ghost appears to be Fred Lightner, husband of Goldie. Reid Shaylor seems to suspect that Fred took a liking to him for fetching sugar for Goldie, and frequented his room for a time after the sighting.

Sean Byrnes tossed in another intriguing possibility concerning the doings in 505. "When we were renovating," he said, "we knocked down a wall and we found a turn-of-the-century .32-caliber pistol sealed in the wall."

Personalities of Ghosts: They seem harmless enough.

Witnesses: Sean Byrnes, manager; Larry Freeman, tenant; Reid Shaylor, waiter in the hotel restaurant and onetime resident; Kathy O'Dell, former employee and resident. Rumors of incidents reported by tenants throughout the history of the hotel.

Best Time to Witness: The time does not seem to matter.

Still Haunted?: Larry Freeman's experience with the sliding door occurred about a month before my interview with him, so he probably still has company.

One might presume that since Goldie Lightner has

left this plane and the hotel that her husband Fred would no longer be hanging around, but who knows? Who is the elderly man whose apparition guests are currently reporting? It might be Fred, but Sean Byrnes points out that many elderly men have lived in the hotel.

Investigations: None reported so far, but Sean Byrnes says bringing in a psychic might not be a bad idea.

Data Submitted By: The above witnesses and Margaret Barber.

The Sise Inn.

17
A New Hotel in an Old New England Mansion
A Sporty Spirit Seems to Fondle Chambermaids, Lock Doors, and Run the Ice Machine

Location: The Sise Inn is located at 40 Court Street in the Downtown Historical District of Portsmouth, New Hampshire. Portsmouth is on Route 95, about fifteen miles north of the Massachusetts state line and about sixty miles north of Boston.

Description of Place: Portsmouth is a charming New England city with a population of 28,000, an old seaport town. The Sise Inn was originally a house built in the Queen Anne style by a prosperous businessman, John E. Sise, in 1881. The house included three stories plus a ground floor. It served as a residence until the middle of this century, and then was used for a variety of professional and commercial purposes.

In the early 1980s, the house was bought by an enterprise called Someplace(s) Different, which owns hostelries in New Hampshire, Maine, and Ontario, Canada. The new owner renovated the original part of the building, maintaining the butternut wood paneling and the Victorian ambience, and built a contemporary addition, complete with a bright atrium that rises some sixty feet. The place is filled with antique beds, armoires, and other furniture, harmonizing with modern touches such as a striking brass elevator door on the main floor. It's the sort of place that provides books, classical cassettes, and such touches as a decorative chess set on a coffee table in the guest lounge.

Carl Jensen.

Art Myers

Ghostly Manifestations: The manager of the inn is Carl Jensen, a Copenhagen native who arrived in Portsmouth by way of twenty years in California. He told me:

> Shirley Cook was our night desk clerk. She moved to Arizona about a year ago. She told me the first story that made me wonder what was going on.
> On the third floor we have an ice machine where the guests can get ice cubes. Shirley was at the desk and she heard the ice machine working. We had no guests at the time. She went up to check it out, and she noticed the door of a suite was ajar. The doors are

always locked when no one is registered in a room. There were four steps leading up from the corridor to the door of this suite. She looked around, and saw that there were ice cubes on the floor by the bin. And there was a trail of ice cubes down the corridor, up the steps, and into the suite. And there was nobody there.

This is Suite 214, and it had a few other peculiarities.

We constantly had trouble with the lock. One evening I checked in a couple who went out to some celebration and came back about two in the morning. When they got up to 214 they couldn't turn the key. They came down to see the night clerk, who went up to see what he could do. He was a very large, strong young man, but he couldn't turn it either. He was afraid if he tried any harder he would break the key in the lock. It was a Saturday night and we had a full house, so there was no other place to put the people.

He called me up and I came over. I thought maybe I could use my emergency key. It wouldn't work, so we called a locksmith. By this time it was four in the morning. He came over, took the key, put it in the door, and turned it. The door opened as if nothing had happened. And for two hours we couldn't turn that key!

Jensen had another tale of Suite 214.

The key was constantly missing. I know that some people will take a key, either forget to turn it in or keep it as a souvenir, but the key to that particular room kept coming back in the mail all the time. Sometimes it was in an envelope, other times it had just been dropped into a mailbox and the address of the inn was on the tag. This didn't happen, at least regularly, with the keys of other rooms. After this happened half a dozen times, I began to think this is a strange coincidence, why just this key? And then all of a sudden it stopped being missing and coming back.

Jensen and I ruminated about what could have happened. Why would so many guests in 214 forget to turn the key in? Did they send it back, or was it some spirit who did it? Did the spirit spirit it off in the first place? The mind reels.

"We've never seen anything," Jensen said, "although we've heard things. And the maids would come to me and say they'd be in a room making the bed and someone would seem to come up behind them and touch them, put hands on their hips. This has happened several times, with different maids and different rooms. One maid opened a closet and felt something was pulling her in."

Jensen tells of a guest who was sitting in his room reading. "He heard a noise and looked up. There was a plant in a pot on the coffee table and he saw it flying off the table. He came down white as a sheet and demanded another room immediately. That's the only time I know of when we had a moving object, although other guests may have had experiences they never mentioned to us."

I interviewed as many employees or former employees as I could catch up with. One was Peggy Brooks, who has been a chambermaid at the inn for four years. She told me of cold spots, of constantly having trouble with the locks of rooms. "One time," she said, "a guest told me someone lay down on the bed beside her. The bed went down as though someone was on it."

Peggy told me she is not completely new to this sort of thing, that when she was a child she lived in a haunted house where one could often smell apple pie baking. A more unpleasant aspect of that particular house was that every so often something would seem to kick the dog. "The poor thing would jump and go 'Yap!'" Peggy said.

Art Myers

Peggy Brooks.

Art Myers

Diane Higgins.

Diane Higgins, function coordinator, told me she had two experiences one day when she began working at the inn, before she had heard anything about ghosts.

"Early one morning," she said, "the elevator just started up, all by itself, from the ground floor near my office, and it went up to the third floor. I heard the doors open. That same evening I heard the ice machine working. This was a different time from when Shirley Cook saw the trail of ice cubes, but the same machine. Maybe the ghost was saying hello. I didn't mention it for a month to anyone, and then I heard that the elevator moves on its own quite a bit."

A couple of night employees told me that their theory is there's something mechanically wrong with the elevator, which is a good way to look at it in the middle of the night.

Anna Bauer, a former front desk clerk, said, "People have told me about things, but I haven't had any unusual experiences myself. I guess I missed everything."

I had an intriguing interview with Dennis Dwyer, a current night clerk. It went like this:

"Have you had any strange experiences?"

"I have, but I don't believe in them. I thought I saw some strange things, but . . ."

"What happened?"

"I saw a rocking chair moving in the middle of the night. It was rocking, and there was no one around but me. It was in the winter so the windows were all shut, there was no draft. It was in the guests' breakfast room. It's a small chair, an old child's chair. It's right next to the front desk, I would have heard anyone in there. I went in to get a cup of coffee and it was rocking. I don't believe in those things, and that's why I find it strange. I can't figure out why that chair would have been moving."

"Did you have any other experiences?"

"We have a tremendously large pair of scissors under the desk. I've never used them, nobody would use them really. One night I was in the parlor and when I came back to the desk that pair of scissors was lying on the check-in book, on top of the desk. Now I never used those scissors, I would never take them out from under the desk. You might say somebody else came and went behind the desk and used the scissors, but I can't see how that could happen without my hearing them, just a few feet away. We have tile floors, and you can hear when people walk on them."

I said, "Let me ask you, when you see a chair rocking and there's nobody around, and you see scissors that have moved, why do you think it happens? You don't seem to believe your eyes."

"Exactly!" Dennis exclaimed. "I always explain it off some way. Because I want to keep my job. If I didn't explain it off I'd be too scared to work there all night."

History: Built as a wealthy family's residence in 1881, and used as a family home till the 1930s, it then became, at various times, apartments, business offices, a halfway house for recovering mental patients, a doctor's suite of offices, a beauty parlor, and a fashion shop. With additions and renovations, it was opened as an inn in 1986.

Identity of Ghost(s): Here the plot thickens. Carl Jensen told me, "The story goes that the Sise family had a butler and a maid who had a love affair that went wrong. The story is that he murdered her and then committed suicide. He is supposed to have hanged himself in his room on the top floor. But there is no documentation for all that."

So I tried for a bit of documentation. I eventually hunted down a lively, entertaining lady named Dorothy Vaughan, retired head of the city library. "I'm eighty-six and I have lived here seventy-five years," she said, "and I have never heard a story like that about the Sise House, that it was haunted or that there was a murder there." She said she had often visited members of the Sise family and others who lived there, so she would know about such things if they had happened.

But she was intrigued by the idea, and began to warm up. "I lived in a house at one time that had a ghost," she told me. "We could hear him walking up and down the stairs. We called him Captain Fry because he had owned the house at one time. My grandmother talked about him a lot. She had conversations with him. She tells of the cat suddenly flying in the air and spitting. My grandmother used to say the Captain kicked the cat."

(Does the ASPCA know about how New Hampshire ghosts treat dogs and cats?)

The first historian I tried told me immediately that he didn't believe in ghosts. This cut the conversation quite short. So I was relieved to run across the more perceptive Miss Vaughan—or, as she preferred to be called, Dr. Vaughan. She has an honorary doctorate of humane letters.

"You know," she said, "there's a big white house two

doors down the street from the Sise house, there are lawyers in there now. My grandmother used to talk about a murder in that house, around 1905. I almost think the man killed his wife. Yes, there *was* a murder there, I can tell you that."

This cheered me up considerably. I have known of several hauntings in which the spirits seemed to have no connection with the places they were haunting. Perhaps they just liked the place, or it was convenient, or there was company there. Could the spirit of a murdered person two doors over have moved to the Sise house when it became an inn, seeking a little diversion? The ghost certainly seemed to be a playful sort, in a variety of ways.

A third local historian, Dick Winslow, perused newspapers for 1905 and thereabouts, but couldn't come up with anything. However, he did send me a newspaper clipping from 1863 about a policeman accused of robbing a corpse. The spirit of the decedent, who was characterized as a "miser," had supposedly come through a medium and fingered the cop. A reproduction of this story appears in the Introduction to this book.

I was not able to discover any verifiable rumor of haunting in the Sise house before it became an inn until I spoke with Carol Wassler, a night clerk. She told me:

I haven't had any experiences myself. Sorry to disappoint you. But a rather strange thing did happen last summer.

A man came in, and he was very peculiarly dressed. He had on a big straw hat and a heavy flannel shirt, although this was in the heat of the summer. He had a bandanna at the neck and he was wearing leather gloves. He was dressed like a scarecrow. We have monitors, so I could see him come in the front door, and he was looking all around. Finally he came up to the desk and he asked me, "Is *she* still here?"

The Sise Inn was a house originally built in the Queen Anne style in 1881 and renovated in the early 1980s.

I asked who he was looking for, and he said, "You know, the ghost." I didn't know what to make of this, so I said, "No, I haven't seen her."

So he looked around and got the feel of the place a little bit. I offered him a piece of candy, and then he walked back down the hallway and stood at the bottom of the stairway, just kind of soaking in the atmosphere, and then he was on his way. He looked like a man in his thirties. I walked to the door to make sure he had left, and I saw him drive off in an automobile. I reported it to Carl and he laughed.

Later, I came to find out that the building was used as a halfway house at one time. Maybe he stayed here then.

Personality of Ghost(s): Is it a he or a she, or both? The hottest witness seems to be the man in the straw hat and bandanna, and he referred to the ghost as "she." On the other hand, who is pawing the maids and trying to pull them into closets? Who is lying down on the beds with female guests? Sounds male. Who is throwing plants across the room, who is snitching keys and mailing them back, who is rooting around in the ice machine and trailing ice cubes down the hall into Room 214 as though for a rendez-vous? Whoever these ghosts are, they seem sporty.

Witnesses: Carl Jensen, manager; Diane Higgins, functions coordinator; Peggy Brooks, housekeeper; Dennis Dwyer, night clerk; Anna Bauer, former desk clerk; Carol Wassler, night clerk; Shirley Cook, former night clerk. The man in the straw hat and bandanna.

Best Time to Witness: Mostly at night, but things also happen during the day.

Still Haunted?: It seems to be.

Investigations: No formal psychic inquiries were reported.

Data Submitted By: Carl Jensen, Diane Higgins, Peggy Brooks, Dennis Dwyer, Anna Bauer, Carol Wassler. Historians Dorothy Vaughan and Dick Winslow. Tip from Tom Bergeron of WBZ, Boston.

18
A Little Museum Where the Ghosts Run Wild and Free
And They Sometimes Go Home with the Help

Location: The Spy House is in Port Monmouth, a town with a population of about four thousand on the New Jersey shore. The museum is right on the water, Sandy Hook Bay, which is adjacent to Lower New York Bay. It overlooks New York Harbor, and on a clear day you can see the towers of lower Manhattan.

To get there take the Garden State Parkway and turn eastward onto Route 36 at that route's northern intersection with the Parkway. In less than ten miles you'll be in Port Monmouth. Turn left onto Wilson Avenue and go as far as you can. The address is 119 Port Monmouth Road.

Description of Place: A three-story wooden house with a basement. It was put together from four small houses—one of them believed to be the oldest house in New Jersey—dating from the 1600s. The building has served variously over three centuries as a home, an inn, a Revolutionary War gathering place for both the British military and the colonists, a pirates' lair, an occasional bordello, and now a museum.

The downstairs contains a grab bag of antiquities—pictures and models of ships, blacksmith tools, Friesian arts and crafts (the Friesians were a Dutch seafaring people, early settlers of what is now New Jersey), spinning wheels, antique furniture. Upstairs, the rooms are devoted to themes—women's activities, wood crafts with the tools of the time, children's rooms, bedrooms. Buttons can be pushed in various rooms and a lecture on the room ensues.

Thousands of people go through the museum each year on school and group tours, as well as on individual, impromptu visits. The museum is open weekdays from 2:00 to 4:00, on Saturday from 1:00 to 4:00, and on Sunday from 2:30 to 5:00. Donations are accepted.

Gertrude Neidlinger.

Virginia Cutler

Ghostly Manifestations: The Spy House is one of the most haunted places I have ever visited or heard about, with innumerable and very active spirits. The place was rescued from being a derelict house on the brink of being torn down and became a museum in the late 1960s. The rescuer was Gertrude Neidlinger, an exuberant lady now in her eighties who is still enthusiastic and in charge. Gertrude was for many years a concert singer who specialized in comedy. "I did with songs what Victor Borge does with the piano," she told me. She appeared at Carnegie Hall and Town Hall in New York, and in Europe and throughout the United States. The Spy House was her answer to the question of what to do when she retired.

She told me she does not see ghosts herself, but senses them and is very aware of the poltergeist things they do. But many people have had more direct encounters with the spirits, both casual visitors to the museum and the staff of local people that Gertrude has gathered to help her run the place.

One of the rather uncommon habits of the Spy House spirits is their tendency to go home with people they like and who might be unwary enough to invite them. I asked Jane Dougherty, a professional psychic who frequents the place, why this is, and she replied, "I think it's because it's a very friendly atmosphere and there's a lot of acceptance. A lot of the people the spirits go home with are psychics or people who have an affinity to the place. It's sort of a family atmosphere there. We treat the spirits as though they are coexisting alongside of us."

One of the first people I interviewed was Joann Maliszewski, a paid employee who does janitorial work. She told me:

The first day I worked there I heard the stove in the kitchen rattling, although I was alone in the house.

Art Myers

The Spy House.

When Gertrude came in, she told me that was just one of the spirits. Another girl, Marian, told me that it was a spirit named Tom. Tom seemed to take a liking to me. A while ago I was going to get laid off, and Tom started ramming the iron down on the stove and making all kinds of noises. He gets upset whenever I'm upset about anything.

Marian had a ghost who liked her named Peter, and she would take Peter home. Marian's favorite is Peter, mine is Tom. She said, "Why don't you take Tom home with you?" I said, "Well, if he wants to get on my bike he can come home with me." My mother is sick, on oxygen. I call her every day from work. On this day when I got home she told me she could hear footsteps in the house. Then she described a ghost—it was Tom. She said he had a long nose, like Pinocchio's, and pointy shoes with black buckles. Later, a psychic who comes to the house a lot, Frank Basile, drew a picture of the way he had seen Tom, and it was the same way my mother had described him.

But he was driving my dog crazy. Having him at my house overnight was enough; I had to get him back to the building here. I sat down on my bed and said, "Tom, I'm sorry but you've got to go back to the house. Everybody misses you." The next morning I took my bike and I said, "Come on, Tom, let's go."

When I got to work I told everybody I had brought Tom back. Gertrude and I were working in the front room and all of a sudden we heard a big bang. We figured that was Tom. But I'm not sure he doesn't pay visits to my house, because the lights go on and off there.

Marian is Marian Dunlevy, a feisty lady who is prone to berate the authorities in her town. "There's an old law that's still on the books and I was indicted as a common scold," she told me. "I had a little dispute with the judge and he gave me 660 hours of community service. I've been helping out at Spy House ever since."

Before long, Marian was pals with Peter, one of the local ghosts. "They have these automatic tape videos," she said, "where you just push a button and the tape comes on and tells you the history of the room or some person." Early in her 660 hours, one of the tapes went on at the other end of the house from where Marian and two other women were working. They heard the tape and went to investigate, but no one alive was there. "A while later," Marian told me, "Gertrude called and asked how things were going. I said okay, but one of the machines went on. Her response was, 'Oh, that's Peter. When he does this it means he likes you, he welcomes you.' He's a young boy and he likes to push those buttons."

Peter dates from the 1700s, Marian told me. He tends to go home with her. A few years ago, she and a friend, Alice Maxwell, were planning a trip to Europe. "Alice was staying temporarily at my house," Marian said, "and her new radio that she had in her suitcase kept going on in the middle of the night."

But let Alice tell the story of her radio. She is a writer, has been a newspaper columnist, and has worked for the Associated Press. She had been spending some time at Spy House setting up an exhibit of Friesian art.

> We were going to Europe, so I bought a little radio. I put the batteries in but didn't turn it on, and I stuck it in my luggage. One night I sat bolt upright in bed and heard music playing. I didn't know where it was coming from. I thought some neighbor must be playing a radio too loud. It would play for a short time and then go off. Every night about 1:00 A.M. this would start. Finally one night I got up to go to the bathroom and I walked by my luggage and I realized the sound was coming from there. I opened a suitcase and took out the radio. It was on the off position. As soon as I took it out, it stopped. I left it out. It would go on again, but every time it was on the off position. I told Marian, "I think we've got a ghost," and she started to laugh and told me the story of Peter, that he turns on their lecture system.
>
> The next morning, Marian went all around her house saying, "Peter, we're going to the Balkans tomorrow and there'll be nobody here." So we think he got into the car when we went over to the Spy House, because the lecture videos started turning on over there. He's a button pusher. Like all males, he's a button pusher.

Another Spy House volunteer who plays host to ghosts is a teacher who asked for anonymity, so let's call her Ginny, which is not her name. She told me she is very psychic, reluctantly psychic. Ginny, now in her thirties, has been a volunteer at Spy House since she was seventeen. She told me:

> One spirit used to come home with me in the back seat of my little Mustang. I feel it was Thomas Whitlock, one of the original Whitlocks. About 1976, I was driving my car home from the place and I felt my hair being flipped up in the back. I went to sleep that night and I felt a tugging on the sheets at the foot of my bed, and a deep man's voice saying, "Come with us, come with us." The sheet was ripped out of my hand.
>
> Another night I woke up and I saw a woman dressed in Puritan-type garb. She was tilted back on a chair, with the two front legs off the floor. The chair and the figure were noncorporeal.
>
> They even went so far as to follow me to my college. This was during a summer session, when I was a secretary in one of the departments. It was at the end of the day. I was leaving, going down some stairs, and my foot caught in my bell bottom. I pitched forward and the next thing I knew my hand was put back up on the railing. They had caught me.

She has had the experience with her hair more than once. She and another girl were working a Ouija board at the Spy House. "We asked for a sign," she told me, "and my hair again got flipped up in the air, and a surge of energy went through my body." She mentioned that an energy surge also went through her when she and her mother, who is also psychic, were participating in a seance at Spy House.

"As I go through the years," she said, "I've just had to turn my psychic awareness off as much as possible to try to keep my level of sanity."

But some people who make no claim to psychic proclivities say they have had unusual experiences at Spy
House. One of these is Eric Dougherty, a member of the
Preservation Society, a group that Gertrude formed to save
the house. He is a computer technician. He is no relation
to Jane Dougherty. When I asked him if he had ever had
paranormal experiences there, he replied cautiously:

> I thought I did. One evening I came out of the house
> and as I came around the corner I thought I saw some
> kids playing in the back. I was going to go over and see
> what was going on when I realized there was no one
> there. It was just for seconds. They weren't dressed like
> we are, of this time. A girl like ran through me. Then
> they were all gone. I felt cold. The boys had high-
> topped pants and suspenders, like Oliver Twist, En-
> glish-style. The girls had dresses, and one looked like
> she had a white apron thing on. They looked like they
> were playing tag. This was in October, and the lights
> were on out back.
>
> They tell me other people have seen them, but I
> didn't know about that at the time. I felt like a fool. I
> didn't want to tell anybody, but I told my wife and she
> told everybody.

At one point in researching Spy House, I began to
look for the most conventional sort of people I could find,
people who were *not* psychic, and I thought I'd try a volunteer named Edwin Banfield, who is a successful businessman. Banfield told me he had never seen or heard a ghost,
but he was aware of things being moved around. "I haven't
seen them move," he said, "but I've seen where they're
supposed to be and they're now somewhere else. Various
artifacts are constantly being moved around when nobody's there."

Art Myers

The bay side of the house.

I asked Jane Dougherty, who is president of the Society of Parapsychology of New Jersey, why the spirits are so numerous and apparent at Spy House. She had already mentioned the acceptance of them by so many of the people who staff the little museum. Now she pointed out the age of the place and the generations of people who had lived there or who had lived in the space before the houses existed, such as Indians. The site seems to have been an Indian graveyard. She mentioned the constant violence— Indian attacks on the early settlers, contention between the English and the colonists, the commandeering of the house for a time by local pirates. There were many violent deaths, mistreatment, even torture within those walls over the centuries. The house was a tavern for a good part of its existence, with the heavy drinking that goes on in such places. All this can be ghost-making.

But then Jane suggested a concept that I had never come across. She said, "I also feel that the proximity of the sea has something to do with it. A lot of hauntings are near the water. It has something to do with the energy."

This struck a bell—in fact, a gong—with me. I have constantly been bemused by the number of haunted lavatories that I have encountered in my pilgrim's progress through the neighboring dimensions. There is a lot of running water in the loo, as the British call this convenience. While investigating restaurants, I have wondered why so many ladies' rooms are haunted. Probably the men's rooms are, too, but men don't talk about it, it's just not macho to talk about spirits. In haunted private homes, the bathroom is seldom neglected by the spirits. An old standby of poltergeist activity is faucets being turned on and off. Self-activating faucets is one way I decide that a place is really haunted. As an indicator, it ranks right up there with mysteriously distressed dogs and cats. I mentioned my faucet theory to Jane, and she agreed it could be part of the picture.

Some time later I was interviewing Gordon Banta, a nationally known psychic who has been at Spy House a number of times, and I asked if he thought being close to water had anything to do with spirit activity.

"It has everything to do with it," he replied. "Your mind is electrical, and what is the best conductor of electricity? Water. So it's easier for spirits to communicate around water. And it's easier for a psychic to be psychic around water. The most phenomenal readings I've ever given have been around water."

I told him about my newly conceived lavatory-faucet theory, and he said, "That's possible. It's definitely possible."

While I was working on this chapter, Richard Senate, a California archeologist and enthusiastic investigator of paranormal happenings, happened to send me a copy of a column on the psychic that he writes for a local newspaper. I was intrigued to note a section titled "The Ghost in the Bathroom," in which he wrote:

> In 80 percent of the haunted houses I have investigated psychic events have occurred in the bathroom. Clearly the number of sightings far exceeds the number of deaths recorded in bathrooms. Why are bathrooms so popular with ghosts? Seemingly the need to visit such a place would end at the point of death. Perhaps old habits die hard.

I think I may know the answer, Richard.

Psychic Gordon Banta now lives in Winter Spring, Florida, but he comes from New Jersey, and he has participated in activities at the Spy House. "The first time I went there," he told me, "I was driving, and just as we got to the House I jammed on the brakes. I thought I had run over a little girl. I was really shook. Then I realized I hadn't, but it was so vivid, so real. She was in the road right in front of the House. She was a ghost. So I tried to talk to her, to see if I could find out who she was. She told me she had been killed there a long time ago. She told me she lived in a house nearby, that she had come over to play and had been run over by a horse and wagon. So I went in and told Gertrude what had happened, and she had a history of this little girl in her notes on the Spy House. She keeps notes of all the things she's researched about the place, and she had this all written down."

Gertrude asked Banta to come back and do a seance. "We held it in an upstairs room," Banta told me. "A woman had her daughter of about twelve at the seance. The spirits came out and everybody in the room saw them. When we went back downstairs the little girl stayed up there. She said a little boy ghost was there and he wanted to talk to her. He told her that he wanted to go home with her. The mother told me later that the little boy spirit came home with them."

Jane Dougherty also told me of a ghost sighting the first time she went to the Spy House. But the sighting was by her mother, who is a skeptic. Jane was a high school teacher who, as she puts it, "got heavily into the psychic." She became a hypnotherapist, and also trains people to use their psychic powers. She told me:

I first went to the Spy House when a TV program was doing a show on me, and they suggested we do it at the Spy House. My mother was sitting outside in her car.

A Spy House lawn decoration.

Art Myers

Another reminder of things past.

When I came out after the film crew had left, she told me about a woman who was standing near the house and staring out to sea. She said the woman looked very upset. She hadn't moved all the time my mother had watched her. That's when I became suspicious. The woman had on a filmy blouse and a long, black skirt. Her hair was held back with a ribbon, and there was a little cap on her head.

I found out later that she had been seen many times. Her name was Abigail, and she was the wife of a sea captain. Her husband died at sea, and she hangs around there waiting for him to return. I have by now contacted Abigail while in trance. She is an earthbound spirit who doesn't understand that she is dead. After her husband died, a relative tried to marry her, and he bedded her, and she has a lot of guilt feelings about that.

Jane has seen innumerable spirits at the Spy House. She feels that many of these sightings are place memories, impingements on space by people who once lived there, and by things that have happened there, rather than the spirits of the people themselves. However, there are also plenty of genuine spirits there who interact with living people.

Along with other psychics, Jane told me about the cellar. It has in its time been used for many purposes, some of them involving fear and distress. It has been a hiding place for people under attack from Indians. It was a place where colonials held, and sometimes mistreated, English prisoners. Jane told me, "It was a place that pirates put people before they killed them. It was an animal slaughter room. It's a terrible feeling down there."

The cellar is not a regular stop on the Spy House tour, but I felt I had to see this place and I asked Gertrude to let me go down there. Obligingly, she removed the padlock on the outside bulkhead and accompanied me down into the depths. She told me about the history of the cellar and about the tunnels that are believed to lie behind the old stone walls, possibly lined with pirate and other treasure. I am not particularly psychic, and I felt nothing unusual in this drear space, but my tape recorder did. My tape recorders are very sensitive to spirits, and give me a lot of trouble while I'm doing books on hauntings. I noticed that this recorder, a new one, was turning very slowly and erratically. Finally it stopped altogether, in mid-cassette. I played it back, and the voices on the tape were very weird. I assume they are the distorted voices of Gertrude and myself, but who knows? I haven't taken the tape to a sound lab to check for intruders in our conversation. In any event, once we were back upstairs the recorder worked fine and has done so ever since.

Jane Dougherty had many other stories about Spy House. One concerned a tourist who came in with a baby in her arms.

She felt a force lift the baby out of her arms as though a ghost were holding it—although it was still in its mother's arms. I think this was Penelope, a woman who lived there and who had died childless.

I woke up one night and there was a figure in my room. At first, I thought it was my daughter, and I asked her what was the matter. Then I realized it was Penelope. When I spoke she disappeared, but I heard someone walk down the hallway into the kitchen and make noises as though they were cooking. It was about three in the morning and I thought—well, I can get up and follow it or I can go to sleep—and I decided to go to sleep. It just happened that one night. She probably came home in my car.

Another in this almost embarrassingly bounteous array of psychic witnesses is Fran Doran. Among various sounds, pounds, bangs, clanks, and other manifestations she has witnessed, Fran told me of being in back of the house with her daughter and grandson one evening and seeing a woman looking out a window at the water.

"Gertrude tells us this is Lydia Longstreet Seabrook, wife of Thomas," Fran said. "She says other people have seen her there. Later, after the house had closed, my daughter and grandson and I were sitting in my car, and we again saw this woman looking out the window."

Spy House seems to be a sort of classroom, laboratory, and playground for the psychic population of New Jersey, and probably no one has learned more from the House than a young man named Frank Basile. "I knew I was psychic when I first came to the House about a year ago," he told me, "but what has been going on in the past year has been extraordinary. I'm really finding out what powers I have."

Frank is thirty-six, unmarried, and lives with his parents. He works at a supermarket stocking shelves. In the past year he seems to have found his identity as a psychic, and from all accounts he has a most unusual gift.

"I've been psychic since I've been a child," he said, "but the House is like a key to a door, opening me up. The more I go there the stronger I get and the more I keep seeing. When I first came here they told me there were about two dozen spirits in the House, but from what I've seen there are many, many more than that."

Many of the apparitions that Frank sees are probably place memories. Or as Jane Dougherty put it, "I think that some of what is being picked up here is energy, not the actual spirits of the people."

Frank says:

> The House tells me stories. I see Indian attacks. I'll see an Indian looking in the window, and the next thing I'll see them busting down the door. They usually come in the back door, which used to be the front door, and they spread out through the House. I'll run around the house, watching. I'll see them clubbing people to death with their hatchets. This actually happened in the history of the House, although I try not to get into the history, so that, whatever I see, I'm not influenced by what I've heard.
>
> In one part of the basement many people were killed. I can hear animals being slaughtered. I saw two men hanging on the walls, being tortured. According to Gertrude, these were British spies. They would be taken down to the cellar to force them to give information.
>
> I've seen the pirate, Captain Morgan, and I've talked with him. I see many pirates in the House. The way they talk—filthy language!

But not all of Frank's observations are so grim. He also sees the spirits that other people in the House are so fond of.

Peter is about eleven or twelve. I can call him and he'll come.

I drew a picture of Tom one day. Tom is a man in his fifties. He has long hair down to his shoulders, a mustache, a real long nose, and pointed black shoes.

The first time I walked into the House I saw a man with a clerical collar sitting in a chair, with a little girl and boy on either side of him. Gertrude said this was a man who had lived there.

One of Frank's most charming accounts concerns the day after a puppet show had been held in the House. Many children had attended. Joann Maliszewski suggested to Frank that he find the ghostly children in the House and see what they had to say about the show.

Frank told me:

I saw Peter jumping up and down with his feet together, and Joann said, "That's the way the puppets jumped up and down." There is another little boy, Walter, who is deaf and mute. He's up in the attic. He's always looking for his Mommy. He came in clapping his hands. Joann said, "Yes, that's what the (live) children were doing." A little girl, Katy, came in from outside. She's got her hands running as you would on the strings of a puppet. I asked the children if they had a good time, and they all nodded. Joann said, "Tell the children that there's going to be more of this." And I actually saw the children jumping up and down like they were saying, Hooray, hooray!

I've never had experiences like this before.

History: The present Spy House building was put together from four small houses built on the site in the 1600s and combined and expanded over the centuries. According to Gertrude Neidlinger, the first house was built around 1648 by Thomas Whitlock, whom she calls the first permanent white resident of New Jersey. He had come to America in 1639 and lived in the area that became Brooklyn. He came to New Jersey to trade with the Indians and to escape Dutch religious persecution on Long Island. The second house, the central portion of the present building, was built for Mary Seabrook, a widow who was Whitlock's second wife. The third house was Daniel Seabrook's house, who was Mary's son, and the fourth house was a Dutch house that was moved to the grounds.

During the Revolutionary War, the Seabrooks turned the house into an inn and tavern to dissuade the British from taking the place over as officers' quarters. According to Gertrude, Lord Charles Cornwallis, the British commander who in 1781 had the honor of surrendering to the Colonial forces at Yorktown, Virginia, often frequented the tavern, along with many other Britishers. "He was a drunken lout," Gertrude says. In fact, she says, his ghost, an arrogant, weaving figure, is sometimes seen. Gertrude intimates the place also operated as a bordello during this period.

The inn was also a gathering place for American patriots. General Washington felt it was an ideal place to set up a spy ring, and this was done. It would be interesting to conjecture that some early Mata Haris operated in the upstairs rooms with British clients. If not, why not? But it is definitely known that the site was an excellent one from which to watch the movements of British shipping in New York Harbor. The house soon became known to both sides as the Spy House. To quote the brochure of the Spy House Museum:

> When a British ship was left shorthanded by mates gone ashore for an evening of merriment, word would be passed to the patriots waiting at the very same inn. A crew in a whale boat was quickly dispatched to sink or damage the understaffed British ship.

The Brits try to burn Spy House.

The British grew irritated with this procedure, and at one time tried to burn the house down. They set fire to the place and went off, destroying all buckets so no water could be thrown on the flames. But they failed to reckon with the doughty Seabrook women! It happened to be washday, and the women smothered the flames with wet clothing soaking in tubs in the sheds.

The house remained in the Seabrook family until the early twentieth century. It was also used as an inn throughout much of the 1800s and into the 1900s.

An exciting interlude occurred when a pirate captain named Morgan and his crew took over the house. This is not the famous buccaneer Henry Morgan, who dates from the 1600s. This Morgan, whom Gertrude says came from a New Jersey farm family, is believed by her to have operated during the early 1800s, and may have occupied the place with the agreement of the Seabrook family. The house, on the water, was an ideal place to hide goods stolen in raids on ships. There are believed to be four tunnels originating in the cellar. They are now hidden behind the stone walls. Some of these tunnels might have been used by early settlers to hide from Indian raids, but others are believed to have been used, perhaps dug, by the pirates to hide treasure. Several psychics have said they are aware of tunnels under the house, and in recent years archeologists working with electronic equipment have verified the existence of the tunnels. Gertrude is seeking a grant to open the tunnels, with their possibility of hidden treasure.

At one point in the pirates' tenure, they raided a French ship and kidnapped a French diplomat and his family. The family was kept in the house for several months, probably for ransom. Gertrude says that a French woman ghost told Frank Basile that the women were raped and strangled and the father beaten to death. Gertrude believes that Morgan eventually went down with his ship in the Caribbean.

A Yankee attack rowboat.

Jane Dougherty says she has been in touch with Morgan's first mate. In fact, Gertrude showed me a video of Jane in trance, supposedly channeling the mate. He seemed to be having anxiety attacks about his noxious career on earth. He was filled with remorse, fearful of leaving the vicinity of the physical plane to go on to higher planes where he felt he might have to account for his professional activities here below. This sort of fear is indeed believed to be a motivating factor with many spirits who hang in on the physical plane and become known as ghosts.

By the 1960s the house had been deserted and was about to be razed. But Gertrude Neidlinger had just retired from show business. After a few weeks of retirement, she felt far from ready to pack it in. She became fascinated with the Spy House, and in 1969 the Middletown Township Historical Society asked her to create a museum. She organized the Preservationists, who act as fund-raisers for the nonprofit venture and help staff the place. And thus the Spy House Museum was born.

Identities of Ghosts: They are so many it would be impossible to make a list without leaving someone out. But the most prominent ones in this account are Peter, the twelve-year-old boy who likes to push buttons; Tom, the man with the long nose; Thomas Whitlock, who is suspected of flipping up young women's hair; the children seen playing by volunteer Eric Dougherty; the little girl whom psychic Gordon Banta saw in front of the house; the little boy spirit who came to Banta's seance and went home with a live little girl; Abigail, the forlorn sea captain's wife, seen by Jane Dougherty's mother; Penelope, the woman spirit who is still mourning her childlessness; Lydia Longstreet Seabrook, who gazes out a window to the sea; Lord Cornwallis, reputed to be still reeling around drunkenly; Indians; pirates, particularly Captain Morgan and his repentant first mate; a deaf and mute little boy who is looking for his mother; a clergyman and two children seen by Frank Basile; a spirit mentioned by Jane Dougherty who has a habit of pinching women, particularly well-padded ones.

Personalities of Ghosts: They vary, as they did in life. However, I heard no accounts of anyone being harmed.

Witnesses: They seem to be countless, many of them visitors. The staff people and others I had contact with were Gertrude Neidlinger, curator; Jane Dougherty, psychic; Joann Maliszewski, staff member; Marian Dunlevy,

volunteer; Alice Maxwell, friend of Marian; Ginny (pseu-
donym), volunteer; Eric Dougherty, volunteer; Edwin Banfield, volunteer; Gordon Banta, psychic; Teresa Malec, Jane
Dougherty's mother; Fran Doran, psychic, her daughter,
and her grandson; Frank Basile, psychic; myself, in the
cellar, where my tape recorder refused to function.

Another possible witness is indicated by what Marian
Dunlevy told me: "There's a mailman who wouldn't deliver
mail to the Spy House."

Best Time to Witness: Almost all of the manifestations
I heard of took place during the day. The museum is closed
at night.

Still Haunted?: It certainly seems to be.

Investigations: These also seem to be limitless, the Spy
House being a veritable magnet for psychically gifted people. It seems a rare day when a psychic—avowed or informal—is not on the premises, checking out the spirits.

Data Submitted By: Most of the above-named witnesses. Richard Senate, who in his newspaper column
commented on ghosts in the bathroom. Tip from A. J.
Rauber, a North Brunswick, New Jersey, investigator of the
parapsychological, from an interview and a story about
him in the *New York Times*, October 29, 1989.

19
The Lady Who
Loathed Liquor
And They Built a Bar in Her Bedroom

Location: The Bull's Head Inn is at 2 Park Place in Cobleskill, an upstate New York village about thirty-five miles west of Albany. It can be reached by I-88, the New York State Thruway, or Route 145, depending on the direction of approach.

Description of Place: This old house, now a restaurant, was built in 1802 in the Federal Georgian style. The doorways are framed with columns, and the posts and beams are of the original solid oak. The oldest building in the village, it borders on the historic district. The main dining room is on the first floor; there is a tavern in the basement and a banquet room on the second floor. The top floor contains an unused onetime ballroom.

Cobleskill is a quaint Dutch Colonial village of about five thousand permanent residents plus thirty-five hundred students when the state university branch is in session.

Ghostly Manifestations: The usual occurrences in haunted restaurants are reported here—silverware, plates, and napkins flying about; various other moving objects; unscheduled noises; an apparition of what appears to be a woman in white.

Some of the staff and patrons are entertained, some are mildly disconcerted, and a few are all-out frightened. As an example of the last, one of the cooks refuses to be in the building alone and then never leaves the kitchen, which she enters by slipping in the back door. She told me she hasn't had any supernatural experiences at the Bull's Head, but she has elsewhere and she's not in need of more.

But the ghost has never hurt anyone, so for most people it's pretty much just an intriguing conversation piece. Kathy Vedder, manager of the restaurant until recently, tells of an experience she had.

> A customer and his wife were sitting at a table in the main dining room and he put some butter in a little dish and the dish picked right up off the table and flew across the room. The man turned white as a ghost. I just picked up the dish and put it back on the table and kept on walking. I said, "Oh you know, these old buildings." He just stared at me.
>
> I've seen things in mirrors, and so have other people. You turn around and there's no one there. It looks like a woman, but it's hard to tell, because as soon as you see it, it's gone.
>
> We have believers and nonbelievers on the staff. You're usually a nonbeliever until something happens to you.

Jeffrey Patterson tended bar at the Bull's Head while he was in college training to be an environmentalist, his present occupation. "I was behind the bar late one night," he relates. "The place was closed, and I was alone. I was

The Bull's Head Inn.

having a drink—which may have something to do with this. Suddenly I saw lights on the wall, as though venetian blinds were opening and closing several times. Then I saw what seemed to be a figure sitting over in the corner of the dining room. It appeared to be a woman in a white nightgown."

This happened about ten years ago, when the restaurant's bar was on the first floor in the main dining room. It has since been moved; bars are now in the basement tavern and on the second floor. But the area where Patterson saw the apparition was, from about 1920 to 1966, the bedroom of Mr. and Mrs. John Stacy. It was then a private house, although they provided bed and breakfast. Mrs. Stacy is reported to have been a strong believer in abstinence and a staunch member of the Women's Christian Temperance Union. Rumor has it that Mr. Stacy was a drinker of sorts, and this was a bone of contention between them. And herein is reputed to lie the ghost's raison d'etre—she is outraged at the use of her home to sell liquor.

Bob Youngs, present owner of the Bull's Head, is sympathetic to the lady but isn't about to turn his restaurant dry to please her. "I guess she'll just have to stay upset," he says.

Several staffers testify that some evenings when the last customer has left and some of them go down to the basement tavern to have a good-night drink they hear someone walking upstairs, although everyone else has left and the doors are locked.

Nathan Corlew, a college student who waits tables and tends bar, says he saw the lady in the downstairs bar one Sunday afternoon, when the tavern is closed. He had gone downstairs to call his girlfriend in North Carolina from a pay phone in the hallway just outside the tavern.

"All the lights were off in the tavern," he relates. "I was dialing the number when I saw something white behind the bar. It was transparent. Then it moved right through the bar, into the room. I froze. I didn't know whether to run upstairs and out of the building or what. Then the thing disappeared. It was a humanlike figure, kind of hovering. I couldn't see a face."

He decided to run up the stairs but not out of the building. Instead he told someone what he had seen and they came back down. He had noticed during his rapid departure that one of the candles on the tables was lit, although he was sure the place was dark when he first came down. It was still lit when they returned.

Nancy Cudmore, a former hostess, has quite a repertory of experiences. One of her most stimulating recollections is the night the old crank-handle phone rang. The place had closed, and she and another staffer were sitting at a table when all of a sudden the old phone, which dates back many decades and hangs on the wall as a decoration, rang as though someone had turned the crank. But there was no one near the phone. The phone isn't hooked up but then again, as Nancy put it, maybe ghosts don't need connections.

"Then we had captain's chairs that swiveled," Nancy relates. "We'd be sitting there and one would just turn around. Silverware would occasionally fly off the tables. In fact, often. We'd hear it in the next room, and we'd find an entire setting on the floor."

Sometimes this could be a boon, Nancy says, telling of a party of late customers who refused to leave. Suddenly the silverware flew off their table.

"Oh, that's Mrs. Stacy," Nancy told them. "It's late and she doesn't like people drinking in here."

They left.

History: The first building on the site, a log cabin, was erected in 1752 by George Ferster. It was burned by Indians in 1778 and again in 1781. The redoubtable Ferster built it again, for the third time, and this time opened it as an inn. It was burned again, but rebuilt in its present form by a prominent citizen named Lambert Lawyer, and re-opened as an inn in 1802, with the name Bull's Head Inn.

The building at various times housed a town meeting place, a courthouse, and a Masonic lodge. In 1839 it became the residence of a prominent businessman, Charles Courter, and over the years it became known as the Courter Mansion. It remained in that family until 1920, when it was purchased as a residence by John Stacy, and in 1966 it was sold to Monty Allen, who reopened the place with its historic name and function. Since Allen's time it has had two other owners, the latest being Bob Youngs.

Identity of Ghost: If it isn't Mrs. Stacy, almost everyone I talked to at the place is mistaken. Whenever anything unusual happens, the standard response there is, "It's only Mrs. Stacy." However, one former staffer who professes an interest in the occult says he wonders if the ghost could be a woman who was burned to death in one of the early log cabin fires.

I made a sincere effort to find out if the haunting of the Bull's Head predated the death of Mrs. Stacy, but three local historians of varying vintage, plus a couple of elderly residents, were unable to tell me, so let's go with Mrs. Stacy.

Personality of Ghost: Seemingly harmless, except for the scary factor.

Witnesses: Bob Youngs; Kathy Vedder; Norman Olsen, historian; Harold Snyder, previous owner; Jeffrey Patterson; Nancy Cudmore; Dana Cudmore, historian; Mary Clist, historian; Colleen Bunzey; Marianne Winters; Nathan Corlew; Roy Melby, bartender.

Best Time to Witness: The manifestations seem to occur at various times.

Still Haunted?: It seems to be.

Investigations: None reported, although Bob Youngs says he'd like to have a seance.

Data Submitted By: The above-named witnesses, plus an article by Alan Ginsburg in the October 28, 1990, *Schenectady Gazette.* Tip received from Kathy Vedder while I was on the Bob Cudmore call-in show over WGY, Schenectady.

20

A Historic House, Full of Eerie Sights, Sounds, and Smells

It's Been a Distinguished Residence, a Hotel, a Chinese Boardinghouse, and "A House of Negotiable Affection"

Location: The McLoughlin House, a National Historic Site and museum, is located at 713 Center Street in Oregon City, Oregon, on the southern outskirts of Portland.

Description of Place: The house was built in 1845 by Dr. John McLoughlin, originally a Canadian physician, who became the chief factor—the current buzzword is CEO (chief executive officer)—of the Hudson Bay Company. He was a moving force in the industrial development of the Willamette Valley, and his two-story finished-lumber house was a mansion in its time among the crude log cabins of most immigrant families.

The house, which has been moved a couple of times, is now in an Oregon City park along with the Barclay House, an 1849 house built by Dr. Forbes Barclay, which is also a museum and also reputedly haunted. The adjacent houses seem to trade ghosts back and forth.

Dr. McLoughlin and his wife, Marguerite, are buried between the houses.

Ghostly Manifestations: I interviewed three people who are or have been staffers at the McLoughlin House and the Barclay House. One is Nancy Wilson, the curator for the past fifteen years. The other two are former tour guides. One is Phyllis Karr, who worked there for four years and is now a writer. She is currently working on a spooky romance novel, and told me, "If you look real close you can see that the museum in my story is very loosely the McLoughlin House." She seems to have picked up a wealth of material in her four-year stint.

The other former guide is Mary Slaughter, who quit twice and now sells real estate, a less unnerving occupation. When I asked her if she would tell me of her experiences at the museum, she replied, "Some I'd be willing to share with you, some I would not. There was one—the last one—when I never went back."

"Mary has been spooked bad," Phyllis told me. "She won't go into the building now."

Their accounts overlap considerably, for they heard and saw many of the same things, sometimes at the same time. Let's start with Phyllis:

> Perhaps my most memorable experience was when I came in one morning and heard the vacuum cleaner on upstairs. I figured it was Nancy—and it was. Then I saw somebody come down the stairs. It was a very heavy tread. I saw a shadow sweep from the bottom of the staircase to the right into the dining room. It was a very tall shadow, and it kind of ducked through the door. I thought it was Nancy. I went into the room and there was no one there. The radio was playing—harpsichord music. This was not unusual, we often play the radio while we're working. Then I realized the vacuum cleaner was still going upstairs. If Nancy had come down the stairs she would not have left the cleaner going. She was still up there. I figured the doctor had

come down to listen to the harpsichord and get away from the vacuum cleaner.

One day the furnace blew in the Barclay House and because there was to be a function there the next day the repair crew had to come that evening. Phyllis met them, took them over to the Barclay House, and then went back to the McLoughlin House, where it was warm, to wait for them to finish the job.

"I was there till after 9:30 by myself," Phyllis told me. "I swear that every piece of furniture in the doctor's bedroom was rearranged. I could hear furniture being dragged. I could hear heavy footsteps on the bare floor. I did not go up there. The guys who were fixing the furnace were very good about coming over and checking on me, because there had been a prowler in the park. While they were in the building there was no noise. But the minute the door closed after them I could hear the furniture being dragged around. And the next morning it was all in place."

Phyllis was the first to mention to me one of the ghosts associated with Barclay House. "There's a little red-haired boy in the Barclay House," she said, "and the furnace people lost a pair of pliers that they had put down in the storage room over there."

She spoke of decorative pieces, such as a tea caddy and a Russian samovar, being rearranged.

You would see them the way they were supposed to be arranged and come back a half hour later and they would be moved. And this is in a place behind ropes where guests can't get to them.

In one bedroom there was a chair that was set at an angle to the corner, and it would often be turned straight.

One small room had originally been Dr. McLoughlin's office. He did not practice medicine after his retirement, but he always took on some charity cases. More than once I couldn't get out of that room fast enough. There was a very disturbing aura to that room. Some time later, a psychic who did not know the history of the house said that someone had died there, probably after an amputation.

There is a dog that haunts the house. There is an office off the dining room with only one door. We came in one morning and there were dog footprints all over that room. This has happened more than once. One of the neighbors had a very friendly dog who would occasionally come in, but she would not go in that room. She'd go to the door and bark.

There's a fellow from Wisconsin who comes to town every year or so to visit with friends and family. I've given him tours a couple of times. He has trouble walking into the parlor, which is where McLoughlin died and where a psychic has said there was a murder, probably during the brothel days. This fellow breaks out into a cold sweat. I've seen the hair on the back of his neck stand up straight when he's standing in the doorway of that room. Physically, he cannot get himself into that room. Yet he keeps coming back. He says, "One of these days I'm going to make it. I've got to find out what is going on." I've heard that in more recent years he was able to go in, but he was in constant motion, rubbing his hands, shifting his shoulders.

The stories could go on and on. I was only there for four years.

After Phyllis, I interviewed Mary Slaughter, but when I replayed the tape I found she had spoken so hesitantly and faintly that I could not make out what she was saying. After some indecision, I called her back and asked her if we could repeat the interview, which she agreed to do. In the meantime, I spoke with her former boss, Nancy Wilson, and Nancy told me that Mary had called her after our first

The McLoughlin House.

interview. "She just about came unglued," Nancy said. Nancy told me she had doubted that Mary would talk at all about her experiences in the house, but she did, twice. Nancy said:

> The first experience I had in the house would be the footsteps upstairs. We now have carpeting upstairs, and you can hear the footsteps go from the carpeting, where they make less noise, to the bare wooden floor. Then you know *for sure* that there's something moving around up there.
>
> You should have seen Mary Slaughter the first time she heard these footsteps. We were eating our lunch. It was just hilarious. I heard them, and I just sat and watched her. Her eyes got bigger and bigger, and then the goosebumps popped out all over her. Finally she says, "Who's upstairs?" And I said, "I don't know. Why don't you go up?" And she wasn't about to move. She

really had a hard time handling these things. She would get just so upset.

One day there was some paint on a sill and I scraped it. I needed something from downstairs and Mary ran down to get it. I was vacuuming up the mess I had made when—tap, tap, tap on my shoulder. So I turned around to see what Mary wanted, except the problem was that Mary wasn't there. I almost screamed, and if I had she would have been gone, I would have never seen her again. She was always so spooked.

There were just simple things. One time I was up in the room that we think might have been the McLoughlins' bedroom and all of a sudden I smelled pipe tobacco. So I moved to another room, and I smelled it there. So I went downstairs, and it followed me. Now, I don't know if Dr. McLoughlin smoked, but his wife was part Indian and there is probably a good chance she did. She was half Cree and half Swiss. Maybe she was watching me work.

And sometimes you'd smell coffee in the house, and there was no coffee in the house.

Both Nancy and Mary Slaughter mentioned a part-time bookkeeper who refused to come into the house and who worked out in the yard because her calculator wouldn't work in the house. I've had many experiences of spirits apparently gumming up the mechanical-electronic works. They seem to play hob with my tape recorders, for example. In *The Ghostly Register* there is a chapter on a haunted restaurant in Florida—Ashley's Restaurant, in Rockledge. While checking out the restaurant, a friend and I had dinner there, and we asked the waitress if she'd noticed anything spooky. "Constantly," she replied. "Last night I was trying to do my money, and the calculator just wouldn't work right. That happens all the time."

Another typical ghostly syndrome at the McLoughlin House is strange doings with money. "It was funny how money would disappear," Nancy said. "We keep our admission money in a desk drawer. One day we were ten dollars short. We took the money to the place where we lock it up, and what was lying there—a ten-dollar bill! Neither of us had put it there. This happened often. Either the missing money would be in the drawer, or a week later you'd be that much over. We got so we didn't even worry about it."

No respectable haunted house would be complete without apports—the appearance of things that seem to pop up from a slightly different dimension. Both Mary and Nancy told me the following story: (here in Nancy's words)

One of the women working in the house lost a button off her sweater. She said it must have happened in the little room where we were sitting. It was a special button and she was kind of upset about it. Well, we looked under the furniture and we looked and looked for that button, and we couldn't find it. And a short time later, Mary looked down and there was a button rolling across the floor. And it was the button off that sweater.

The little red-headed boy at the Barclay House, we blame him for everything that happens. I've never seen him, but I know two women who have, and he was so really formed for them that they called the police because all the doors were locked and they couldn't figure out how he had gotten in. They were women who were working for the Chamber of Commerce when they had their office here.

We always blamed him for taking things. There was an older man who was helping me, and we brought some things from the McLoughlin House to the Barclay House and set them on some steps and went to lunch. And right on top of one of the boxes was a pair of garden clippers. When we came back the clippers were gone. We never found them at that time. I found them a couple of months later in a room upstairs, in a box of books. That was bizarre.

Did Phyllis tell you we had a little boy with his family, and she was taking them through? The boy was about seven and there was a littler one, about four or five. They were upstairs and the older boy was looking over the bannister and he said to Phyllis, "Is that little boy supposed to be downstairs by himself?" Phyllis was fast on her feet and she asked what color his hair was. And the little boy said, "Well, it's redder than my brother's." The parents were looking up at the ceiling, acting like this little boy had some kind of psychic power, that he was always doing things like that.

I could go on and on.

"Please do," I said.

There's the thing about the portrait and the day McLoughlin died, in September. It happens about twenty-two minutes to ten in the morning. This has happened many years. It's a good-sized oil painting of him, with a big wide gold frame. That's the only day in the year this seems to happen. Evidentally the sun hits the frame, but it only lights the oval of his face. I have tried to find out the exact time he died, but I can't, but I did find out that he died in the morning. It's really eerie. I have sat and watched it. The oval of his face glows. It's bizarre."

Mary Slaughter mentioned that one year they pulled the shade the night before the anniversary of McLoughlin's death, and that the next morning the shade was up and the sun was on the portrait.

Nancy Wilson went on:

McLoughlin's rocking chair is in an upstairs room, and we have had four or five people say they saw it rock when nobody was in it.

We have had a couple of teachers, men who didn't know each other, who have called and said they saw a woman looking out the window of that same room when they were jogging by. They wondered if we had mannequins in the house. And other people have reported seeing a woman in that room, the southeast bedroom.

One woman told a guide it was so nice that we had someone in costume. She had seen this woman going up the stairs, and her gown was so pretty. But there's no one here in costume.

We were selling an 1840s painting of Mount Hood by a well-known artist recently, and two people came from the *Oregonian* for a story. The photographer went upstairs while the reporter was talking to me. Pretty soon he came downstairs, and he said he was looking in a room at the top of the stairs and he thought he heard the reporter's footsteps coming up the stairs, but when he looked down the stairs nobody was there.

I called the photographer, Bob Ellis, and he confirmed the incident. "My interest was piqued," he said, "let's put it that way."

Nancy continued.

I've seen a shadow twice of someone. One day I had been upstairs and was coming down and something went crash in the hallway. There's nothing up there to fall. I looked back up the stairs, and I glimpsed a shadow going into McLoughlin's bedroom, ducking to go through the doorway. So that's why we think it's McLoughlin, because he was so tall he had to bend to go through doorways. The shadow had just stood up, as though it had dropped something and bent over to pick it up.

And one time when I unlocked the front door to
come into the house the shadow went around the bottom of the stairs into the dining room. I heard the
footsteps and saw the shadow at the same time.

Just little things . . .

Mary Slaughter's stories are the same as Nancy's and
Phyllis's—the footsteps, the smells of pipe smoke and
coffee brewing, the one day in the year when McLoughlin's
portrait lights up, the bookkeeper who worked on the
books out in the yard, the admissions money that would
disappear and reappear, the missing button that she suddenly saw rolling across the floor.

"I quit twice," she said. "The first time it was because
a friend of mine thought it might not be a good place for
me to be. When I told Nancy I was leaving and handed her
the keys to the house, the banjo clock in the dining room
stopped. That's an oldtime pendulum clock. I went over
and started it going again. I quit, but I went back a couple
of years later."

I had been told—by the other women and by Mary
herself—that she did not want to talk about the event that
caused her to leave the second time. However, she did tell
me this much:

I invited three Indian friends, two women and a man,
to see the house. I took them in on a Monday, when it
was closed. They got just a few feet in and it was like
something had hit them, all three of them. I said, if you
don't want to go any farther it's all right. But they said
no, they wanted to see the place, so we went into the
dining room. And one of the crystals that decorate the
candlesticks on the table was dancing. This had happened before, a number of people have seen it happen.

They heard knocking on the walls. I could not hear
that, but all three of them did. We went upstairs, and

the man felt he was being drawn toward the bannister. We decided it was time to leave, so we did.

We went to a restaurant and we were talking about this and the Indian man said his throat was starting to close. You could see him being physically affected by it. The Indian ladies pulled out some healing crystals and gave them to him and he came out of it.

They talked to me at length about not going back. I didn't know what it was, and they didn't either, but they felt there were a lot of entities in the house.

I never went back.

History: Born into a Quebec farming family, John McLoughlin was nineteen when he signed on as a physician for the North West Company, which merged with the Hudson Bay Company. McLoughlin rose in the hierarchy of the merged company to become its most important representative in the Northwest. Despite his British background, he threw his weight to the side of American dominance of the area and became an American citizen in 1851.

His house, built in 1845, became a landmark. It was known locally as "the house of many beds" because of the hospitality the McLoughlins offered to just about anyone passing through Oregon City. McLoughlin died in 1857. His daughter sold the house and it became an elegant hotel.

"It then became the property of the owner of a woolen mill," Nancy Wilson relates. "He hired Chinese to work in the mill and they lived in the house. During the Depression of 1886 the people ran them out because they wanted the jobs they held. They ran all the Chinese out of Oregon City, and that happened in many cities. Then the place became a 'house of negotiable affection.' "

I congratulated Nancy on her turn of phrase, and she said the term was not original, that she saw it in an advertisement for a restaurant in a building that had once housed a brothel.

The building then became an apartment house. "The house was abandoned for many years," Phyllis Karr said. "It was a way station for hobos. Rather than have it torn down, it was moved to its present location. It's been a museum since 1909, and is the oldest museum in Oregon."

Identities of Ghosts: Indications are that there are many entities in the house. The primary candidates are John McLoughlin and his wife, Marguerite. Another conspicuous entry is the little red-headed boy who seems to primarily inhabit the Barclay House.

Psychics have sensed the spirits of Chinese people. Bernadine Dobey, who checked out the building recently with a group of dowsers, told me she sensed a protective spirit, an Indian. The McLoughlins had Indian servants. There is the woman seen in the window by two joggers, and the woman in the period gown seen by a tourist. Psychics have in the Barclay House sensed the spirits of Dr. Forbes Barclay, its builder, as well as a woman and a relative of the Barclays known as Uncle Sandy. And there is the dog who leaves footprints on carpets in the McLoughlin House, and who the present tour guides suspect belonged to the little boy and who comes visiting.

Personalities of Ghosts: Some seem benign. Others, such as those encountered by Mary Slaughter's Indian guests and the constant visitor from Wisconsin, don't seem so amiable. There is believed to have been violence, perhaps murder, in the house during its days as a bordello and possibly during its time as a refuge for hobos, and there was certainly much fear and distress during the expulsion of the Chinese. The little boy seems mischievous. Some of the disembodied occupants seem merely to be seeking attention from us mortals.

Witnesses: Nancy Wilson, curator; Phyllis Karr, former guide; Mary Slaughter, former guide; Bob Ellis, the *Portland Oregonian* photographer; two women who worked in the building when it housed offices of the local chamber of commerce; many other people who have worked in the house, as well as many visitors.

Best Time to Witness: The witnesses have had their experiences when the museum is open during the day, or in the evening. No one seems to have camped there all night.

Still Haunted?: It seems to be.

Investigations: Suzanne Jauchius, an Oregon psychic, first told me of the house. She said she went there once and was aware of Dr. McLoughlin sitting on a bed in the room he died in.

Nancy Wilson says:

> Many people who claim to have some psychic powers make comments when they go through the house. We had one woman who was brought here unofficially by a man from another museum. She said she was a well-known psychic from the East Coast who was out here hiding, trying to rest. There has been a lot of renovation here, and she picked up on a doorway that has been closed in. I'm quite sure that the furniture in the parlor and dining room is set up backward, and she mentioned that.
>
> The most interesting thing she came up with was that she was very disturbed by one room that is set up

as an office. She said there were little people huddled there. They were speaking a language that she did not understand. She said they were not Indians. The chances are she was picking up on the time and the area that the Chinese were gathered into when they were being taken out to be put on a boat and sent to Portland. I asked her if they were Orientals, and she said, "Yes, I think they are, but why are they here?" It was really kind of bizarre. She said, "They are so frightened."

We have no idea who the little boy is, but a woman who was a friend of the Barclays' daughter, Katy, told me that a little boy had died in the Barclay House. Her name was Mildred Mendies. She was elderly when I knew her. She said that as a teenager she had come to visit Katy and she slept in Uncle Sandy's room after he died, in his bed. And she said that on several instances when she was crawling into bed and getting ready to go to sleep he would come through the wall, sit in his chair, look to see who was in his bed, and get up and leave.

A group of dowsers who came to the house said that they found spirit paths from the McLoughlins' nearby graves into the house. One of the dowsers, Chuck Darby, told me he found two ghosts, and by asking his pendulum determined they are the McLoughlins. He said he followed one ghost all the way up to a bedroom and then found him again downstairs. Darby said that by using an L-rod a dowser can follow a ghost. "The rod points straight forward," he said, "and it changes where the ghost changes path. You can check out a ghost because if you check out a living person the L-rod will go out when it hits their auras. The same thing happens when you hit a ghost, because a ghost is energy too, just like a living person."

Another dowser, Mike Doney, told me, "We follow the L-rods. It's the very same technique a dowser uses when following a water line, or a utility line, or something of that nature. It's the way the rod swings."

This was the first I had heard of spirit paths, but a friend of mine, Enid Hoffman, a psychic and a dowser, said there are such things. The paths at McLoughlin House might have developed because the McLoughlins were buried only about twenty feet from their house. Enid told me she has found spirit paths in the hallways of homes.

"One I remember," she said, "was a man whose wife had been very ill. They had bedrooms at opposite ends of a hall. When they were alive, he had walked back and forth tending her. When he died, his spirit kept going back and forth on that path he was used to."

Data Submitted By: Persons listed as witnesses. Various dowsers. Material from the National Park Service's brochure on McLoughlin House. Articles in the *Portland Oregonian*, September 7, 1989, and October 26, 1989.

21
The Haunted Radio Station
A Few Apparitions Hither and Yon

Location: KWJJ, a country music radio station, is housed in a mansion in an affluent residential area in the southwest section of Portland, Oregon. The address is 931 Southwest King Street.

Description of Place: The Wilcox Mansion is something of a showplace in Portland. It was built in 1893 by Theodore B. Wilcox, a milling, shipping, and banking magnate, and served as a residence for the Wilcox family for many years. During World War II it housed a Soviet purchasing mission. It then became a school of music and dance, founded by Ariel Rubstein, an eminent concert pianist, a Russian emigre. The mansion was purchased in 1959 by Rod Johnson, who moved his radio station from downtown Portland. Although now under different ownership it still has the same call letters. It is a large station with the maximum legal wattage. It has a staff of twenty-six people.

Although the station uses all five of the mansion's

floors, as well as the basement, there seems to be room left over for public use. The current station manager, Michael Kern, told me, "We allow the public to use our dining rooms. People have weddings here. And we give informal tours for people."

The place is a beautiful Victorian residence, the first two levels built from sandstone, the upper stories from wood. The interior contains ornate mahogany woodwork, crystal chandeliers, nine marble fireplaces, gilded wallpaper in the main entryway. A legacy from its music school days, there are two grand pianos, one on the third floor, another on the first floor.

Ghostly Manifestations: I first heard of KWJJ while working on the previous chapter, about the McLoughlin House in Oregon City. I was interviewing Nancy Wilson, the curator, when she told me about a haunted radio station in Portland. She knew about it from experience. Her husband, Larry, is a radio engineer and occasionally has worked at KWJJ. One evening she accompanied him, and while waiting sat in a bay window on a landing of the main stairs, reading. All of a sudden she saw something rather offbeat.

"I saw a woman servant, in a black uniform with a white hat, walking along in the upstairs hall," she told me. "She went a little way and then she was just gone, she disappeared."

Nancy felt the woman probably dated from around the 1920s, for her dress was not long; it went halfway down the calf. Nancy was not overly startled, for at the McLoughlin House she lives with ghosts, but she was curious. A short time later the evening shift DJ, Rick Taylor, came along. Nancy told him what had just happened, and he wasn't at all surprised. "He started telling me about experiences he had had there," Nancy said.

Rick now does his disc jockeying at rival Portland country music station KUPL. He had excellent recall of some strange evenings at KWJJ, but then, these things are not easily forgettable.

"I've seen what appeared to be a ghost twice in there," he told me. "I worked five years in the mansion, and I worked evenings a lot by myself. From my studio I could see into an area where there was a grand piano. One night I saw this person walking around the piano, a guy wearing a white suit and a white hat. I thought, that's kind of weird. He just kept walking around the piano. Finally I went out to see who it was, but there was nobody around. When Berry Burks, the announcer who worked the midnight-to-six shift, came in I told him what I had seen and he said, 'I've seen that guy late at night. It's a ghost. I don't let it bother me anymore.'"

Rick saw the ghost another time, still walking around the piano. And at one point he heard the piano down on the main floor playing, although to his knowledge there was no one in the building but himself.

He had tales of doors that were locked or unlocked when they weren't supposed to be, of lights that went on and off mysteriously, but my favorite of Rick's adventures concerns a time he had repaired to the men's room. As any reader of my volumes on ghostly places must have noted, ghosts love bathrooms. Rick has one of the great bathroom stories.

"I was sitting in one of the stalls," Rick said, "with the door open. I felt this cold breeze come in. There was a cabinet with four doors in front of me. They were piled full of teletype paper and toilet paper. I got up and opened the cabinet doors to see if there was an air vent in there that was open. I couldn't see anything so I turned around and sat down again. And all four cabinet doors shut at the same time! I got out of there fast."

I spoke with Berry Burks, who followed Rick on the air at KWJJ and now does so at KUPL. "I saw an old man three times," he told me. "He looked like he might have been in his mid-seventies, maybe a little older than that. He had white hair. There's an attic there where they keep a lot of the memorabilia of the station, and it used to be a record library years ago. That was where I saw him twice, but I also saw him once in the main lobby downstairs. He was dressed in dark clothing, nothing out of the ordinary. He looked at me once, and we locked eyes, and he went away."

I asked if the apparition's clothing was of any particular period, and Berry replied, "It's hard to tell because I didn't see enough detail. I was just kind of blown away by the fact that he was there. He had trousers on and a shirt. If I had to name a color, I'd say he was wearing dark brown pants and a dark olive green shirt."

I mentioned that Rick had told me that his ghost was wearing white clothing and was continually walking around a piano. Berry replied, "I never saw him near a piano. I'd just see him for a second or two. I would be going around one corner and he'd be going around the other."

I suspect these are a couple of different ghosts. After all, it's a big old place, plenty of room.

At one point I contacted George Sanders, who was general manager of the station several years ago. He is now an author living in North Carolina. The interview started slowly. Sanders hadn't seen any ghosts. To prime the pump I asked if he'd ever experienced things moving around. "No," he said, "I just used to wish the employees would move around a little." This was a funny line, but it wasn't much help. But then he began to warm up, and before long he was really winging them in.

"There's a huge chandelier in the main entry hall," he said, "and it used to shake. It would shake and quiver at the damnedest times. It would do it at night. I used to think it must be a truck going by, but we discounted that because there are more trucks going by in the day and it didn't do it then. It would shimmer and shake. You'd come down the stairs and you'd hear this tingling sound. And then it would stop. And you'd go to your office and it would start again. I remember thinking it would have to be a convoy of huge trucks to cause this, because the house is huge and heavy, and it's set back from the street. There was no way the chandelier could be affected by the wind, and it wasn't earthquakes."

I am always encouraged when interviewees, presumably uninformed about parapsychological phenomena, tell me of incidents similar to those I have run into in other hauntings. It gives me confidence they can't be making these things up. Sanders went on to do this twice. First, he told me of a picture being hung upside down, a phenomenon that figures in a haunting in a hotel in San Diego (*The Ghostly Gazetteer*); second, he told of the mysterious disappearances and reappearances of an object, similar to the distinctive cigarette lighters that kept popping up in Tombstone, Arizona, in the first chapter of this book.

"In my office," he told me, "I've interviewed five presidents." He had an ongoing relationship with John F. Kennedy, and had a signed photograph of Kennedy and himself on the wall of his office. Following the Kennedy assassination, the picture was turned upside down two or three times. At first Sanders wondered if this were some kind of ghoulish joke, but he doubted that. "No one on the staff was disrespectful of Kennedy," he said. But then he mentioned something that indicated to me even more strongly that this was not being done by someone with a very bad sense of humor. The upside-down picture hung flat against the wall, just as the picture had in the San Diego hotel. Sanders said:

> I hung that picture myself. The wire was geared to hang the picture right side up, but when it was upside down those times it was flat against the wall. That doesn't seem possible. I'd keep trying it, I'd turn it around, but it wouldn't hang flat against the wall. In fact, when it was upside down it wouldn't stay hung at all.
>
> There was another thing that I thought at first might be some kind of a gag. Out of nowhere, on my desk there appeared a circular, plastic emblem of the Virgin Mary. I assumed that one of the guys on the staff had done it. I settled on the owner, Rod Johnson. So I'd take the thing and put it someplace for him to find. I'd hide it in his office, like in a book or whatever. He would always claim he never saw it. But the thing would always return. It would be on top of my desk, or I'd find it in a drawer. I thought we were playing a game.
>
> Rod flew his own plane, so one time I got some glue, the kind that when you glue something you can't take it off, and I glued it to the outside of his plane. He claimed, and I know he wasn't lying, that he never saw it there.

At this point in the story I found myself questioning a couple of things. Why was Sanders so sure Rod Johnson wasn't kidding him? Why was he sure the emblem hadn't fallen off? I was making skeptical noises when Sanders slipped me the clincher. He said, "It's now here in my house in North Carolina. I do not remember anyone giving it to me. About six months ago, it showed up way in the back of a drawer of my desk." He said the desk had never been in the radio station, it was strictly an East Coast desk.

This certainly sounds like an apport, an object that pops in from another dimension, presumably materialized by a spirit.

Another star witness is Michelle Helm, who works in marketing at the station. She gave me a story that reminded me of a ghostly cat who left indentations and warm spots on beds in a house in New Jersey, duly recorded in *The Ghostly Register*.

"About three years ago," Michelle said, "there was a girl who worked here named Beth Kent. One time she came into my office with an armful of papers to put into a file cabinet. She went to put them down on a chair, and then she stopped, and she looked at me with a very peculiar look on her face. I asked, 'What's wrong?' And she said, 'It was like I couldn't put them down, as though there was something there.' She put the stuff on top of the file cabinet instead of on the chair. I walked over to the chair and felt it, and it was warm. I reached over to a chair that was next to it and felt it, and it was cold."

Michelle had another good account, but allow me to lead into it with a story from Rick Taylor, the ghost-spotting disc jockey. "One time," he told me, "they hired a young couple to come in to clean the house. I don't remember their names, because they were only there for one night. The gal went down into the basement to find some cleaning products and she heard some very heavy breathing. She came up looking white as a ghost. Her husband and I went down there and we couldn't find anything. But they quit that night."

Michelle Helm told me, "The sales department used to be located down in the basement. It was pretty much of a dungeon down there, but there were cubicles for the sales staff. Beth Kent worked there. She said she'd be typing along and periodically out of the corner of her eye she would see like a figure go by, but when she looked it would be gone. She figured he must be friendly because he never like knocked anything over or did anything to her. But the thing of it is that that area where he was walking by went to the entryway of a tunnel that connected the mansion with the carriage house."

Just another ghost following a familiar path?

History: The mansion was built in 1893 by Theodore B. Wilcox. The last Wilcox to live there was Theodore B. Wilcox, Jr. During World War II the building housed a Soviet purchasing mission. In 1949 it was purchased by Ariel and Eleanor Rubstein, who created a school of music and dance there. Ariel Rubstein, a Russian emige, was a concert pianist who had been director of a music school in New York City.

In 1959 the building was purchased by Rod and Betty Johnson, owners of KWJJ. They moved the station from its location in downtown Portland. In 1973, the station was taken over by Park Broadcasting, a New York State corporation that owns several stations.

George Sanders, general manager for the Johnsons, told me, "It's a house filled with history because of the kind of people who come and go. Some of the most famous people in the world have been in that building."

Several U.S. presidents have been interviewed there, as well as other eminent people. I also spoke with Ariel Rubstein, who is now in his nineties. The hauntings were news to him, he said, but he mentioned some of his famed musical friends who had visited him there. They included Artur Rubinstein, Sergei Rachmaninoff, Jascha Heifetz, and Gregor Piatigorsky.

Identities of Ghosts: The most easily identifiable seems to be the woman with the servant's dress. She probably was a servant for the Wilcoxes. The two men seen by the two DJs seem to be different spirits. The one in the white clothing might have been a musician, an impression occasioned partly by the eccentricity of his dress and partly because he kept circling the upstairs grand piano, and may have been playing on the one downstairs.

Concerning the elderly man in everyday clothing, the first person I interviewed was Michael Kern, present manager of the station, who told me, "We know that Theodore is roaming the halls here. It's just a fact and nobody worries too much about it. We never see him, but there are always things that are moved, lights are turned on when nobody's been near them, doors are open when they've been locked, and there are lots of noises here and there. It's an ongoing thing and we just accept it."

I asked who Theodore was and he replied Theodore Wilcox. Well, there were two Theodore Wilcoxes, senior and junior. My hunch is that it's Junior, who died in 1961, rather than Senior, who died in 1918. My theory is that business magnates who date from the 1800s aren't as likely to walk around in their shirtsleeves, even in their own mansions.

Who the vague apparition often spotted by Beth Kent in the basement is might be anybody's guess. She never got a good look at it; it might be either of the Wilcoxes, a servant, or a visiting spirit who took up residence.

Personalities of Ghosts: None of them seem to be bothering anybody, unless you count Rick Taylor's experience in the men's room.

Witnesses: Michael Kern, present station manager; George Sanders, former station manager; Nancy Wilson, curator of the McLoughlin House in Oregon City, who was visiting KWJJ one evening; Rick Taylor, former DJ at KWJJ, now with KUPL; Berry Burks, former DJ at KWJJ, now with KUPL; Larry Blumhagen, former DJ at KWJJ, now with KMXI; Michelle Helm, employee in the marketing department of KWJJ; Beth Kent, former employee at KWJJ.

Best Time to Witness: Most of the accounts involve the evening or night hours, although there are also incidents during the day. Manifestations are possibly more noticeable after hours, when only one or two people are in the building.

Still Haunted?: It seems to be.

Investigations: No formal psychic inquiries were reported. However, during the 1980s the station held a number of Halloween parties for its clients, and psychics were often brought in for entertainment. Nobody I interviewed seemed to recall whether these psychics became aware of the local spirits, or whether they stuck to predicting business and country music trends.

Data Submitted By: The above-named witnesses. Also Betty Johnson, former owner, with her husband, Ron, of the station; James Opsitnik, former manager of the station; Ariel Rubstein, former owner of the building, where he conducted a music school; Sanna Sterling Hern, former sales manager of the station. Articles in the *Portland Oregonian*, February 21, 1942, and March 16 and 17, 1961.

22
The Ghost Who Wasn't— or Was She?

A Little Girl Who Is Reputed to Haunt a Theater—and How Her Story May Have Started

Location: The Orpheum Theater is situated at 203 South Main Street, in downtown Memphis, Tennessee.

Description of Place: The theater dates from the 1920s, when movie theaters were built very large and very ornate. Although of rather nondescript beige brick on the outside, inside it's quite grand, with two-thousand-pound chandeliers and much gold leafing. It seats 2,600 people and currently hosts concerts and touring Broadway shows, among other entertainments.

Ghostly Manifestations: This is a two-part story.

Part One: Mike Curtis, onetime manager of a haunted theater in Tupelo, Mississippi, included in *The Ghostly Gazetteer*, mentioned that he had heard of a theater in Memphis that was reputed to be haunted by a ghost named Mary. He gave me the name of a man who had been the manager there many years ago, Elton Holland. Holland had been there when the theater was called the Malco. It was the flagship theater of the M. A. Lightman Company, which owned several theaters in the South. Holland went on to become vice president of the company and is now retired. I called him, and he gave this delightful account of Mary, the ghostly little girl of the Orpheum.

This is the weirdest phenomenon I've ever come across. About thirty years ago we had a youngster there—I'm not going to tell you his name because I don't want to embarrass him. This kid started out with me as a teenager. He loved the theater business. All he did was change light bulbs, which was a full-time job. He didn't want any money, but I gave him a little token of our appreciation. He just wanted to be around theaters. He stayed with the theater in charge of maintenance after the present people took it over.

I wanted him to be careful, because he was very nonchalant on the ladders, these perpendicular ladders that went up the high walls. He didn't pay any attention to what I said. He'd be careful for maybe a couple of hours and then all of a sudden he became an acrobat. I wanted to make an impression on him. And in my younger days I liked to play jokes.

We had a fifth floor that we called the gallery. We had a night watchman, and one night he heard a scream and he realized he must have locked someone up in the gallery. Whoever it was came down five flights of stairs in total darkness and hit the doors that were the entrance to the gallery so hard he knocked them off their hinges. He just kept running out onto the street. It took maniacal strength. He must have been scared to death. We never found out who he was.

With the background of this real episode, I told my young employee that the frightened man must have seen Mary. I took him around and showed him the broken doors. Then I made things up as I went along. I said that Mary was a little girl who had been in a stage show during the Depression. Her mother had been in the gallery and was so proud of Mary and excited that she had fallen off the balcony and been killed. And that every once in a while, when the moon was right, Mary would come back and look for her mother. Mary had a white dress on.

This is how the whole thing started, and it has built up. The TV stations picked it up years after I had left the theater. The young man added his variations to it. It was written up in newspapers. It was just a snowball thing.

I was just trying to make an impression on him, hoping he'd be more careful when he was climbing around changing light bulbs. That's how the whole thing started. If anyone sees Mary it's more than I have done, and I was there about twelve years.

Everyone who has written up Mary has talked himself into actually seeing her. It's kind of hilarious, because these people are supposed to be pretty sophisticated. It comes up about every five years, and my wife and I have a big laugh about it.

Part Two: There are reporters who are tempted to let well enough alone, and do. But I am the compulsive type who never knows when to stop researching, even though it might spoil a yarn. So I plunged onward.

I called the theater and spoke with Shannon Bolton, the public relations person. Shannon wasn't so sure there really was a ghost, but as a PR person who was she to debunk a great publicity ploy? She had what seems to be the current word on Mary's origins. Mary, according to this doctrine, was a twelve-year-old girl who was killed in an accident in 1921 in front of the theater that was on the site in those days. It was called the Grand Opera House and was demolished when the building that is now called the Orpheum was put up in 1928. The spirit of the little girl, it is said, was attracted to the theater and made it her home. When the new building was erected, she stayed.

Well, things like that do seem to happen.

Shannon also had a variety of other Mary stories, such as:

- The late actor Yul Brynner supposedly saw the little girl wearing her white dress and sitting in her accustomed seat, C-5. He was playing in *The King and I* at the time. Brynner was reputedly quite psychic.
- In 1977 several members of the cast of the touring show *Fiddler on the Roof* thought they saw Mary in her traditional seat. After opening night they convened in the balcony where the seat is to hold a seance, and reportedly felt that they made contact with little Mary.
- Workmen have seen a theater door fly open and then shut. And it opens outward, so it doesn't seem to be the wind.
- Shannon told me, "There was a man who worked here—some people say he made up a lot of stuff—but he loved to talk about Mary. He thought she was wonderful." Could this be Holland's young bulb snatcher, grown older?
- Shannon told me about a housekeeper who told of having tools mysteriously missing, and later finding them in the toilet. This does sound like the sort of thing a child ghost might do.
- One time an alarm went off in the theater. The police came and brought dogs, but the dogs refused to go into the theater. They stopped at the front door and lay down stubbornly. This was in recent years, Shannon says.

The last two items sound particularly interesting to a veteran ghost writer such as myself. Things of this nature *do* seem to happen in haunted places, and it would take a certain amount of sophistication about the occult to invent such stories.

Wait a minute, I'm convincing myself!

Shannon provided me with two press stories about Mary. One was published by *Memphis* magazine in October 1979, and was written by David Dawson. The other was by one Doug Morris, whose byline identified him as *Journal* City Editor. No one I contacted in current Memphis journalistic circles seems to know of a newspaper called the *Journal*, but there must be or have been one somewhere thereabouts.

Morris quotes a bulb changer whose name I won't give either, since Holland didn't. The bulb man admits he's never seen Mary, but he constantly felt her around him, he says. He felt what he describes as a "cold, eerie feeling, like getting into a bathtub of cold liver. Once you feel it you'll never forget it."

That I can believe.

Morris also tells of a Memphis State University parapsychology class that checked out Mary and felt she was there.

Memphis magazine quotes a woman to the effect that a group she was with saw a little girl dancing in the lobby, who suddenly disappeared. And an organ repairman tells of an "unsurmountable" problem that developed when he was repairing the Orpheum's organ late one night. He gave up and went across the street with a couple of friends for coffee, and when they returned the organ was fixed.

And so—Holland's account is a delightful spoof, and probably the way a lot of this got started. Perhaps I should have stopped there. But I wondered if there might be a few other ghosts in the old Orpheum. It seems like such a natural place to be haunted. In fact, Shannon told me that she had heard there are seven ghosts, this based on the investigation by the student parapsychologists.

"I'm not really sure I believe it," Shannon said, "but when I give tours to the school children they love it."

History: The building was erected in 1928, replacing another theater that dated from the 1890s. It was used as a vaudeville theater and later as a movie house. When big movie houses became white elephants, a nonprofit organization called the Memphis Development Foundation took over the theater. The Foundation's aim is to help the city's downtown area to prosper. The land is leased from the city.

Identities of Ghosts: Could it be little Mary, come "alive" from Holland's tale? And how about those other six disembodied spirits?

Personalities of Ghosts: Harmless enough. Probably just a bunch of freeloaders, in on passes.

Witnesses: Let's give them a break and not use their names.

Best Time to Witness: Take your pick.

Still Haunted?: Who knows?

Investigations: The Memphis State parapsychology class; the *Fiddler on the Roof* cast's seance; Yul Brynner's observations while counting the house; many print and electronic journalists; and who knows what hopeful psychics may have wandered in looking for Mary?

Data Submitted By: Elton Holland; Shannon Bolton; articles in *Memphis* magazine and the mysterious *Journal*.

23
A Very Publicly
Haunted Restaurant
Deep in the Heart of Texas, the Ghosts
Put on a Dinner Show

Location: The Catfish Plantation Restaurant is at 814 Water Street in Waxahachie, Texas. The town is thirty-five miles directly south of Dallas on Interstate 35.

Description of Place: Waxahachie, population about twenty thousand, is basically an upscale bedroom community for Dallas, but it also has an interesting and unusual past and present. Tom Baker, with his wife Melissa, the owners of the Catfish Plantation, says, "It was famous for cotton in the late nineteenth century: that's what built the town up. It's filled with large gingerbread Victorian houses. It's come to be a tourist town, known for historical homes. The courthouse is the most filmed courthouse in the United States."

In recent years the town has been the setting of some outstanding movies. Dallas is a regional film center, and Waxahachie is a colorful place to shoot. Among notable films made there have been *Places in the Heart* with Sally Field, *Tender Mercies* with Ellen Barkin and Robert Du-

Melissa and Tom Baker.

vall, and *A Trip to Bountiful* with Geraldine Page. The well-known TV and movie writer and producer Horton Foote is from Waxahachie and does movies there. A well-known national children's television series is produced there.

Waxahachie is about to become a center for the world of physics: it will be ringed by the famed supercollider. This will be a fifty-four-mile circular tunnel and a $5–6 billion project. "To the physicist," says Tom Baker, "this will be what the microscope is to the biologist. They'll take protons and electrons and shoot them around the circumference of the circle. We have many Nobel Prize winners coming here. There are two or three thousand scientists already here working. Facilities are being built just outside of town that will be the size of a large university campus. There are a lot of interesting things happening here."

All in all, not quite the image one is likely to have of a small Texas town.

Ghostly Manifestations: When the Bakers bought the house in which they started the Catfish Plantation in late 1984, ghosts were far from their minds. What they had on their minds was Cajun cuisine. The place, built in 1895, had been a private home for many decades. In the years before the Bakers bought it, it had housed three unsuccessful restaurants. When they bought the house, nothing was said about ghosts.

"When things began happening," Melissa says, "we kept it quiet for a long time; we didn't talk about it. But it got to a point where I wanted to know if other people had had experiences in there. I had heard that some things had happened when they were restoring the place."

She asked the owner of the immediately preceding restaurant, a physician, and he denied anything like that. She asked the two women who had owned a restaurant there before the doctor, and they denied anything unusual.

"So after that I stopped my questioning," Melissa says. "I was afraid rumors would start about us crazy people asking questions. As it turned out, after the ghosts in the place got publicized people began coming forward and saying they knew of things that had happened."

Melissa and Tom had for several years been employees of Southwestern Bell Telephone. He was a manager, she was a service representative. They had two small children and lived in Dallas. After they had owned the restaurant for a time, they moved to Waxahachie. Melissa got her introduction to highjinks a couple of months after they had bought the place. Tom was still working at his job; she had quit and was commuting to Waxahachie.

One morning she arrived and let herself in with her key, to find her first ghostly manifestation:

There was a pot of coffee made for me. It was fresh coffee. It hadn't been made the night before. I could tell from its consistency that it was fresh, and from the level in the coffeepot, and it was hot. No one else has a key to the place. Of course, that wasn't frightening, and I didn't at the time think of it being a ghost. I thought it was a prank.

About two or three weeks later, I came in in the morning and I found a big stainless steel iced tea urn sitting on the floor. That's not where we keep it, we keep it up on a shelf. And all the coffee cups had been taken off the shelf and piled inside the urn. Again, I thought this was a trick. Yet I had locked the place up when I left the night before and was the first one in in the morning.

After that we began having employees come to us and tell us there were coffee cups flying across the rooms. Or that somebody had been hit in the head with a piece of cheese and they'd turn around and there'd be no one there. One time we had a can of freeze-dried chives sitting on a shelf in the kitchen, and people saw it leave the shelf and go flying across the room and scatter the chives all over the floor. We had these constant reports of employees seeing movement.

We have a stereo in the dining room, and the station would change from one end of the band to the other when no one was near to change it. Lights would go on and off, water faucets were going on and off. We were having refrigerator doors open and close a lot.

We kept it quiet. We didn't talk about it with customers at this time. We were afraid that if this got out it might hurt our business. And we really didn't know if we had a ghost or not.

Often people are reluctant to reveal that their home or place of business has a ghost or a few rambling the premises. While I was writing this book I heard of a large

The Catfish Plantation Restaurant.

catering place in New Jersey that was reputed to be haunted. I contacted the owner, but he declined to cooperate. "A lot of our business is weddings," he said, "and I don't want the girls to be afraid that a ghost will come to their weddings."

Early on in my career as a ghost writer I heard of a house in East Hartford, Connecticut, where the ghost of a woman from a century or more ago wandered. Her husband had brought his mistress home, and his wife had committed suicide. The husband and mistress had continued to live there till they died of old age. The wife remained, an earthbound spirit. A famous parapsychologist, Karlis Osis, gave me a great comment: "She wouldn't go to heaven because her husband might be there." But I never was able to use it, since the people who owned the house wanted to sell it and were most desirous of keeping the ghost quiet.

But sometimes public enterprises such as restaurants, hotels, and museums—although perhaps initially wary—find that a friendly haunting is very good for business, and this is what happened with the Catfish Plantation. They now hand out pamphlets to diners about the ghosts, and one customer mentioned to me seeing the ghosts advertised on a billboard. But back in 1985, Tom and Melissa were keeping a very low profile concerning their mysterious residents.

"Tom never believed all this at this time, anyway," Melissa told me. "He was still working at his job in Dallas and wasn't down here a lot. I'd go home and tell him these tales and he thought we were just a bunch of crackpots."

Both come from conventional religious backgrounds. Melissa was Catholic and Tom was Baptist. "It took a while for me to believe there was something going on," Tom says. "I come from a very conservative background. My father was in the military and the civil service. I have a bachelor's degree in economics from Southern Methodist University, my master's degree is from there, and I worked for seventeen years for Southwestern Bell. All of which is to say that ghosts were the least of my thoughts."

But Melissa, deep in the heart of Waxahachie, was getting very antsy. She wanted to know what was going on. She recalls:

> Tom said to me, "If you lose one customer, you'll be the next ghost floating around Water Street." But against my husband's wishes, I called a talk show in Dallas. They had a writer on who had written a book about the supernatural, and then they asked for callers. I called and asked if there was somebody in the audience who could tell me if a ghost could cause coffee cups to fly across a room. I didn't give the name of the restaurant or where we were. I just listed the things that had been

happening, and then I hung up. A parapsychologist then called in to the station and said what I had described were signs of a classic haunting, as he called it, that we should have a professional in.

We had a lady who came to work for us as a waitress by the name of Helen Cain, and she had a daughter who she said was psychic. Not a professional; she just had that gift. Her name was Ruth Jones. Helen wanted her to come to the restaurant one evening after it was closed and hold a seance.

So one night Ruth Jones held a seance. She told me:

We come from a country family, and the old ways have always been taught to us. It's something we've always been able to do.

When I first heard about this I thought it might be a publicity thing, but when I went there all sorts of things began happening. It was all supposed to be done in fun, with young people who worked there around the table. But one of the boys began trembling and grew very pale, and the girls began crying. There was knocking on the walls and dishes rattling in the kitchen. The candle on the table came up like an explosion of light. The kitchen door came open by itself, and she just wandered in, the young one. She was dressed in a sort of wedding gown.

The "she" is presumably one of the three ghosts who are said to inhabit the Catfish Plantation. Her name is Elizabeth. Whether the others at the seance could see her I am not sure, but Ruth says that she could, that she often sees spirits.

The other two ghosts are reputedly Caroline, an elderly lady who had lived in the house and died in 1970, and Will, a farmer who lived there during the Depression years.

At this point, Tom Baker was flipping his wig:

I thought everybody was crazy, but I let them do their
thing—I let them have their seances and talk. But then
I personally began to have some experiences. I finally
went to a seance and a door swung open. The telephone
rang and there was no one there. Each of these things I
thought was set up. But the next day I began to wonder.
I had left there really negative; I had treated it as a joke.
I must have really irritated whatever was causing this,
because that morning when I came in the ceiling of the
room where they had had the seance was covered with
water. It was totally covered—the old metal ceiling.
There's an attic above the room, but there's no ready
way to get up there. I have to bring a ladder from home
and go through a hole in the ceiling—it's about twelve
to fifteen feet high. So I got the ladder and went up
there and I found that a plastic pipe coming off the air
conditioner had been cut. The only time I've ever had
water on the ceiling was that night after the seance. So
I walked away from that feeling that something funny
was happening around here.

The next thing was one night at home I was lying
in bed asleep and I heard a piano play. The next morning I asked Melissa and she said she had heard it too.
There was no one else in the house.

Melissa said, "I had been dreaming of the ghost, because so many things had been happening. At this time we
only knew of Caroline."

(It might have been Caroline who had made Melissa's
early pot of coffee; Caroline was, during her life, according
to psychics, a great one for having tea parties; she was now
unaware she was dead and was very upset when no one
came to her parties.)

Melissa continued, "I asked her in the dream to communicate with me, and in my dream she was going to play the piano. When the keys tinkled it woke me up. Tom was still asleep. In the morning he asked me if I had heard the piano playing. It was just playing some weird notes."

About this time the Bakers were contacted by two parapsychologists and psychics who had heard of their problems. They were Dwanna Paul and Carol Williams, who give classes and do research under the name Invisible Friends. They brought in a crew of helpers with devices such as temperature gauges, laser light beams, cameras equipped with infrared film, and sound equipment. Melissa was immediately impressed with them. She had been half expecting some sort of weirdos, but they and their group seemed like substantial, professional people. She was even more impressed when Dwanna immediately asked her who Mattie was. Dwanna told Melissa that Mattie, a step-grandmother Melissa had been close to, was standing beside her.

"I was raised Catholic," Melissa told me, "and there were always prayers for the guardian angel. I thought, this is like a guardian angel."

Dwanna and Carol and their group came often to the restaurant without any fees, for the place is a gold mine of interest for students and researchers of the psychic.

"The first two seances were conducted by Ruth Jones," Melissa said, "and then there were four or five by Dwanna. We'd get a bit of information each time, like a puzzle. Dwanna gave me the names of Elizabeth, Caroline, and Will. She gave me the causes of death and the approximate times that they died. Elizabeth was strangled on her wedding day. Dwanna said the murderer was a previous lover, and I thought it was a male. But other psychics now have told me the murderer was a woman, so that could have been her bridegroom's previous lover."

(Unless Elizabeth was a lesbian, I suggested. No use ruling out anything.)

Elizabeth's last name was Anderson, psychics said. Her father was the builder of the house. Melissa told me she has had people doing research to check some of this information. It is already established that an Elizabeth Anderson lived in the house in the early 1900s.

Melissa continued:

Caroline died of a stroke. She lived here with her husband Clem from 1953 till the day she died in 1970 at the age of about eighty. Her last name was Mooney and her maiden name was Jenkins.

Will was an old farmer who lived here during the 1930s. He's wearing overalls.

[The area, now a residential neighborhood, was then farming country.]

With Elizabeth we get the scent of roses, touching, cold spots, and some movement. Caroline is the thrower and slammer. In the seances it has come out that she spent a lot of her time during her life in the kitchen, preparing dinner for her family. When they don't come home now, she gets very angry. When she sees all the strangers in her house she starts throwing things.

We're not licensed to sell alcohol, but you can bring alcohol in and we do have wine glasses and frosted beer mugs for the patrons. The wine glasses sit up on a shelf in the kitchen, and we have a hard time purchasing them fast enough to keep up with the rate of speed that Caroline breaks them. She slams doors, and she's the coffee cup thrower.

Elizabeth is often seen as an apparition in the front window. It's a bay window that looks out on the street. She stands at this particular window, which looks down the street, where you could see anyone coming from town, and she looks out this window.

A number of people say they have seen her there, of which more later.

Will is the quiet one, Melissa says. He seems to hang mainly around the porch. "Police say they have seen a man standing on the porch," Melissa says, "but when they get close he disappears. I can pin things on Elizabeth and Caroline, but Will doesn't seem to do much. He probably contributes to some of the cold spots."

The security system often goes off, but when the security people investigate the place is empty. Which reminds me of some immortal words entered not long ago in the archives of the Cape Cod town of Sandwich, Massachusetts, involving a haunting in *The Ghostly Gazetteer*. A local policeman, Jim Foley, had been called to this house so often that he wrote in the town archives:

> It is highly recommended that any officer entering this house act according to his or her feelings. In other words, if you feel like running, please do so. Screaming will also be allowed. It is requested, however, that upon exiting the house you at least slow down long enough to open the door and not go through it.

Others of the Catfish Plantation's features are cold spots and the chiming of a clock. Cold spots—called psychic cold—are supposed to signal the presence of a ghost. This is a standard ghostly manifestation. The restaurant seems to be replete with cold spots.

"Sometimes I'll be standing at a table," Melissa says, "telling ghost stories to customers, and a cold spot will come around. And the customers will be able to feel it."

A lot of these cold spots, Melissa feels, can be attributed to Elizabeth, who is a toucher. She is the ghost who seems to be reaching out to people. She is seen as an apparition more often than the others. She has been known to follow customers home.

"One night," Melissa relates, "I was counting the money and doing my paperwork and I got this cold sensation on my right hand. It was just on that hand. I feel Elizabeth was holding my hand while I was working. This went on for about fifteen minutes."

Adding to the ghostly ambience of the place is a clock that shouldn't be chiming. It's one of three antique clocks that the Bakers bought at an auction. "They don't work," Melissa says. "They have missing parts. They were simply purchased for decorative purposes. One of them, the time changes on it. And it chimes. Not on the hour, but it will chime, chime, chime, chime, chime. It might not chime for weeks or months. Sometimes there are customers there. Usually, once it starts chiming you'll feel cold spots in the room."

As in so many haunted places, the ghosts like to play with electricity. Lights flicker in the dining room. A light goes on in a broken-down refrigerator that had been put aside and unplugged. Not to mention the electric coffee maker that was Melissa's introduction to the ghostly delights of her new place of business.

And, another common parapsychological manifestation, doors are often found locked or unlocked, whichever they are supposed not to be.

The Bakers are convincing people—educated, friendly, earnest. To an investigative reporter who after decades of interviewing people has some confidence—possibly over-confidence—in his ability to spot phonies and con artists, the Bakers certainly seem very believable.

But I also believe in covering as many bases as possible, so I have interviewed a number of people that these things are purported to have happened to. After the Bakers got into the spirit of their ghostly environment, they began to urge patrons to tell them of things that had happened, and they often recorded the customers' names and how

The owners of the Catfish Plantation invite their patrons to share their ghostly encounters.

they could be reached. These records were made available to me.

First, however, let me relate an intriguing incident in which, unfortunately, there is no ready way to contact the people involved—they got out of the restaurant too fast. They were a young couple with a baby. Melissa told me:

> They were the only ones in the restaurant. It was a cold day and kind of moist outside, and there was a mist on the window. I had just been by their table and I commented on how pretty the baby was. I asked what its name was, and they said Alicia. And I went on.
>
> About five minutes later, the waitress came to me and said, "The people with the baby are frightened. They think they've had a ghost experience." The

mother said she was eating and something on the window caught her eye. She looked at it and "Alicia" had been written on the window. They left without finishing their meal. They told me they thought this was a very lovely place and they enjoyed their meal but they would never be back again.

Tom was there that day and he told me: "I went in, and I saw the writing on the window and the scared look on these people's faces. They were scared to death, and they got up and left."

Playing devil's advocate, I asked Tom if he was sure the people hadn't done it themselves.

"No, I'm not," he replied. "In fact, all this stuff I try to explain it like that."

While researching this book, I came across more than one place in our fair country where the ghosts seemed to go home with people. One is the Spy House in New Jersey (Chapter 18), where a number of spirits seem to go home on occasion with their favorite mortals. And the Willard Library in Evansville, Indiana (Chapter 6), where a spirit went home with her favorite children's librarian until the unseemly roar and dust caused by renovations was over with, a period of several weeks.

This sort of thing seems to have happened in Waxahachie, and it also happened to a person who had felt sympathy with one of the ghosts. She is Dorothy Poole of Fort Worth, who, with her daughter, Nancy, had had lunch at the restaurant on a day that, by chance, the national TV program "A Current Affair" was shooting there. Ms. Poole told me:

All the way home my daughter and I were talking about how we felt sympathy for that girl [Elizabeth] that all those strangers were there in her house making jokes about ghosts and so on. We didn't participate in the conversations because we were feeling a little offended at how people were taking it so lightly.

That night about 11:30 I had fallen asleep in my bedroom and I heard someone whisper, "Here you are." I turned and looked over my shoulder and there was this young woman standing there. She had something in her hands. I thought at first it was a doll. It was as though she was handing it to me. Then I realized it was a powder box in the shape of a lady. That's something people had in those days. I remember that my mother had one. Then she vanished. She was standing between me and my digital clock, and while she was standing there I couldn't see the clock, but when she vanished I could see that it was one minute after twelve. I was not asleep. I know I was awake.

Ms. Poole wrote a letter to the Bakers about her experience. In it she said:

At first Nancy and I had planned not to mention this experience to you since the media seemed to be making such a circus of the situation, but then we decided it does concern you to have all the pieces to fit together, and we feel you are seeking to understand rather than exploit these residents in your restaurant.

In her account to the Bakers, she gave further details about the encounter:

I sleep alone in a water bed. . . . I saw a young woman, about twenty, standing there near me. The water bed must not have existed in her dimension or she would have been standing in it. I looked at her just from the waist up and did not notice her footing, but I saw her face quite clearly. It was a face I had never seen before

but would recognize if I should see it again. The figure
standing there reminded me of an old sepia photograph—all rosy beige tones rather than any bright col-
ors. Her most striking feature was her gentle, earnest
brown eyes. Her hair was light brown, straight, thin,
and worn close to her head rather than being curled or
fluffed out. Instead of being pulled back severely it was
draped around her face in a sort of scalloped effect to
soften the hairline. I was born in 1920, so I vaguely
remember people of that time period and have seen
family pictures to remind me how women looked then.
It is possible she would manifest herself in a form that
would be familiar to me, or possibly I would perceive
her in that guise; she may not necessarily have an
earthly body in her present situation. She wore a beige
or ecru dress with a moderately low round neckline and
a touch of lace and embroidery. Her dress was what
would have been called an afternoon frock. It was not a
wedding dress, nor was it white. She was not unhappy
or distressed in any way. Poised and serene are words
that best describe her.

Ms. Poole then described the apparition's reaching out
a china figurine, a powder box, as though to offer it as a
gift. She concluded her letter with a quotation from Thorn-
ton Wilder's book, *The Bridge of San Luis Rey*—"There is
a land of the living and a land of the dead—and the bridge
is love."

She added, "I consider it a very touching compliment
that Elizabeth reached out to me to span the bridge."

Melissa Baker told me of a young customer who felt
that Elizabeth followed him out of the restaurant, and who
brought her back. His name is Jay Freeman. I called him,
and this is what he said:

Yes, that did happen. Henry, a friend of mine, and I

would go there every so often after work. The spirits were quite active that night. Several cold spots were felt. I've never seen things in the act of moving, although I've seen the after-effects of their having been moved.

Henry and I left and went out the door toward our car. We suddenly felt this cold. So we walked across the street, and it wasn't there. We walked back, and it was there. So we walked back up the steps and I opened the door and said to Melissa, "I brought someone back for you."

The door was open; a strong wind was holding it open. And as I said that, the door slammed shut, against about a fifteen- or twenty-mile wind.

The restaurant was closing for the night, Freeman added, and everybody, including the staff, had gotten into their cars and were about to pull away. They looked through the big front window and could see a door swinging back and forth inside.

Another story at the restaurant concerns two customers who saw a sort of formless wraith floating up against the ceiling. They were Sandra Porch and her thirteen-year-old daughter, Mary. I contacted Sandra and she told me:

We were sitting having dinner. It was about six o'clock, still daylight. This was about six weeks ago. We were looking into the next dining room. Above the top of the door there was like opaque smoke, just sort of floating. My daughter saw the same thing. Then it disappeared, but it was gone too quickly to be smoke. I looked, took my eyes away for a moment, and it was gone. It was a sort of grayish white, no form or body. After it disappeared, I went over and looked up, but there was nothing there.

I knew there were supposed to be spirits there,

that's one of the things they advertise with, but I never expected to see anything. I don't know if I saw an apparition, but I wouldn't say that I hadn't, either.

Interview with Marvin Wright, vice president for sales of Larkin Products, a large Waxahachie manufacturer of oil-field equipment:

I don't know if I saw a ghost or not. This was before they started advertising that they had ghosts. I hadn't heard about anything like that. We had some out-of-town guests and we were taking them to dinner. When we pulled up in front of the Plantation, I saw this lady sitting at a table, through the window. Someone said there was a sign that the restaurant was closed tonight. I said, it's not closed, I just saw someone sitting in there. And when I looked again, she wasn't there.

I didn't think any more of it till they started advertising that the place is haunted. I saw it the other day on a billboard. But this happened to me before anything was said about it being haunted. We had pulled up right in front of the window, and I saw her sitting at a table there. Six or eight months later I ate there, and by this time they had a little pamphlet they handed out about the ghosts. When we left, I told them what I had seen.

A similiar account is given by Sean Burress, a computer programmer whose wife, Rane, works at the restaurant. He came late one evening to pick her up. While she and her friend, Helen Cain, who also worked there, were standing outside waiting for him they thought they saw Elizabeth looking out the front window. They told him of this when he arrived and they got into his truck. He was most doubtful, and drove the truck back with the lights off, hoping to prove to the women a thing or two about creative imagination. He parked the truck and walked up to the window. He describes seeing a short young woman dressed as Elizabeth is supposed to be dressed. He could not, however, see her face, he says, although he was quite close to the window. He does mention that he departed quickly.

Melissa told me of a particular employee named Shirley Oliver, a dishwasher and busgirl, who seemed to have a special relationship with the spirits. "She had a lot of experiences," Melissa said. "She would see apparitions." Shirley figures in the following account.

Melissa told me:

> There was a lady sitting in the restaurant having dinner with her mother. Her mother had gone to the rest room, and she was alone at this moment. Something fell on her table. She looked and found a ring on the floor. She kept it. She thought maybe we had rigged the house for tricks. She got the ring home and cleaned it. It had a blue stone and she found some initials on the inside of the band.
>
> She called me and said she had an experience in the restaurant but that she was a Baptist and did not believe in ghosts. She said the initials looked like *CEL* or *GEL*. Or maybe it wasn't an *L*. The last letter was straight; it could have been an *L*, but the bottom part was worn away. It could have been a *J*. Caroline's married name was Mooney, but we didn't know her maiden name at the time; since then we've found out that her maiden name was Jenkins."

I told Melissa it might have been an apport, something that materializes out of the blue, apparently from a slightly different dimension than the one we're accustomed to. "Yes," Melissa said, "I've learned that word since that happened."

I called the lady, who spoke freely but asked that I not reveal her name:

> Yes, I saw this ring fall from the ceiling. It landed on the floor. I took it home, and then called them and told them about it. I went back and showed them the ring. They thought it belonged to one of the lady ghosts that lived there, which I don't believe in.
>
> This ring is kind of old and tarnished. I took it to a jeweler and then to an antiques dealer. I thought there were initials in it, but they said the marks only meant that it was a gold-plated ring. The stone wasn't real.
>
> When I went back to the restaurant, one of the cooks came out from the back. She said that it was her ring. I took it that maybe she had flung it off her hand. That's what I'll leave it at. I don't believe in these things at all. I believe in evil.

Melissa Baker, however, has a different reaction to the happenings at her restaurant. She says, "I always had a fear of death. It really disturbed me to think of dying, or my parents dying. And now I truly believe that there is life after death, that there is something that continues on, that this body is strictly physical. There is a spiritual world after we die. It's much easier for me now to deal with someone dying, because it's not final."

History: The house was built in 1895 in a farming-residential area of Waxahachie by a man named Anderson who had a daughter Elizabeth. According to local legend, in the early 1920s on her wedding day, Elizabeth was strangled in the house by a lover—either hers or the groom's. A second spirit, Caroline Jenkins Mooney, died at about the age of eighty, in 1970. She had lived there with her husband, Clem, and their family. The least active spirit, Will, is believed to be a farmer who lived in the house during the Depression.

In recent years, the house has been used as a restaurant, three times unsuccessfully, but since 1984, under the Bakers, successfully.

Identities of Ghosts: They are believed to be Elizabeth, Caroline, and Will.

Personalities of Ghosts: Elizabeth comes across as sweet, reaching out, loving to touch people, often appearing as an apparition. Caroline sometimes seems angry, probably because strangers are using her house. She is described by Melissa Baker as "the thrower and the slammer." Will is mostly just there. He is usually seen on the front porch, and also, Melissa suggests, probably contributes to the cold spots that pervade the place.

Witnesses: Tom and Melissa Baker, owners; Ruth Jones, medium; Helen Cain, waitress; Dwanna Paul and Carol Williams, mediums; Chris Berry, former cook; Rane Burress, an employee, and her husband, Sean; Shirley Oliver, employee; Marvin Wright, patron; Jay Freeman, patron; Dorothy Poole and her daughter, Nancy, patrons; Sandra Porch and her daughter, Mary, patrons; a patron and her mother who prefer to remain anonymous.

Best Time to Witness: Manifestations seem to occur at any time.

Still Haunted?: It certainly seems to be.

Investigations: Seances held by Ruth Jones and by Dwanna Paul and Helen Cain and their group of researchers; many psychics have dropped by informally to

sample the cuisine and the spirits; the restaurant has
become a staple of the media, both local and national.
Dallas TV stations have done shows on the place, as has
the national TV program "A Current Affair."

Data Submitted By: Interviews with most of the above-
named witnesses; numerous newspaper articles; manu-
scripts by Lissa Proctor and Dorothy Poole; videos of TV
programs; tip from Richard Bolton of San Diego.

24
Is the Onetime Mayor of Seattle Haunting This Theater?
Along with a Few Other People with Leftover Life to Live

Location: The Harvard Exit Theater is in downtown Seattle, Washington, at 807 East Roy Street.

Description of Place: The Harvard Exit is an art movie house specializing in foreign and classic American films. It is housed in a three-story red brick building that started life in 1924 as the home of the Women's Century Club, an organization with a feminist orientation that still meets twice a month in the building. Since 1968, however, the building has been a movie theater.

In the building's early days, some of the members of the women's club lived in the building. There was an auditorium on the main floor. Sometime after the conversion of the building to a movie house, another auditorium for film showings was built into the third floor, giving the theater two screens. The second floor is now used for administrative purposes.

Ghostly Manifestations: The theater and its spirits have been the subject of innumerable newspaper and magazine articles, as well as television and radio shows. Some of them, particularly the TV shows, have been superficial, obtuse, and derisive. But others have been done from an intelligent and serious point of view, with a sophisticated awareness of the psychic.

An example of the latter is "Seattle in Vogue," a cable TV show produced by J. R. Benight and Jane Riese. This talk show covers many subjects, but Benight and Riese told me they are both somewhat psychic and like to do programs on the occult. They brought in a medium for their show on the Harvard Exit. Another example of enlightened TV treatment was a show produced by Shirley Enebrad for KOMO's program "Town Meeting," for which a well-known California psychic, Sylvia Brown, was imported.

Benight, Riese, and Enebrad were of considerable help in my preparing of this chapter, but let's start with a skeptic, Allen Blangy, district manager for the chain that now owns the theater and onetime manager of the Harvard Exit. In steering me to Blangy, Benight said, "It's kind of a case where Blangy feels he doesn't believe in ghosts but he doesn't have a choice."

Blangy was not about to go bananas over ghosts, as a woman in Selma, Alabama, once put it to me, but like the lady he had to admit something funny was going on.

> I've heard lots of stories, but most of them I figured were drug-related to begin with because they came from the sixties when the movie theater was run by a wild bunch of hippie types. I didn't really believe too many of the stories I heard, although there were a few people who were more . . . well, straight . . . and who had some stories.

I personally never experienced anything that was out of the normal. Except that there *was* something I thought was odd. I was closing the theater one night, and I heard people in the auditorium on the third floor. We had been closed for a while, and I thought they must be just sitting there talking. But there was nobody up there. But when I went in I heard the side exit door open and close. I went over to make sure it had closed tightly. It hadn't, but when I pulled on the panic bar there was someone on the other side tugging back. I kept pulling and pulling. My assistant was down the hall so I called to him to come over. I had managed to pull the door shut, but I didn't feel comfortable to open the door and confront these people by myself, because I thought it odd that they would have been tugging against me. So we opened the door together, and there was nobody there. We were on the third floor and the only way down was a metal fire escape that makes a lot of noise when you go up or down it, and there had been absolutely no noise. So I couldn't figure where these people could have gone. It was pretty bizarre. It was real spooky.

I had employees who had experiences. Our offices are on the second floor. One night this woman was up there closing out the books. We were all down on the main floor, and we heard her screaming and running down the hall. We ran up to see what was wrong, and she was shaking and very upset. She said she had seen a translucent female figure hovering in the air at the other end of the hallway.

Blangy gave me some background on the Women's Century Club. "The club is still in existence," he said, "but they refuse to talk to anybody about ghosts; they're pretty sensitive about the issue."

I had already interviewed Benight, and I commented, "I suspect it's the ghosts of a few of their former members."

"That's what I keep thinking," Blangy said.

Then he flipped to his on-the-other-hand mode. He told me of a young woman who claimed to have seen an apparition one night in the balcony of the main auditorium. "But she was young and had just discovered alcohol and drugs and seemed to be partying a lot at the time," he said. I thought this was a cute way of putting it, but was later told by reliable informants that this woman is straight as a string. Blangy also told me of a former theater manager who described various striking experiences, but indicated that her employees played tricks on her, although in light of my subsequent research this seems unlikely.

He told me that at one time during the early incarnation of the building as a theater, a manager was reputed to have opened up to find that one of the projectors was running a film on the screen to an empty house. Why not, I thought hopefully, why shouldn't ghosts like movies? Blangy didn't know what movie was playing, which disappointed me. But he had another explanation for this unusual film event.

"The problem is," he said, "that the owners of the movie theater at that time were pretty crazy people and I can imagine them putting something on the screen to watch, and going to answer a phone and then walking out the building, forgetting the movie was on. They were real scatterbrains."

I thought this was another fetching explanation, a nice memorial to that dear departed decade, the sixties. But I liked the movie-loving ghost theory better.

At this point, Blangy flipped back to his but-maybe-there-is-something-there mode. "You've got a mixture of stories," he said. "Some are based on the fact that it's known the place is haunted, so people play up on that, and then other experiences are truly sort of odd."

In fact, he became quite creative, I felt. Although I'm trying to fit the information I collected on the Harvard Exit into the chapter format I've been following, I must here prematurely reveal one of the suspected ghosts. She is none other than the onetime president of the Women's Century Club, who also became the first and only woman mayor of Seattle. Her name was Bertha K. Landis.

"One thing I noticed about five years ago," Blangy said, "was when one of the skyscrapers here, Smith Tower, decided to put a little museum in their building and have an exhibit on this woman mayor. I saw a newspaper article that mentioned that when the people were setting up the exhibit they kept having odd things happen—stuff being shifted around, and visions of a ghostly woman figure. It triggered in me the thought that there had not been any sightings at the Harvard Exit for a while. I wondered if the ghost had moved over there because there were more of her personal artifacts there."

Fortunately, at least according to some of my informants, she seems to have moved back.

One of my star witnesses is Alice McCullough, a young woman currently working her way through college by cleaning houses. But a few years ago she was spending her nights cleaning the Harvard Exit:

> I worked there for four and a half years, and my family has worked there about twenty-two years. I'm the youngest of a big family. My sister Jeannie worked there when it originally opened as a theater. She was in charge for a while. And my brother Michael has been the janitor there for twenty-two years. So I've pretty much grown up in and around that theater. I grew up hearing stories. My sister had several experiences, and I had one about four years ago.
>
> At the time I was janitoring, as well as working

there as a regular employee. One night about half an hour after I got there I was vacuuming and it was real loud and I had the radio on, and I got this sense that someone else was in the building with me. There's a balcony and there are offices off it, so I assumed that someone had come out of the offices and was trying to get my attention. I turned off the vacuum and turned around, and I saw this figure with an old-fashioned dress, real transparent. It didn't last very long, but then I didn't stay there very long, either. I looked away from it and left the auditorium. I didn't see a face or hands, just the clothing. That's the only time I've ever seen anything, although over the years you often felt that you weren't alone, that there was something there.

Alice suggested that I contact Janet Wainwright, who had been manager of the theater before Allen Blangy. "She's the person who has had the most experiences," Alice said. "She's a personal friend of mine, and she would tell me things. She would come in to open up and there would be a fire going in the fireplace in the lobby. Furniture would be rearranged in the room. Sometimes it would be in a circle around the fireplace. And a woman would be sitting there reading a book. She was definitely not a human; you could see through her. She would turn, look at Janet, smile at her, close the book, turn off the lamp, and walk out of the room."

I had heard this story before. From Alice McCullough, it was at least secondhand, but I tried to get it firsthand and called Janet Wainwright. She was pleasant, but firm about not being interviewed.

"People call me eight, ten times a year about this," she said, "but I just don't want to discuss it anymore with anybody. I've had some really negative experiences from having spoken about it."

I felt guilty in pressing her, but not enough so that I

didn't try to pursue the subject a little. I asked her if she had had the experience in the lobby that Alice told me about.

"Yes," she replied, "I had different experiences, but that one was the most notable."

"And you saw an apparition of a woman?" I asked.

"That's right, but I really don't want to describe it. I was fairly open about it, and other experiences, for a long time. Then a television station did a story on the ghost at the Harvard Exit and I became involved with it, and I was disgusted by what they did and vowed that I would never talk about it again.

"But I'll tell you this, I think that whatever is there is a very positive energy force."

Jeannie McCullough, Alice's older sister, told me she started working at the theater in 1971. She said:

> It was a small theater then. Now it's part of a big chain out of California. I worked there about seven years. I've always felt a presence there, and I've worked with people who have seen a female presence. Two women came rushing to me because they had these experiences. One [not Janet Wainwright] saw a woman standing in front of the fireplace, and you could see right through her. The other came rushing down from the second floor because she had seen some presence in the hallway. [This predated by many years the arrival of Allen Blangy and his similar experience with a frightened employee.] I just calmed them down. I'm not afraid of that stuff. I think it's very real, it's part of the spiritual world. I've always felt very positive toward the presences in that building. I never was frightened at all.

Jeannie told me that in the early 1970s a woman lived on the third floor and taught psychic practices. "The women in those workshops had incredible experiences," Jeannie said. "I'd be downstairs when they came out after their class was over, and they really had experiences. A lot of people have used that building to connect with spirits."

Jeannie's sister Alice told me:

> At one time there was an apartment on the third floor and a woman there used to have seances. One time the woman came down and told my sister a spirit had come through who wanted to speak to her. My sister had had a best friend who died of a brain tumor. This woman claimed my sister's friend had come through and wanted to talk to her, and apparently they couldn't go on with whatever they were doing because my sister's friend was interfering. My sister was stunned, but she didn't want any part of it, so she didn't go up there. Jeannie thinks that what this woman was doing up there might have stirred some things up. This woman was into heavy-duty psychic type of work.

History: The reports of the haunting of the Harvard Exit seem to go back to the very beginning of the building's use as a theater. I made an effort to contact women in the Women's Century Club to see if there were haunting reports when it was a full-time club building, but gave up when I was told I was wasting my time, that the women were highly threatened by intimations that the place housed spirits, and that they would refuse to speak about the matter.

Investigations: The first investigators I spoke with were J. R. Benight and Jane Riese, who produce a TV talk show called "Seattle in Vogue." They told me they are both psychic themselves and that in the past they have taken psychics into the Harvard Exit building. On this occasion, they brought one along. Benight said:

We actually talked with some spirits. The first we talked with was an older woman. She was very stern, kind of like the way you would imagine a stern grandmother to be, the kind who wags her finger at you. She was really brash at first. I wasn't sure if we were going to get along or not. Toward the end we sort of softened up. I got the feeling she had been part of the Women's Century Club. She wanted to know why we were there and we told her. We asked if the ghosts there realized they were dead, and she goes, "Oh yes." I asked if she was aware that she didn't belong there, that she needed to move on, and she got really pissed about that. "We like it here, this is our home," she goes. And she says, "You wouldn't want to leave your home in the middle of the night, and neither do we."

The next spirit we talked to was that of a man. He was murdered on the site before the building was erected. I understand that there was a house or something there, and there was a brawl over something. There is a record of there being a murder there. He called himself Peter. He was kind of goofy, very light-hearted.

There was a third spirit from whom the channeler was getting an accent and ways of speech that seemed like early American speech, kind of an English accent, but not the accent you would hear nowadays from someone from England.

Then there was another thing there. It wasn't really a ghost, it was more of a thought form, and we talked to it. It was a first for me, I'm telling you. The thought form was there to watch over the building, I gathered. I felt very uncomfortable with this thought form: it was kind of dictatorial. I got the feeling that it was formed over a long period of time, and not just from one person but from a group of people. I think it was built from a group of suffragette women.

When Benight spoke about a thought form, I thought

it might be apropos to speak with a psychic I know who has had considerable experience with such entities. He does much work with difficult hauntings, and I recall an experience he had had in Utica, New York, with a thought form. I wrote about this dehaunting in *The Ghostly Register*. His name is Roger Pile and he lives in Branford, Connecticut.

Roger told me this:

A thought form basically comes from mass energy. A thought can create matter. Therefore, a thought form can be created from mass energy, usually of a negative nature. Hatred, jealousy, all those energies are negative and therefore heavier than the positive thought form and would be closer to the physical. They would react very much like earthbound spirits.

The difference between a thought form and an earthbound spirit is that the thought form has no personality as such. They can be very arrogant. They think they are totally unable to be destroyed or dealt with. In a case I worked on recently in New Jersey we encountered thought forms because of negative energy that had to do with drugs. There were thought forms all over the place. It took some effort to destroy them.

Thought forms have energy, substance, and consciousness and must be dealt with differently than earthbounds, elementals, or demonic forces. You must reverse the energy pattern of the thought form. It knows what you're up to, so it's going to be resisting with all its strength. So you have to bring in that inner light, because light always banishes darkness. That reversal of energy explodes the thought form. It actually explodes into positive energy and scatters throughout creation.

There are positive thought forms but they are much, much lighter and therefore are not as visible as the negative thought forms, which are closer to this earth and are at the same vibratory level as earthbound spirits. So that's why you don't ordinarily encounter positive thought forms, although you could encounter them in moments of inspiration because you have raised your consciousness.

Jane Riese told me she had had a parapsychological experience at the Harvard Exit a couple of weeks before she and Benight did their show:

We went to see a movie, *Green Card* with Gerard Depardieu. We were just ordinary people going to a movie. I felt something in my hair, as though someone was toying with the hair over my neck. This went on for about ten minutes. The movie came on and we were watching it. We were sitting toward the back of the theater. I kept getting this flicker out of the corner of my right eye, in the direction of the exit door, up front to the right of the screen, at a slightly lower level than the screen itself. It was like a little light flare, or something. J.R. poked me in the ribs and said, "Do you see something down there?" Then I could see it in a kind of silhouette form, although more translucent. It was the figure of a man, in profile, quite distinguished in his demeanor and bearing, looking up at the screen watching the movie. He had a rather portly belly. He was dressed in a suit, an old-time sort of suit. J.R. kept seeing the flitter; we were seeing it in slightly different ways. I sensed an eerie thing about that exit door, which was separate from the ghost. There was something weird about that door. This guy, this entity, was an affirmative spirit, I felt. I didn't feel threatened by him or anything like that. It might have been Peter, although I did not get the feeling that he was a rough, macho kind of guy.

Allen Blangy told me:

I get quite a few calls from psychics and parapsychologists about the Harvard Exit. There were some guys I let camp out in the building. They set up tape recorders, they hung magnets in doorways, they brought in a person who was more perceptive of spirits. They told me they had left recorders going all night long and then listened back to them, and there would be strange noises they would pick up. They said there was a ball of energy in the third-floor auditorium. They said it would move across the auditorium and move out that same exit door that I had trouble with. They tried to photograph it. Over a period of several weeks they observed it and could see it actually appear and move, usually late in the evening. They were quite excited about some of the tests they did. They claimed that a magnet in a doorway began to revolve wildly—not like some air currents were moving it, but like somebody had spun it around. They were doing a book on haunted places in the Northwest.

Sylvia Brown, the California psychic who appeared on the KOMO-TV show on the theater, told me, "There's a woman there who dates back about forty years. People have said they see a woman in a long dress, but I think what they saw is an actress in a period costume. This is a very short woman, with dark hair, wearing a high Empire blouse with the mutton sleeves, like they wore in the Victorian period. But I felt that she wasn't of that period but must have been wearing this for some suffragette skit."

Sylvia said she felt there was a violent death in the building in the early 1940s, that this woman was suffocated there. I did not hear anything like this in the biography of the building from any other source.

Identities of Ghosts: There seems to be some consensus that one of the spirits is Bertha K. Landis. Landis was president of the Women's Century Club and also president of the City Federation of Women's Clubs. From 1926 to 1928 she was the first and to date the only woman mayor of Seattle. She may fit the profile of the stern grandmother of Benight's recollection.

I checked with the research department of the Seattle public library and was told that Landis did not die in the building from suffocation or anything else. She died at her home, then in Michigan, in 1975. I asked the librarian if she seemed, in her pictures, to be a small woman. "No," she replied, "she seems to be a good-sized woman."

The librarian read me a headline of a story about Landis, presumably an obituary: "She Believed in God; She Fought for Morality."

Other candidates for spirits in the Harvard Exit are:

- Peter, the ghost whom Benight called "goofy" and "light-hearted," who may have met his end in a house on the site before the present building was erected.
- The distinguished, portly gentleman whom Jane Riese reports seeing watching the incomparable Depardieu go through his paces on the screen. He hardly seems the goofy type, but who knows?
- The fellow who Benight said had what sounded like an early American accent. (The channeler was a direct voice medium, Benight told me, so the accent was quite apparent. Benight gave the medium's name as Richard Dupris. I was not able to catch up with him for an interview, but Benight said Dupris was in trance throughout the session anyway, so he would have little or no recollection as to what had happened.)
- The thought form that Benight felt had been created from the vibrations of what he called suffragette women in the building, although according to Roger Pile thought forms abound when drugs are being used in a

place, and according to Allen Blangy the Harvard Exit was a swinging place in its early days.

• There is also Jeannie McCullough's suspicion that the psychic workshops conducted at one time by the woman in the third-floor apartment might have stirred up something.

• Sylvia Brown's short woman in the Victorian stage costume, who Brown testifies met a violent end in the building.

Personalities of ghosts: Some of the people who have worked in the building feel sure that the entity or entities are positive. Others aren't so sure. Psychics who have investigated the building report a variety of spirits with a variety of personalities.

Witnesses: J. R. Benight and Jane Riese, TV producers and psychics; Richard Dupris, psychic; Shirley Enebrad, TV producer; Allen Blangy, former manager of the Harvard Exit, present district manager of the chain that now owns the theater; Janet Wainwright, former manager of the theater; Jeannie McCullough, former manager of the theater; Alice McCullough, former employee of the theater; Sylvia Brown, psychic. A number of other people who have worked at the theater.

Best Time to Witness: Manifestations have been reported at all times, but primarily at night.

Still Haunted?: The most recent witness I became aware of, Alice McCullough, had an experience about four years ago.

Data Submitted By: J. R. Benight, Jane Riese, Shirley Enebrad, Allen Blangy, Jane Wainwright, Alice McCullough, Jeannie McCullough, Sylvia Brown, Roger Pile, the research department of the Seattle public library. Assistance from Richard Senate.

Index